HISTORY
AS APPLIED
SCIENCE

HISTORY
AS APPLIED
SCIENCE
A Philosophical Study

by WILLIAM TODD

University of Cincinnati

Wayne State University Press, Detroit, 1972

901
T636h
1972

Acknowledgments

The following have granted permission to reproduce copyrighted material:
The Clarendon Press, Oxford: J. L. Austin, *Philosophical Papers* (1961); New American Library, New York, N.Y.: *The Way of Life,* translated by R. B. Blakney (1955); Oxford University Press: R. G. Collingwood, *The Idea of History* (1956); The John Day Co., New York: *The Way of Life According to Lao Tzu,* translated by Witter Bynner, © 1944 by Witter Bynner; The Macmillan Co., New York, and G. Allen and Unwin Ltd., London: Arthur Waley, *The Way and Its Power* (1934); Edward Arnold Ltd.: J. Huizinga, *The Waning of the Middle Ages* (1924); Seeley, Service, and Co. Ltd., London: Oscar Parkes, *British Battleships* (1936); Theosophical Publishing House, Wheaton, Ill., and London: *Tao Teh King,* translated by Elizabeth Mears (1922); Harper & Row, New York: Alan Bullock, *Hitler: A Study in Tyranny* (1964); Prentice-Hall, Inc., Englewood Cliffs. N.J.: Crane Brinton, *The Anatomy of Revolution,* © 1938, 1952; Wesleyan University Press, Middletown, Conn.: Charles Tilly, "The Analysis of Counter-Revolution," *History and Theory,* Vol. 3, © 1963; Lady Julia Namier, holder of copyright: L. B. Namier, *Diplomatic Prelude, 1938–1939,* published by The Macmillan Co., London (1948); The Open Court Publishing Co., LaSalle Ill.: *Lao Tzu's "Tao-Teh-King,"* translated by Paul Carus; John Murray Ltd., London: *Tao Te Ching,* translated by J. J. L. Duyvendak (1954); Barnes & Noble Inc., New York: Marcel Granet, *Chinese Civilization* (1957).
Part of the material in Part II, Section 5, is taken from William Todd, "Counterfactual Conditionals and the Presuppositions of Induction," originally published in *Philosophy of Science,* Vol. 31, No. 2, April 1964. It is reprinted with the permission of the publisher.

In writing this book I was often helped by the comments of students in my philosophy of history course at the University of Cincinnati. In particular, I have profited from many discussions with Mr. Michael Wolfe, a member of that class. I am also much indebted to Mrs. Mary Todd and Miss Lucy Eaton for the typing and indexing.

CONTENTS

Introduction 9

1 TYPES OF HISTORY 13

1 / Scientific Chronology 16

2 / Social History 24

3 / Detailed Political History 29

4 / History of Technology 39

5 / General History 53

6 / Textual Criticism and Historical Translation 66

7 / Statistical History 80

8 / Economic History 91

9 / The History of Ideas 99

10 / Piecemeal History 116

11 / Evaluative History 122

12 / Systematic History 133

13 / Conclusion 152

2 A METHODOLOGY FOR HISTORY 161

1 / Models in Mathematics and the
Social Sciences 162

2 / Games 181

3 / The Uses of Models 193

Contents

4 / Operations Research and History   197

5 / The Problem of Counterfactuals   203

6 / Historical Understanding   226

    Notes   241

    Index   245

8

INTRODUCTION

This book has in part the traditional objective for philosophers of history: the examination of the arguments that historians use, the conclusions that they arrive at, and the premises that they start from. In the course of this examination the philosopher generally goes on to define the relationships which he takes to hold between history, the various empirical sciences, and literature. Many philosophers have concluded that the historian's task is very similar to that of the empirical scientist except that the historian is primarily concerned only with special cases of more general laws, as opposed to the laws themselves. Other philosophers, such as Collingwood, have thought that the job of the historian, and of his reader, is to re-enact a historical situation in his own imagination.

Although these positions are often taken to be contrary, much of the present study will consist in an attempt to show that they can be reconciled. This will be done by suggesting a new methodology for the historian which will enable him to discover empirical facts, but which will also allow him to achieve the kind of historical understanding that Collingwood and his followers have emphasized. Moreover, it will be argued that this methodology preserves the most important features of historiography as it presently exists. The object is only to give the historian a systematic framework in terms of which he can carry out the familiar sorts of investigations but which will allow him to push them farther than is presently possible. In particular it is hoped that this will enable the historian to better substantiate conclusions which are sometimes more detailed and sometimes more general than the ones to be found in most historical work.

It is crucial for both the objectives mentioned above that we examine samples of actual historical work. Only then can we claim to have given an analysis of what the historian is actually doing, and only then can we suggest a methodology for making historical research more efficient and more thorough. The first part of this book therefore consists of an analysis of a set of samples taken from the work of contemporary historians. Of course, no small set of examples can be exhaustive, and, in any case, I will not claim that there is any single procedure which can be called "the historical method." Rather, there is a loosely-knit "family" of features, most of which characterize any given piece of historical writing. Moreover, I will not attempt to give any account of the way in which some historians seek to use history to establish quasi-metaphysical theories. For example, no account is given of the way in which a Hegelian or Marxist historian might view the progress of history as the unfolding of hidden contradictions, and no account is given of the reasons an ancient Chinese historian might have for thinking that history repeats itself in cycles centered on the founding of dynasties. Rather, our attention will be focused on the working historian who takes as his objective nothing more grandiose than that of discovering what happened at a particular place and time, at least where this concerns a set of people (either individual persons or masses of people) and certain human institutions.

In fact, the kind of reasoning used generally depends on the kind of history being done and on the kind of evidence available. The samples of historical writing are thus chosen so as to maximize the contrast in the subject matter dealt with, the kinds of evidence available, and the extent to which our general knowledge of human nature is presupposed. My method in this section of the book will be to look for features that characterize all or most of the samples despite these contrasts.

While a number of common features will be noted, two will have crucial importance. The first is the presence of counterfactual assertions in the premises and conclusions of historical arguments. A counterfactual statement is any hypothetical statement which has a false antecedent such as "If Lyndon Johnson had run in 1968 he would not have been elected" or "If water froze at 40° F, Boston harbor would be closed during the winter." Historians often deny any interest in counterfactuals and say that they are interested only in what did happen, not in what might have happened under other circumstances. While historians are right in refusing to try to find out what would have happened if, say, all Europeans had shared a single native language in the eighteenth century, I will argue that historians constantly commit themselves to counterfactuals of a more modest sort. This does not constitute any difficulty since counterfactuals are also essential to ordinary life and to science, and we will see that there are systematic ways of justifying the sorts of counterfactuals that historians need. This fact about historiography is not really very surprising. Historians ordinarily claim to be establishing causal connections between events, and it is widely recognized that causal connections lead to counterfactuals. If I claim that my partner's sneezing caused me to miss a putt, then I am implicitly claiming that if he had not sneezed, I would have done better.

Secondly, it will be argued that evaluative judgments are essential to historiography taken as a whole. Again, historians often say that they are taking an "objective" approach which is independent of any ethical evaluations of the historical figures involved. Again, they are quite right in rejecting the sort of history parodied in *1066 and All That,* in which the history of England is divided into the reigns of "good" and "bad" kings. But once again, I will argue that there is a particular class of non-moral evaluative judgments which historians do customarily make, and which can be arrived at in a legitimate way.

The second part of the book will show that the relatively new science of operations research is akin to history in many ways, and that it can be used to illuminate the procedures of the historian. While the object of operations research is to predict the future and to aid planners in making decisions, the methods of operations research can also be turned on the past. Operations research proceeds by constructing models, and the models can as easily be of the past as of the future. It is, in fact, just this application of operations research which I will suggest as a paradigm of historical method. The main object of the second part of the book is then to show just how we can arrive at the counterfactuals and evaluations implicit in the samples of historiography contained in the first part.

part 1
TYPES OF HISTORY

In choosing examples of historiography I have limited myself to contemporary historians for two main reasons. First, it would be hard to improve on Collingwood's account of the historians of the past.[1] My attempt is simply to do for contemporary historiography what he has done for the historiography of past ages. Secondly, great advances have been made in historical method in relatively recent times. I am not trying to give a history of historiography, but instead want to depict it as it now stands. In my choice of examples I have also tried to get as much diversity as possible combined with the highest possible quality. Consequently, these examples of historiography include all sorts of writing, and they deal with different kinds of subject matters.

My historical selections are all examples of what Collingwood would call scientific history as opposed to scissors-and-paste history. That is, they do not merely quote authorities and pass on information accumulated by earlier historians; they treat their documents simply as evidence and do not assume the truth of what the sources assert. However, where Collingwood sometimes seems to suggest that a scientific historian never accepts anything on authority, one finds in reading an actual history that there is always a certain body of knowledge accepted without question. A historian of the twentieth century does not, for instance, take the trouble to establish that the First World War actually occurred. The scientific method is reserved for controversial matters about which the historian is trying to make his contribution; in between controversial points he simply relies on general background knowledge.

The historical passages shortly to be discussed deal with controversial points either in the sense that there is present disagreement on them among historians or in the sense that the points made contradict an established tradition in history. In some cases the points may be made so well that they are no longer controversial, but all of them were once controversial.

In my survey I will not really suppose that each historian has his own peculiar method which can be delineated. Still, the choice of such different *kinds* of history makes it inevitable that different methods will be used in different cases. Further, the historians chosen will not all even reach conclusions of the same sort. Some will be trying to establish single facts or fix a date, others will be explaining historical events already known to have occurred; still others will overtly make normative evaluations. Many of these differences will be traceable to different sorts of sources. There is a great difference between dealing with a period for which there are so few extant documents that even the simplest facts must be established by an elaborate chain of inferences, and dealing with subject matter, such as twentieth century Europe, where there is more material than anyone can read. Apart from the extent of the available sources, it also makes a difference what sorts of sources they are. If one's sources are archaeological fragments, one gets one kind of historical writing; if one's sources are magazine articles and newspaper editorials one gets quite a different kind of writing; if the sources are ship designs with marginal notes one gets a still different kind of history, and so on.

Two good historians dealing with the same subject matter and using the same sources may write two very different histories, but it is likely that if they do so it is because they are trying to answer different questions. If they are trying to deal with the same questions, again using the same sources, the same considerations will be relevant for each, and they will have to argue in the same general way, even though they may ultimately reach different conclusions. In the same way that an experiment in science throws light on a given problem regardless of the identity of the experimenter, the same historical sources will be relevant to the same historical problems whoever the historian may be. Thus, we will not be studying the personal idiosyncrasies of a dozen different historians, but rather the ways in which a dozen different sets of subject matters and questions may be approached.

As Collingwood points out, the scientific historian approaches his sources with a question already formulated and tries to wring the answer out of the sources. In the finished narrative the questions that are asked may not be presented as such, and it may not even be easy to reconstruct them. We will attempt to supply these missing questions. Moreover, historians seldom present complete arguments as such, letting us see exactly what their premises are. Thus, when a historian arrives at an important conclusion we will try to see whether it is supported by an argument in the strict sense, and if it is, to supply the missing premises and reconstruct the argument leading to the conclusion. In a few cases, where we cannot really speak of the conclusion as being arrived at by argument, we will try to see how the conclusion *is* reached.

1 Scientific Chronology

For the first example I have chosen some passages concerning ancient China from Marcel Granet's *Chinese Civilization*.[2] Ancient China presents peculiar problems to the historian which are probably more difficult to overcome than those encountered in the study of, say, ancient Greece. While the civilization is undoubtedly ancient, the sources are very limited for several reasons. One of the reasons is that many of the ancient books were burnt by the order of the emperor, Ch'in Shih Huang-ti in 221 B.C. A more basic reason is that the Chinese have always attached religious importance to their own history. They have long theorized and philosophized about their history, and ancient Chinese historians often altered history to make it accord with theory. Westerners think of this as forgery but to the Chinese it did not appear as something dishonest; rather they assumed that the theory was correct and, since the history did not agree with it, they concluded that the history must be incorrect. For instance, it was a widely held theory that the founder of a dynasty must be a great hero and that his virtue is passed down through generations, gradually diminishing so that the last king of a dynasty must be a great villain. One can easily see how such a theory can dictate history. In this and many other cases the alteration of the texts is made without any more being said about the matter, and the present-day historian is left to decide what is original text and what is alteration of one sort or another.

The first passage to be analyzed concerns the fixing of dates in ancient China. Granet's starting point is a history written by Ssu-ma Ch'ien, the greatest of the ancient Chinese historians, in the second century B.C. One of

Ssu-ma Ch'ien's main sources was the Ch'un ch'iu (the Annals of the State of Lu) which begin in the year 722 B.C. Ssu-ma Ch'ien, however, gives dates back to 841 B.C. based on certain extant lists of reigns which included indications of their duration. Using the same general sources, the traditional history of ancient China, he could have gone still further back but did not do so, judging the process to be uncertain. Granet raises a specific question: Is it now possible to go back further and give dates before 841 B.C.? Actually, there are two chronological systems to be found among the Chinese. One, adopted and perfected by Pan Ku, the historian of the first Han dynasty (206 B.C.–8 A.D.), places the accession of the dynasty in question, the Chou, in 1122 B.C. According to the other tradition the victory of King Wu, the founder of the dynasty, over the previous dynasty occurred in 1050 B.C. The second tradition agrees with the chronology presupposed by Ssu-ma Ch'ien even though he does not attempt to push it back as far as that. The second king of the Chou, King Ch'êng, is supposed by the second chronology to have ascended the throne in 1044 B.C. If we then take the dates which Ssu-ma Ch'ien gives and add up the lengths of the reigns of previous kings we also come out with 1044 B.C. as the date of accession of King Ch'êng. It is in this way that Granet shows that Ssu-ma Ch'ien's chronology is of the second sort.

At this point another source enters the picture; 1044 B.C. is also indicated as the date for King Ch'êng in the *Annals Written on Bamboo*. These annals are a seemingly legitimate third source since neither Pan Ku or Ssu-ma Ch'ien was able to use them. They have only been known since 281 A.D. when they were discovered in a tomb closed since 299 B.C. Granet is willing to concede the authenticity of the story of their discovery (this is a sub-investigation in itself). One might suppose that the agreement between Ssu-ma Ch'ien and these annals would support the second system of chronology. Many lesser historians would have jumped to the conclusion that 1044 B.C. is the date of the accession of King Ch'êng. However, Granet argues in a different way at this point. The dates given in the *Annals Written on Bamboo* allow us to infer in the first place that a particular system of chronology had a certain vogue in ancient China and it could easily have been powerful enough to influence Ssu-ma Ch'ien, who was writing some two centuries later. Granet then infers not that 1044 B.C. is the correct date, but simply that Ssu-ma Ch'ien accepted a traditional chronology, perhaps the only one known to him. That is, it is much more likely that Ssu-ma Ch'ien accepted a going chronology than it is that he had some independent evidence of the date of King Ch'êng's accession. This assumption also explains why he himself hesitated to assign dates before 841 B.C.: he knew that his chronology was just based on tradition and he did not want to press it too far. Thus Granet does not accept what the *Annals Written on Bamboo* say, but instead argues *from the fact that they say what they do* to the existence of a certain chronological tradition. His conclusion, then, is that they do not corroborate this crucial date.

In fact, Granet then goes on to adduce evidence contrary to this chronology. There was an ancient theory that the span of life of a sage is a hundred years, and it was part of the theory that a sage attained his full powers at the age of fifty. In accordance with this theory the ancient historians worked very hard to show that Shun, an ancient mythical emperor-god, became vice-sovereign at fifty, and they also thought that Confucius became vice-minister at fifty. The number five hundred being a "grand total," they wished that number to play a part in the history of the world analogous to the role of fifty in the life of a man. Hence there arose a theory that a sage must appear every five hundred years. Apparently, following the theory, Ssu-ma Ch'ien and the *Annals Written on Bamboo* make Confucius and King Ch'êng's tutor, the

Duke of Chou, live exactly five hundred years apart. Both sources had a motive to fix the gap between the two sages at five hundred years. Further, Ssu-ma Ch'ien was also a biographer of Confucius and would have been particularly inclined toward any chronology which would tend to glorify Confucius—it would certainly have made it easier to convince his contemporaries that Confucius was actually a sage. In addition, Granet points out that Mencius (372–289) was active in propagating the glory of Confucius, and he vigorously promoted the belief that a sage must appear every five hundred years. Further, since his work served to fix much of the historical tradition, he might easily have influenced both Ssu-ma Ch'ien and the annals, and he must also have had a stake in the chronology that places King Ch'êng at 1044 B.C. Granet concludes that the chronological tradition from which the annals draw inspiration was tainted by theoretical presuppositions. By a different process of reasoning, he comes to the same conclusion as Ssu-ma Ch'ien and assigns no dates prior to 841 B.C.

Granet's argument, while not stated explicitly, is easily reconstructed. One premise is, of course, that there is no reason why wise men should appear every five hundred years; indeed, it is unlikely that they would. This premise clearly rests on scientific evidence even though it is so general that it would be difficult to say which science it is drawn from. It is partly a statement to the effect that a certain correlation—that between births of wise individuals and five-hundred-year time spans—has not been established in any science. It is also clear that this theory conflicts with what is known psychologically about the random occurrence of very high levels of intelligence. Another premise is that the five-hundred-year theory was popular at the time that the principal sources were written. This premise is a historical one and could be the subject of a separate inquiry. Of course, if an ancient source asserts a theory, then the theory must necessarily be ancient. Hence, this sort of inference is reliable and we can question it only by questioning the date of the source. That Granet has less to say on this subject reflects the fact that the historian cannot question all his sources at once. Some have to be assumed to be genuine, and, if this hypothesis allows us to explain the data, it is confirmed at least to some degree. The procedure here corresponds exactly to that of an empirical science. The most crucial premise is a psychological one about ancient Chinese historians: that they could not resist the temptation to change chronology to make it fit a theory. Granet takes this premise as obvious and it *is* obvious to any sinologist. So many other examples of this tendency have appeared that it is not implausible to suppose it to have been operating here. If one had independent evidence to the effect that the historians concerned were fanatically interested in keeping dates accurately, the matter would be otherwise, but in fact all the available evidence indicates that the opposite tendency was at work. Hence, Granet is arguing from an implicit psychological law about the ancient Chinese in general and ancient Chinese chronologists in particular. The law, which might still have to be qualified, has nevertheless been confirmed inductively by other cases and its acceptance is justified even though the number of favorable cases is not as great as would be required in empirical science, and no statistical procedures are applicable. Such laws are all that the historian has to work with, however, and they are better than nothing; hence they are used. It now follows that the chronology placing the sages five hundred years apart has probably been doctored. On one theory of induction it would follow *deductively* that *it is probable* (to some degree) that the chronology has been doctored. On another theory of induction the conclusion would follow only inductively, but it would contain no probability qualification. Either theory is satisfactory for present purposes, and, whichever one chooses, the practical upshot is that the chronology cannot be used as a premise from which to infer further historical conclusions. At this point most historians would be willing to admit that the *Annals Written on Bamboo* do not give us a solid foundation from which to assign dates, but Granet, not satisfied, pursues his attack on the *Annals:*

> Further, these traditions, since the discovery of the *Annals,* have been worked over more extensively than we can fully appreciate. What we do know is sufficiently serious. When the tomb in which the *Annals* were buried was opened, after almost 600 years, a part of the strips of wood on which they were written served as torches. The remaining bundles were first "scattered at random". The characters which could be read on them were "in a writing long fallen into disuse". The strips, once more gathered together, remained for a long time "in the secret archives". We possess an inventory of them. It shows *progress* achieved *by the successive editions.* This inventory teaches us that the *Annals* opened with the Hsia dynasty and attributes to the Hsia a longer duration than to the Yin (the dynasty between the Hsia and the Chou). The text, as deciphered and put in order by scholars, makes the Yin dynasty, on the contrary, longer than the Hsia, and begins with the reign of Huang-ti (an ancient god-king who was originally supposed to have lived before the beginning of either dynasty). The *Annals,* said the first who saw them, claimed that K'i, son of Yu the Great (founder of the Hsia dynasty), had killed Yi, the minister and successor designated by his father, in order to seize the throne from him. This declaration was contrary to the canonical tradition according to which K'i is a saint, and which makes Yi die in an honourable way. The *Annals,* revised edition, state that Yi dies a natural death and that the sacrifices to him were offered by K'i. [P. 55]

Another curious point about the *Annals* is that an eclipse of the sun is mentioned for a date which works out to the autumn of 2155 B.C. According to astronomical calculations there was an eclipse on that date. One might take this remarkable accuracy as tending to establish the reliability of the *Annals,* but Granet draws the opposite conclusion. The story surrounding the eclipse is of a mythical order and, considering the inaccuracy and sketchiness of all other reports of the period, it is overwhelmingly unlikely that this one event could have been recorded accurately when nothing else was. Granet thinks instead that later Chinese historians of at least the seventh century A.D., who knew how to calculate the dates of eclipses, simply added the date to the text. The record might be believable if the eclipse had just been listed as occurring in the reign of a particular king, but the dating of it almost to the month is too much and causes us to be suspicious. This inference is also interesting in that it illustrates the historian's use of the findings of natural science. Granet concludes ironically:

> It is evident that the text of the *Annals* has only become correct thanks to the labour of centuries, with the most perfect sincerity. These labours were inspired by the idea that canonical tradition cannot err. On the other hand, errors may slip into the manuscripts in the course of their transmission. To rectify these adventitious errors by using the latest teachings of science is to re-establish the text in its first purity. [P. 56]

Granet has, in effect, destroyed any reasons one might have for preferring the second system of chronology to the first and he concludes (pp. 56–57) with the remark, "We must resign ourselves, as Ssu-ma Ch'ien had already done, to leaving without dates all the periods anterior to the year 841 B.C."

In these passages, Granet has been interested primarily in whether dates can be fixed and a chronology established. It is sometimes said that chronology is not history and that it can only count as a sort of prelude to history, as if establishing a chronology is merely a matter of writing down dates for events, and does not involve any sort of historical explanation or understanding. The passages just discussed should convince the reader that there is no basis for this opinion. Granet's reasoning is as subtle as that used by any historian anywhere even though his conclusion is only about dates, and is a negative one at that. He is actually questioning his sources in the most careful way, and he arrives at a conclusion which is surprising to one who has only a superficial knowledge of the period. Such a person would have accepted the agreement between Ssu-ma Ch'ien and the *Annals* in the first place. Granet has actually written a sort of sub-history, all in order to establish a conclusion about the fixing of dates. This sub-history concerns the practices of Chinese historians and annalists, it involves a conclusion about what they did in the way of altering texts, and it includes a hypothesis as to why they did this. Granet's sub-history involves all the usual elements of historical explanation and understanding in very high degree, but these elements here play an unusual role in that they are means to an end rather than an end in themselves.

Of course, the fixing of dates is not really an end in itself either, since it has obvious applications; it is often necessary to have a chronology to establish which persons were contemporaries and to establish the order in which events took place. Then, too, it is important to discover all the respects in which any ancient text is unreliable since this may help other investigators to interpret the source. Further, the ancient sources in this area are so few that it is necessary to investigate each one as thoroughly as possible. For these reasons the history of ancient China affords some particularly good examples of the interdependence of various pieces of research. At the most basic level is the collecting of the sources and the deciphering of the ancient language. Next comes the editing of the texts to remove later additions, and then the establishment of whatever chronology is possible. The next stages involve the removal of mythology and the comparing of differing accounts. The final stages consist in the reconstruction of the past from the differing accounts, the explanation of what happened and the writing of the narrative. It should be obvious that one cannot really distinguish these stages in the actual work of a historian, and one cannot proceed steadily from each stage to the next. In some cases, the later stages have to be presupposed in order to edit a text or even to decipher some of the characters involved. For example, one might have to know the ideology of the people in power at a particular time in order to know in what direction they might have doctored a given ancient text. Indeed, one might have to know this even to know what meaning was attached to a particular word or character appearing in the text. Consequently, there are no general rules for the historian to follow in dealing with this or other periods.

2 Social History

Our next example is a passage from Granet in which he is trying to reach conclusions, not about fixing dates, but about the peasant customs of ancient China. In particular he is interested in the ancient Chinese winter custom of the inhabitants shutting themselves up in their villages (even separating the sexes) and "hibernating" along with the animals.

In the vast plains of classical China, the soil, hardened by the dry frosts of winter, no longer accepts man's labour. The Chinese peasants then considered it to be, as it were, in sanctuary. While they themselves took their rest, they granted rest to "all the creation". They began by inaugurating a season of universal retreat. They sang "O Earth, come back to your place!—Waters! return to your depths!—Creatures of the summer, stir no more!—Trees, plants! return to your pools!" This invocation can be readily understood from the standpoint of the poor farm-labourers, who were obliged every year to reclaim the fields which had been snatched again by a rebel nature. They explained this resumption as a kind of advance and retreat. Grouped together in species, all creatures came back to rest in a winter refuge. "The water begins to freeze, the earth to harden with frost . . . . . The rainbow is hidden and we see it no more. . . . . . Heaven and earth no more have intercourse. Winter has set in. . . . Guard the bridges and the fences! Close the roads and the paths! . . . . . . Do not uncover what is covered! Open neither houses nor buildings! Let everything be closed and everything shut up! . . . .Emanations from the ground might escape and spread! . . . . .The hibernating animals might die!" When the hibernating animals shut themselves up in their retreats, men also shut themselves up, to assist in the universal retirement. "If a peasant has not gathered and garnered his harvests, if a horse or a bullock or a domestic animal be left to wander, he who takes possession of them does no wrong." The rights of property do not hold at a distance, or rather, when winter comes to put as it were the barrier of a divorce between human labour and the ground, every species is put out of the reach of every other. All outside contact is forbidden. There is then a universal ban, a general dispersion, a rupture of all related life. On the other hand, beings of the same nature who can remain in company, are drawn yet closer together. Penned up according to species, men and things are busied during the retreat in re-establishing their specific genius. Restoring themselves in the company of their kind, they arm themselves with the forces which, when spring has come and the rights of sanctuary have been removed, will allow of a general resumption of contact. Then, with an offering of leeks, lambs, and a black bullock, they can say farewell to the genius of the cold: breaking the ice, they can "remove the barriers which are opposed to the reign of warmth" and call down hail and thunder; they can chase away the genii of drought, and, after a first ritual ploughing, they can once more open up the ground which is renewed by rest.[3]

Here Granet's premises consist of passages taken from ancient literature and his conclusion concerns the customs of men and the feelings surrounding those customs. His main conclusion is that the peasants believed each species of being to have a specific genius which could be restored only by rest and contact with the same species, and which might be destroyed if let out of its hibernating place and put in contact with members of a different species. The sources quoted do not in themselves tell Granet as much as this. One says that hibernating animals might die if emanations from the ground were to escape and that houses and buildings must be closed. Granet then infers that if the ancient Chinese believed that the hibernating animals must be closed in the earth to preserve their health and also believed that men's houses must be closed, then they must have further believed that a man who wandered outside in the winter would come to harm. That is, the ancient Chinese believed that natural elements and animals had to be closed off in winter for their own good, and since they emulated nature by closing themselves off, a reasonable reconstruction of their thinking and feeling is that they compared themselves to the hibernating animals and believed that their own hibernation was necessary to their own well-being. Thus Granet concludes that the ancient Chinese thought of themselves as a part of nature and, since they believed everything in nature to have its specific genius, it is reasonable to conclude further that they believed man to have his own specific genius which would be restored by the winter retreat in company with his fellows.

The reasoning here is entirely different from that displayed in the first passage. There the conclusion was reached strictly by argument and the basic premise was a psychological law about Chinese annalists which was believed to hold. Here the reasoning is by analogy, but it is not an analogy which Granet draws; it is an analogy which he supposes the Chinese to have drawn between the hibernation of animals and their own winter retreat, and between themselves and nature. In the absence of definitive sources, how then does he know that they made this analogy and regarded themselves in this way? Of course, part of his information goes beyond the sources quoted and consists in his general knowledge of the period. However, the most important part of Granet's procedure is his imaginative identification with the Chinese peasant farmer. Thus he says, "This invocation can be readily understood from the standpoint of poor farm labourers who were obliged every year to reclaim the fields which had been snatched again by rebel nature." He is saying in effect, "Put yourself in the place of these peasant farmers and look upon winter as snatching from you your fields. If you then think of yourself as competing with natural forces and you notice that everything else alternately rests and acts, you will think of yourself as alternately resting, to store up the genius, and then acting in order to exercise it." By putting oneself through these thoughts and feelings one can see why the peasants went into a winter retreat more extreme than would be required just by the onset of cold weather. This is not a matter of reasoning from general laws. It is a matter of asking, "If I were in that position, how would I feel and what would I do?" The only assumption on which it rests is that human nature is constant enough so that we *can* understand people so far removed from ourselves. But, if we do not make this assumption, we will never be able to understand the ancient peasants or their social customs. The situation is analogous to that of the cosmologists who are faced with the question of whether to assume that the basic laws of physics and chemistry hold everywhere in space or just in our own locale. Some, like Bondi, assume the universality of such laws, not because they have evidence for such an assumption, but because they think that the investigation would be quite hopeless in the absence of such an assumption. Similarly, the historian has to assume the universality of certain basic features of human motivation and behavior in order to hope to be able to understand persons far removed from his own culture.

The process just described is very similar to what

Collingwood calls the "re-enactment of the past." Collingwood describes as follows what the historian must do to
achieve understanding when, for example, reading the
edict of an ancient emperor:

> Merely reading the words and being able to trans-
> late them does not amount to knowing their historical
> significance. In order to do that he must envisage the
> situation with which the emperor was trying to deal, and
> he must envisage it as that emperor envisaged it. Then he
> must see for himself, just as if the emperor's situation
> were his own, how such a situation might be dealt with;
> he must see the possible alternatives, and the reasons for
> choosing one rather than another; and thus he must go
> through the process which the emperor went through in
> deciding on this particular course. Thus he is re-enacting
> in his own mind the experience of the emperor; and only
> in so far as he does this has he any historical knowledge,
> as distinct from a merely philological knowledge, of the
> meaning of the edict.[4]

While I wish to take advantage of Collingwood's insights
into the methods used by historians, this notion of re-
enactment is, for him, closely associated with idealist
metaphysics. In order to avoid any such connotations, I
will generally refer to this process as "sympathetic identification" as opposed to "re-enactment of the past."

By this means Granet is trying to explain a phenomenon which he already knows to have existed. There is
independent evidence that the Chinese did shut themselves up for the winter, each sex separately, but in this
passage he is trying to see *why* they did. Hence he is
giving a non-psychological explanation of behavior. It
need not be implied that the behavior of the peasants is
impossible to explain psychologically, but it is just that
psychology has not yet given us precise general laws of a
sort which could be used to give such an explanation. We
might, of course, look to sociology or anthropology for an
explanation, and we might find that other peasant societies have acted similarly under similar conditions. That

would help us in showing that the hibernation did take place, but we already know that more directly, and we are not trying to establish that fact. On the contrary, we are trying to explain it and, in the absence of the required psychological generalizations, the only way in which we can do it is by sympathetic identification. However, it should be noted that, in our first sample, this technique was much less prominent. In some samples to be considered later it will play a still less important role.

It is, of course, the lack of raw data about ancient China which in the end forces Granet to rely so heavily on sympathetic identification. We will see later, most notably in Charles Tilly's study of the Vendean counterrevolution, that it is possible to reconstruct ideologies by statistical methods. If, for example, we had records that some Chinese villages "hibernated" for the winter while other nearby ones did not, we could try to correlate this difference with other recorded differences between the two sets of villages. These techniques are, however, seldom available in ancient history.

3 Detailed Political History

For our next example we turn to recent times and Alan Bullock's *Hitler, A Study in Tyranny.*[5] While this is a biography in form, a biography of a figure like Hitler necessarily involves great chunks of straight political and military history. In fact, the passages chosen are more representative of political history than biography and deal more with von Papen than with Hitler. After the elections of November 1932, none of the German parties was able to form a parliamentary majority and the Nazis had actually lost ground. The chancellor, Franz von Papen, was head of a "presidential cabinet," appointed by the

president, Paul von Hindenburg, and he was not theoretically dependent on parliament. However, in parliamentary matters Papen was aligned with the relatively small
Nationalist party which had another leader, Hugenberg,
whom Papen was unable to influence in many important
matters. Needing to form a coalition to stay in power,
Papen then approached the Nazis and Hitler. But Hitler's
condition had always been that he be chancellor and that
he be a presidential rather than a parliamentary one.
Since neither Papen nor Hindenburg was prepared to
accept his conditions, negotiations soon broke down. At
this point Kurt von Schleicher, the minister of defence,
made a move for power himself, and both he and Papen
approached Hindenburg with alternative plans. Papen's
plan involved his continuing himself as chancellor and
suspending the constitution; Schleicher thought that this
was unnecessary and that, if he were appointed chancellor instead of Papen, he could split off part of the Nazi
party under Strasser and form a coalition. Schleicher
finally won out by arguing that the army had lost confidence in Papen and that it would not support him in
suppressing the disturbances and riots that would be
occasioned by Papen's continuing as chancellor. Thus
Hindenburg was forced to appoint Schleicher instead.
The latter then had as much difficulty as Papen had previously had in getting support from the other parties, and
the stage was set for Hitler's rise to power. Up to this
point there is a fairly clear and noncontroversial historical
account of what happened, but Papen continued to play
a role and entered into a political relationship with Hitler.
The controversial nature of their relationship forces Bullock to make a decision about Papen's intentions.

Bullock asks this question: what was Papen trying
to accomplish in the interim between his own chancellorship and that of Hitler? His conclusion is as follows:

> Up to the very evening before the announcement
> of Hitler's Chancellorship, Papen continued to balance
> two possible plans. Either he could become Chancellor

himself, with the support of Hugenberg and the Nationalists, in a presidential cabinet and dissolve the
Reichstag for an indefinite period; or he could take the
office of Vice-Chancellor in a Hitler Ministry, which
would aim at a parliamentary majority with the help of
the Nationalists and possibly of the Centre, dissolving the
Reichstag if necessary in order to win a majority at fresh
elections. In the second case, guarantees of various sorts
would have to be obtained against the Nazis' abuse of
power, they would have to be tied down by their partners in the coalition and the President's dislike of having
Hitler as Chancellor would have to be overcome. Though
he still insisted on the Chancellorship for himself, Hitler
was now prepared to enter a coalition and to search for
a parliamentary majority, but there was room for a great
deal of manoeuvring and bargaining on the composition
of the Cabinet and the reservation of certain posts—the
Foreign Minister and the Minister President of Prussia,
the Ministers of Defence and Finance—for the President's own nominees. [Pp. 246–247]

It should be remembered that, since Papen had
great influence with Hindenburg, he could probably have
controlled the President's choices. Bullock's evidence for
his view hinges on a secret meeting between Papen and
Hitler at the house of a Cologne banker, Kurt von Schröder, in January 1933. Bullock follows the account of the
meeting given by Schröder at the Nuremberg trials at
which time Schröder also stated that the idea of the meeting was first broached to him by Papen. Bullock describes
the events:

Hitler took with him Hess, Himmler, and Keppler,
but the talk with Papen, which lasted for two hours, was
held in Schröder's study with only the banker present
besides the two principals. First, misunderstandings had
to be removed: the sentence on the Potempa murderers
and Papen's behaviour on 13 August. Papen slipped out
of the responsibility for Hitler's humiliation by putting
all the blame on Schleicher for Hindenburg's refusal to
consider Hitler as Chancellor. The change of attitude on
the President's part, he said, had come as a great surprise
to him. But what Papen had really come to talk about
was the prospect of replacing Schleicher's government:

he suggested the establishment of a Nationalist and Nazi coalition in which he and Hitler would be joint Chancellors. 'Then Hitler made a long speech in which he said, if he were made Chancellor, it would be necessary for him to be the head of the Government, but that supporters of Papen's could go into his Government as ministers, if they were willing to go along with him in his policy of changing many things. The changes he outlined at this time included elimination of the Social Democrats, Communists, and Jews from leading positions in Germany, and the restoration of order in public life. Papen and Hitler reached agreement in principle so that many of the points which had brought them in conflict could be eliminated and they could find a way to get together.' After lunch Schröder's guests stayed chatting together and left about 4 p.m.

Next day, to the embarrassment of both the participants, the meeting was headline news in the Berlin papers, and awkward explanations had to be given. Papen denied that the meeting was in any way directed against Schleicher, and, at his trial in Nuremberg, he not only repudiated Schröder's account as entirely false, but claimed that his main purpose had been to persuade Hitler to enter the Schleicher Cabinet. There seems no reason to suppose, however, that Schröder gave an inaccurate report; perhaps Papen's memory played him a trick for once! [Pp. 243–244]

Bullock remarks that Papen repudiated Schröder's testimony at Nuremberg, but in his memoirs (which Bullock lists in the bibliography of his revised edition) Papen not only gives a different account of proceedings but also gives some evidence for his account which does not rest entirely on his own testimony. The first difference is that where Bullock says that Papen suggested the meeting to Schröder, Papen says that Schröder suggested it to him. In fact Bullock's account here does seem unlikely because he has both Papen and Keppler, the Nazi contact man, suggesting the meeting to Schröder at the same time, apparently by coincidence! More important, Papen's account of his intentions, which Bullock never gives, is as follows:

This was the casual beginning of a meeting which caused as much controversy as anything I have done. At the Nuremberg Trial the prosecution described my lunch with Hitler as the beginning of our plot to bring the Nazis to power. This is an almost unbelievably naive interpretation; most of the political parties had been prepared at one time or another during 1932 to consider a Cabinet with Hitler as Chancellor. Perhaps I can now put the facts straight once and for all.

I must have been asked dozens of times why this conversation with Hitler ever took place. The answer is simple. The Nazis had 195 Reichstag seats, and remained a major political factor under the Schleicher Government. I still had serious doubts whether Schleicher would ever succeed in splitting the party, and even if he did, he would only command a highly unstable majority. Constitutional reform was still as necessary as it had ever been, and the required majority was still not available. There was evidence to suggest that if the party did split, the non-Government wing would probably team up with the extreme left; which, for tactical purposes, they had often shown themselves prepared to do. Schleicher and I had always shared the opinion that this was a development to be avoided at all costs. It still seemed to me far better that the whole Nazi Party should be saddled with the responsibilities of Government in coalition. By December, Schleicher's plan was already proving itself unworkable. Strasser had, in fact, broken away from the party, after angry scenes with Hitler, but not a single member of importance had followed him. It seemed to me that all the current rumors concerning the weakness of the party were greatly exaggerated. Hitler had restored discipline with his usual ruthlessness. Their finances were supposed to be in a bad state, which was hardly surprising considering the sums that had been spent during the November election. But financially the party had always managed to keep its head above water, whether the funds came from industrial circles or from abroad—a topic that I shall deal with later.

I thought there was still a possibility of persuading Hitler to join the Schleicher Government. A number of leading Nazis were convinced that the losses in the November election meant that the strength of the movement had passed its peak and that they would be well advised to join the Government now. I had not the slightest intention of causing Schleicher difficulties and thought rather in terms of picking up the threads of my discussions with Hitler in the previous August.[6]

Papen goes on to say that Keppler's correspondence with Schröder lends credibility to his account, and he also defends himself against the charge of having arranged some of the financing of the Nazi movement.

We cannot suppose that Bullock really thinks that Papen's memory "played him a trick"—apparently he did not want to say (simply) that Papen was lying. The difference in the two accounts is, of course, considerable. If we believe Schröder, Papen's intention was to get Hitler to help him dump Schleicher and get back in power. If we believe Papen, his motive was to help Schleicher preserve his own regime through Hitler and that he acted as he did because he and Schleicher agreed on basically the same economic program and the same program of constitutional reform. It is an interesting case of conflicting testimony because both motives are plausible; someone in Papen's position could easily have acted in either way for either reason and we can imaginatively identify with him whichever explanation we accept. There are two possible Papens and we do not know which one to identify with. And until we know, the method of sympathetic identification will not work here. It worked much better in the case of the Chinese peasants whose attitudes in their conflict with nature are much more predictable despite both their great distance from us in time and the scarcity of documents. In the Papen-Schleicher situation there is a multitude of available documents but they tend to cancel each other out. Even after we have digested them, we still do not know how to imaginatively reenact Papen's role at this juncture. One part of the difficulty is that we are dealing with an individual instead of a whole class of persons and are trying to reconstruct his motivation in much greater detail than would be attempted for a whole class of persons. The other part is that Franz von Papen was a much slicker individual than the average Chinese peasant appears to have been.

The question of Papen's intention at this crucial moment in history must therefore be decided on external evidence rather than by sympathetic understanding. The historian's first inclination would be to look for evidence of Papen's general veracity or lack of it. In fact, Bullock does apparently catch Papen in a lie on a related occasion. Bullock says that during this period Papen was still influencing Hindenburg, was still living next door to him in Berlin, and was a frequent and welcome visitor in his house. Although Papen denies having much contact with Hindenburg, there is an affidavit in support of Bullock's version from Meissner, Hindenburg's state secretary. Meissner apparently had no reason to lie. Further, Papen himself claims that there was a close relationship between himself and Hindenburg, and in the circumstances it seems unlikely that he would never have visited his neighbor. Bullock does not ignore Papen entirely as a source since he quotes the remark which Schleicher is said to have made to Papen when it seemed that Papen was to remain as Chancellor: "Little monk, you have chosen a difficult path!" (p. 236). This quotation occurs in Papen's memoirs,[7] and it seems likely that Bullock got it either from that source or from Papen's testimony at Nuremberg. Another argument against Papen is that he was actually on trial at Nuremberg and, even though he was acquitted, he was under a great pressure to dissociate himself from Hitler's rise as much as possible and would naturally have denied any complicity. Even when writing his memoirs he was still under pressure of this sort and, in any case, would not have wanted to contradict his testimony at Nuremberg. Thus, if Papen's account is untrue, one can readily imagine a motive for its untruth. This possible motive does not, of course, show it to be untrue, but it is one of the steps in the argument being constructed. On the other hand, as Bullock remarks, there is no such reason for disbelieving Schröder. He, too, must have been under pressure to dissociate himself from the Nazis and he could not have liked admitting that negotiations aimed at putting the Nazis in power took place in his study. Thus one cannot imagine any motivation for his distorting the truth *in this direction.* Hence the conclusion of the reconstructed argument would be that Schröder is telling the truth and Papen is not where they differ.

Two sorts of justification could be given for Bullock's inference. First, we might appeal to the psychological law, or supposed psychological law, to the effect that witnesses never distort the truth in a way unfavorable to themselves. Of course such a law could merely be probabilistic and it would suppose, for instance, that witnesses are in general able to detect what will put them in a better light and what in a worse. Granet appealed to a similar law in dealing with the ancient Chinese annalists, but there he dealt with a relatively large class of unknown persons; Bullock is dealing with two individuals of whom he knows quite a lot. Were he to use a law of this sort, he would forfeit the advantage of knowing individual peculiarities. In the case of the annalists Granet had no such information in the first place and would have lost nothing by arguing from such a law, but in this case Bullock would lose quite a lot and it is not clear that the appeal to such a generalization would add anything. Thus he is more likely to have used another method, which I will now describe.

We saw before that there are basically two Papens that fit the evidence and that they are such that we can understand either one. However, Schröder is considerably different. We can sympathize with a man who, amidst the confusion and emotional strain of Nuremberg and under the threat of perjury, would simply tell the truth about a past episode, particularly if it did not look as if he were going to be convicted of anything. The only part of his story that might be suspect on these grounds would be

Schröder's statement that Papen had suggested the meeting to him rather than vice versa, but this is not the crucial question. If we suppose that Schröder was lying and Papen telling the truth we cannot see how to put ourselves in Schröder's shoes at all, at least without inventing circumstances for which there is no evidence. But on the hypothesis that Schröder was telling the truth and Papen lying we can imaginatively reenact both their roles. Hence the latter hypothesis is to be preferred. The issue here is so confusing and so important, however, that Bullock would have done better to present Papen's side of the dispute more fully.

There is a certain analogy here with what is called "the method of hypothesis" in science. Let us assume that two hypotheses have the same antecedent probability. Suppose, however, that a particular prediction, p, is more probable on the first hypothesis than on the second. Suppose, further, that p turns out to be true. It then follows that, taking this p into account, the first hypothesis is more probable than the second one because it yields this true prediction. Taking g to represent general background information, exclusive of p, we can represent the matter as follows:

Premise 1. $P(h_1, g) = P(h_2, g)$
Premise 2. $P(p, h_1 \cdot g) > P(p, h_2 \cdot g)$
Premise 3. p is true
Conclusion: $P(h_1, p \cdot g) > P(h_2, p \cdot g)$

Thus, one can say generally that a hypothesis on the basis of which we can explain a particular fact is, all other things being equal, preferable to a hypothesis on the basis of which that fact cannot be explained, or can be explained only by adding *ad hoc* hypotheses.

It can be seen that the same process is involved here in Bullock's history except that the ability to understand or sympathetically identify takes the place of the ability to explain. Thus, a hypothesis which allows us to understand a historical figure is, all other things being equal, preferable to a hypothesis which does not allow this understanding or which requires *ad hoc* hypotheses. An example of such an *ad hoc* hypothesis in the present case would be the following. If we take the view that Papen is telling the truth, we cannot then understand, under ordinary assumptions, why Schröder would lie. One could, however, square the theory with the facts by further supposing that Schröder was at this point overcome with a sense of guilt at having had any association with the Nazis at all; this might have then led him to exaggerate his own role in the rise of Hitler. Alternatively one could adopt the different *ad hoc* hypothesis that Schröder, at the time of the Nuremberg trials, was still proud of his association with Hitler, and that he was trying to exaggerate it. However, as long as there is no independent evidence for either of these "extra" hypotheses, they have the same status as the superfluous epicycles of Ptolemaic astronomy, and should be avoided if at all possible.

We can now draw a somewhat closer parallel between the method of hypothesis, as used in science, and Bullock's reasoning in this case. In the case of a more complex scientific theory the prediction, p, would probably not be a simple statement which is directly confirmed or disconfirmed in any clear-cut way. Rather, confirming it would likely be a matter of constructing a model resting on plausible assumptions consistent with the hypothesis and which is such that p is either true of the model or is likely to be true in the simulation or game which comprises the model. However, when one understands a historical figure in the sense of being able to put oneself imaginatively in his place, then one should be able to sketch out the general principles on which he acts and to say what factors would influence him and what his motives would be in certain crucial situations. Once one has come this far, one has some of the information which would be required to set up a model in which there would be counterparts of, say, Hitler, Papen, and Schröder. The behavior of these counterparts would then be determined by the rules of the model (game). This sort of thing will be explored in more detail in Part II, but it is worth noting here that what really separates Bullock's reasoning from a scientific use of the method of hypothesis is his lack of an explicit methodology and the fact that he cannot investigate the situation in the detail characteristic of a scientific model.

What is most lacking in this sort of history is what we might call a "preparatory reorientation" on the historian's part. To make the necessary sympathetic identifications he does not have to assume imaginatively the values and beliefs characteristic of an alien culture, nor does he have to learn to read his documents, such as the records of the Nuremberg trials, in any special way, as he would have to do with the ancient Chinese annals. Further, in contrast with the next sample, he does not have to know or master any special body of technical knowledge. Rather, what he draws on most heavily, in sifting through masses of generally accessible and reliable documents, is his common sense knowledge of politics and the behavior of people in cultures much like his own. The conclusion is not that this sort of history is less important than the other sorts, but that it minimizes the role of certain peculiar historical methods.

4 History of Technology

We now turn to a very different sort of history, Dr. Oscar Parkes's history of British battleships.[8] This is not a history of the parliamentary manoeuvres which went into the building of the battleships or of the effect that they had in international politics; it is not even a military history since it does not include the engagements in which the ships took part. It is actually a history of the design of British battleships and the developments therein. To some it might seem that an account of the technological developments involved in the building of battleships, railway engines, and assorted other machinery is not really part of history at all, but is a part of engineering. However, even the most restrictive definitions of the scope of history limit it only to the history of human actions which influence human events on a large scale and which are in turn determined or influenced by human decisions. The designing of ships is undoubtedly a human action and, if the design is for a battleship, it may have the most profound influence on human affairs. Further, the decision to design one sort of ship rather than another is a human decision and, in most cases, one that a fairly large group of people have to arrive at together. Participation of many people implies many different motives and the possibility of negotiations, even of intrigue. In short, all the elements present in any other sort of history are present here although, as we will see, present in rather different proportions. The reason for regarding this sort of history as belonging only to the penumbra of history is that it requires specialized knowledge that most historians lack. Since many historians specialize in international relations, or in the domestic politics of one or more countries the paradigm for history has been political history. Since historians are likely to know less about economics, warfare, philosophy, science, and technology, these other areas are often thought of as being less "history" than political history. Even the sort of history that depends extensively on detailed archaeological knowledge or on detailed linguistic knowledge is sometimes thought of as being somewhat removed from the central core of history. However, part of my thesis is that historical knowledge always involves knowledge of some other sort. Even the most limited sort of undiluted political history always involves some psychology and sociology; it is just that often the sort of elementary psychology or sociology involved is classed as common sense knowledge rather than as belonging to those particular fields. Thus the illusion arises that there can be pure history unmixed with anything else. I have therefore chosen a field that is very unlike political history to illustrate the wide range of subject matter falling under history. In the passage to be considered, Parkes is talking about the design and construction of the battleship *Dreadnought,* the first really modern battleship, which made all others of the time obsolete. Parkes notes in the first place that the idea of the design was not peculiarly British and that in some ways it was anticipated by both Italians and Americans. However, the British were the first to complete such a ship by a margin of several years and Parkes's question concerns the reasons for the *Dreadnought*'s having been built when she was. His basic answer is that the men responsible for building her acted from a variety of motives but that these motives all coalesced in the ultimate design and order for construction.

Before we trace Parkes's explanation we will consider a few background differences between this study and the ones we have dealt with previously. A characteristic of this one is that the problems the historical personages were concerned with are much more clearly defined than either those Papen and Hitler were trying to deal with or those confronting the ancient Chinese peasants, if indeed, the peasants were consciously trying to solve any problems at all. With Papen we never really knew whether his problem was that of trying to keep himself in power or that of effecting a reform of the Weimar constitution. However, the problem of the men behind the *Dreadnought* was how to build an improved battleship which could defeat existing battleships under certain specified conditions. All that they did or recommended was based on certain facts about armor, gunnery, speed, rate of fire, and so on. Further, these facts were very largely known; it was not primarily a question of establishing detailed facts but of balancing one consideration against another. Similarly, it was not a conflict between those who favored the status quo and those who wanted to make changes, except, perhaps, in one small instance, and it was not a matter of various individuals being committed to various policies for personal reasons. Almost all of the people in responsible positions were committed to building a new sort of battleship which would be superior to the existing ones. Further, none of them had time to become closely identified with one among the various possible designs, and no one's prestige depended upon the adoption of one of these designs. All the principals, of course, had their theories, but they were not publicly committed to maintaining their views in the way that politicians are, and they were free to alter or give up their theories in a way that politicians are not. In fact, the deliberations of the design committee were marked by an unusual exchange of views and mutual adjustments of opinions. As Parkes does not have to establish the motives of the principal figures, his problem is quite different from Bullock's. He has no difficulty about assessing testimony or even establishing the reliability of sources, which are largely sets of memoranda, including design sketches, and articles in which the main figures put forward their views as to the advantages and disadvantages of various kinds of ships. Only in the case of Sir John Fisher's statements is there any reason to suspect insincerity. Parkes's main job as historian is therefore to assess the technical facts and developments which first led people to take seriously a design of this sort, and then to trace the focusing of opinion which led to the order for construction.

We will now briefly compare the *Dreadnought* to her predecessors. The *Lord Nelson* class was the last class of British battleships laid down before the fall of 1905 and constituted the most modern and powerful ships afloat until the *Dreadnought* was launched. The latter was somewhat larger being 17,900 tons to the *Lord Nelson*'s 16,500 tons, but she was very much longer being 490 ft. to the *Nelson*'s 410 ft.; the increased length accounted in large part for the *Dreadnought*'s improved speed of 21 knots to the Nelson's 18 knots. The *Dreadnought* had an even greater speed advantage over most other contemporary battleships, and this was one of her most important features. She was, however, best known for the layout of her main armament. At this time battleships carried two classes of heavy guns; for instance, the *Lord Nelson* had four 12-inch guns and ten 9.2-inch guns as well as assorted smaller guns for use against torpedo craft. The *Dreadnought*, on the other hand, had ten 12-inch guns and no other guns apart from small 12-pounders; also unlike her predecessors, a very large proportion of her main armament (8 guns) could be fired *at once* broadside at a single target. The fame of the ship is therefore a result of the fact that she was the first really fast battleship and the first big ship with a unified main armament. The American battleships of the *Michigan* class were designed at about the same time as the *Dreadnought* and embodied similar principles; however, delays in their construction postponed launching until 1909. Soon after the appearance of the *Dreadnought* all the other major powers, recognizing that she had made all their battleships obsolete, followed suit in building similar ships. This fact greatly influenced and intensified the arms race since other countries had to build up fleets of "dreadnoughts" in order to keep up with England. Since these ships cost almost two million pounds each and involved such other expenses as those entailed by the widening of the Kiel Canal and the construction of new docks all over the world, this policy had important financial and economic consequences. Thus the advent of the dreadnoughts was a major event in the history of the world, and Parkes attempts to explain their appearance in the years immedi-

43

ately following 1906, and in particular their first appearance in the British and, to a lesser extent, the American fleets. His explanations fall into two main classes. First, some changes actually took place at about this time in naval technology and naval tactics which made the new designs feasible and desirable. These might be called the "physical causes." Secondly, he traces the development and spread of new ideas among naval officers and navy departments which tended to favor the dreadnoughts. Some of these ideas hinged on the new technical developments while others had been current for some time but took on new meaning.

The first of the important technical innovations was the torpedo. Although it had been in existence for some years, at about this time it came to be generally relied upon as a practical instrument of war; and by the early twentieth century torpedo boats were being built in large numbers to carry it. Submarines were at the same time becoming a practical possibility and enhanced the torpedo threat still further. These developments meant that in any fleet action which took place at close range the large ships lost their decisive advantage over small ships, particularly torpedo boats. Since a battleship of 16,000 tons could easily be sunk in the night by a torpedo boat of a few hundred tons and proportionate value, the torpedo boat quickly became the favorite weapon of the "underdog" navies. This threat particularly worried the British, who had by far the world's largest investment in battleships—i.e. potential targets for torpedos. It thus became particularly important for the British to build battleships which could fight at long range; hopefully, far out of the range of torpedos.

The second main technical development of the time was the improvement of gunnery, which made long range gunnery possible. This improvement was not so much the result of new equipment but of new practices developed primarily by Captain Percy Scott in the British navy and by Lt. Commander Sims in the United States navy. Thus, in certain standard short-range gunnery tests, the percentage of hits rose from thirty-one percent in 1899 to seventy-nine percent in 1907; improvement in short-range tests was matched by a proportionate increase in the accuracy of long-range gunnery. This information as to the possibilities of long-range gunnery was fully available only to the British and American navies, who had made the improvements, conducted the experiments, and seen the results. The great difference, from an admiral's point of view, between hearing by rumor that "the so-and-so navy is getting hits at ten miles" and seeing it done from his own ships constitutes a part of Parkes's explanation for the first appearance of dreadnoughts in England and America. It is interesting to note that the steps involved in Parkes's inferences and explanations are so convincing and sound that some might not be noticed at all. However, we will examine them to see what historical method is being used.

It was obviously advantageous under the circumstances to build battleships which could fight at great ranges and be out of the way of torpedos. Further, the improvement of gunnery made it possible to fight at these ranges. Also, if one's battleships can hit the enemy at greater ranges than they can be hit in turn, a capability that the British had, it is to their advantage to fight at the greatest possible range. Moreover, these considerations are so obvious that any competent naval officer or naval official would have been aware of them. Therefore, in the absence of contrary considerations, the British navy would have been inclined to build battleships capable of fighting at long ranges. It is equally obvious that ships of superior speed can choose the range at which they want to fight and can consequently choose a long range. Hence the naval officials concerned must have concluded that the ships of the future would have superior speed. Since this was one of the *Dreadnought*'s most important characteristics, it is reasonable to take this feature of her design to be a consequence of the British navy's realization of the tactical advantages to be gained by it. It was mentioned above that there might be contrary considerations, and the two most important ones are basically financial. First, there is always a risk in experimenting with any sort of new ship and the process is bound to be expensive even if successful. Secondly, since one country's initiative, if successful, would be emulated by everyone else, one would have to be prepared to keep up, on a large scale, what one had begun. This concentration on increased speed and long-range gunnery would involve an even greater financial outlay which might be ruinous for some navies. However, since the British navy had the largest resources, these considerations had less force there than abroad although it was not negligible even in England. Thus Parkes can go a long way towards explaining one of the most important features of the *Dreadnought* without even mentioning the people who decided to build her. The existence of certain factors which must have been well known can in this sort of history replace to some extent the examination of documents which actually record their influence.

However, the desire for speed in battleships was not peculiar to the Anglo-Saxon navies; it extended even to navies which were not as impressed as the British by long-range gunnery. Thus the Italian naval architect, Vittorio Cuniberti, recommended the building of a 17,000 ton battleship with a speed of no less than 24 knots which would mount twelve 12-inch guns. Writing in 1903, he actually anticipated the *Dreadnought,* but his proposal was made for very different reasons. Cuniberti thought that a single 12-inch hit would be fatal to an enemy battleship if fired from short range and correctly placed. The 12-inch gun also, of course, had longer range, but Cuniberti was more interested in its power to penetrate thick armor at short range. He therefore wanted a fast battleship which could get to the decisive range quickly before being damaged too heavily by enemy gunfire; an overwhelming fire could then be delivered at that range. His reasons for wanting an all-big-gun armament consisting entirely of 12-inch guns had nothing to do with long-range firing. On the contrary, he wanted as many 12-inch guns as possible to maximize the probability of getting a decisive hit as quickly as possible at relatively short range; he dispensed with the traditional medium-caliber guns on the grounds that they could not deliver a fatal blow at the decisive range and would therefore be of little use. Still, articles such as Cuniberti's tended to reinforce the desire for speed in naval circles at the time, and the fact that different persons wanted speed for entirely different reasons (some to get close to the enemy and others to keep from getting close) did not reduce the power of the idea.

Returning to the British, one of the chief proponents of the dreadnought idea was Sir John Fisher, who became First Sea Lord in 1904. However, in 1906 Fisher was still a highly controversial figure. He had probably done more to liberalize the British navy and to make it more efficient than anyone else in its history. Inevitably, many of his schemes impinged on established interests and earned him dislike and distrust. Although there was a certain amount of automatic opposition to anything that he proposed, the Board of Admiralty was favorable to Fisher and he persuaded them to place an order for a battleship with the following characteristics:

Speed: 21 knots.
Armament: 12-inch guns and antitorpedo-craft guns. Nothing between. 12-inch guns to be as numerous as possible. No guns on main deck, except a-t-c guns if necessary to place them there.
Armour to be adequate.
Must be capable of using docking facilities at Portsmouth, Malta, and Gibraltar. [P. 472]

To avoid some of the expected opposition to a new sort of battleship, a committee on design was appointed, including many of the most respected naval officers of the time as well as some illustrious figures from civilian life. This committee was representative of the navy at the time and the members were largely convinced of the need for a faster ship. Only one member, Philip Watts, the naval constructor, wanted to build an enlarged *Lord Nelson*. Perhaps he would have preferred to modify an existing design instead of starting from scratch. It was more difficult to decide on the armament for the new ship (how many big guns and how they should be arranged) and here a number of theories had to be dealt with and a compromise obtained. Although the Cuniberti theory had some supporters in England, and even Fisher was intrigued by it, the committee had determined to build a ship to fight at long range; even so (on this assumption) there were two distinct theories of gunnery which both had powerful adherents. One was that of Captain Scott, who was convinced that the only way to get accuracy at long range was to fire salvos instead of single shots. Salvos can be spotted easily at long range and the range can then be corrected for subsequent salvos. To fire salvos it is necessary to calibrate all the usable guns so that their shots fall within a small area and make a cluster of splashes. Since guns of mixed caliber cannot be calibrated together, the adherents of this school of gunnery wanted all big-gun armament. Fisher, on the other hand spoke against firing salvos:

> Now the result of all long range shooting has gone to prove that if we wish to make good shooting at 6,000 yards and above, the guns must be fired slowly and deliberately, and the shots marked preferably one gun at a time. Hence the use of a larger number of guns disappears but the advantage of a few well-aimed guns with large bursting charge is overwhelming. . . .
> The fast ship with the heavier guns and deliberate fire should absolutely knock out a vessel of equal speed with many lighter guns the very number of which militates against accurate spotting and deliberate hitting. . . .
> Suppose a 12-in. gun to fire one aimed round every

minute. Six guns would allow a deliberately aimed shell with a huge bursting charge every ten seconds.

Fifty per cent. of these should be hits at 6,000 yards.

Three 12-in. shells bursting on board every minute would be HELL! [P. 469]

But it is a consequence of Fisher's theory that only a relatively few guns at a time are usable at long range and, if the number of guns was to be cut down from the *Lord Nelson*, enough weight was saved so that they could all be big guns. Thus the two theories had the same implications as far as an all big-gun armament was concerned and both led indirectly to the *Dreadnought*. It is true that on Scott's theory the greatest possible number of big guns would be desirable while on Fisher's theory there would be no point to a really large number of guns; however, considerations of weight limited the maximum number of guns in any case and narrowed down the possible areas of disagreement.

On the necessity for high speed Fisher was motivated by other factors besides the ones already mentioned. He put it this way:

> The most advanced thinkers in the Navy and those having the greatest personal experience of the sea have come to the definite conviction that the battleship is really dead. No one need fight a battleship except with submarine boats or destroyers, and the sole function of a battleship in future wars is to be sunk. They can defend nothing day or night with certainty.
>
> But this new battleship now proposed will not only be a battleship but a first class cruiser superior to any but the very latest, hence for years to come she will be useful since whether battleships are or are not used in the future her speed will always make her of the greatest value. [P. 469]

It is unlikely that any of the other responsible persons were much influenced by this consideration, but it is a historical accident that the single most important figure in the Navy, who held unorthodox and original views, nevertheless came to the same conclusions as the others, albeit for different reasons.

Parkes points out that Fisher held still another un-conventional view which had the same net upshot as the more conventional one:

> Fisher was not a member of the Committee, but acted as chairman. The first meeting was on 3 January 1905 at the Admiralty, when the Fisher-Gard designs "E" and "F" came up for consideration. In the Report these are described as having been prepared chiefly in

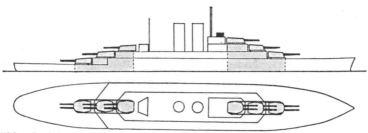

Fisher-Gard design 1. Battleship "E" reciprocating engines. $550 \times 85 \times 26\frac{3}{4}$ ft. $= 21,000$ tons. Twelve 12-in. 21 knots.

accordance with the strong recommendation of Admiral Sir Arthur Wilson, whose opinion had been asked for by the Board. Wilson had pointed out that the unfailing outcome of all fleet manoeuvring in an action is that it becomes a *broadside* action; and that therefore the acme of battleship design would be one in which all guns fired on either broadside. Note that there was never any suggestion as to the real origin of "E" and "F", and this example of agile diplomacy representing Admiral Wilson as a strong advocate of all-centre-line turrets was typical of Fisher's methods in submerging his own personality and fathering his projects on to someone who had been persuaded into an expression of approval for them. Fisher evidently sponsored the superfiring gun designs with the idea that they would provide a maximum *axial* fire, being a strong advocate of this form of attack. In his *Memories* (p. 121) he states:

> "I am an apostle of 'End-on-Fire,' for to my mind broadside fire is peculiarly stupid. To be

obliged to delay your pursuit by turning even one
atom from your straight course on to a flying enemy
is to me to be the acme of an ass."
He was therefore prepared to let "E" and "F" go forward
as broadside designs, preferring to withhold his own
opinion on their possibilities for concentrated axial fire.
[Pp. 472–473]

It again turns out that Fisher and his colleagues had completely opposed ideas as to the best way to fight a battleship action; but, again, it happens that designs "E" and "F" provide not only great broadside fire but also great axial fire, so both sides favored the same design for different reasons. Some further technical difficulties appeared and the designs had to be altered but the pattern is clear.

Parkes's explanation of the appearance of the *Dreadnought* has several parts. First, the design satisfied the need to exploit the new developments in naval tactics and technology which had taken place. Secondly, where conflicting opinions were held by large or important groups within the navy, the result was not a controversy which bogged down in inaction; rather, a design was eventually adopted which satisfied all the parties at once to a large degree. This need not have been the case and was in some sense a "historical accident." The third part of the explanation is of an entirely different type. Here Parkes argues that Fisher's diplomacy was in part responsible for the adoption of the design; that is, Fisher avoided disputing opposing points of view when he saw that their eventual upshot would be in the direction that he wanted. This wiliness may have been the sort of thing for which so many disliked and distrusted him. Still, as Parkes says, it may have accounted for the finding and adoption of a design which satisfied everyone to such a high degree. Even without Fisher the *Dreadnought,* or something like her, would probably have been built but the *Michigan* might have come first. Apart from his discussion of Fisher, Parkes has been able to give most of his account by referring to facts rather than to personalities. Such things as.

sketches of gun layouts and statistics about long-range firing tend to replace the usual sorts of testimony and documents.

We are now in a position to see what sets this kind of history apart from the other kinds and what makes it seem peculiar to the professional historian. In this respect it may be compared to the history of mathematics, which belongs to the same genre. In both cases the historian deals with purposeful human activities and constructions and is writing history in the way that he would not had he decided to write a "history" of nature. However, once the constructions reach a certain degree of complexity, like battleships or Hilbert spaces (which have an infinite number of dimensions), they generate their own rules and dictate their own development quite apart from the original intentions of their inventors. For example, a battleship may, like the British *Captain*, turn out to be unstable and capsize in a gale to the horror of her designer. Similarly a mathematical system may turn out to have inconsistent axioms, or may have a dependent axiom. Complex constructions, whether naval or mathematical, will always turn out to have features not originally anticipated, which nevertheless follow according to fairly strict rules from the original design or axioms. These features, originally unnoticed, determine much of the subsequent history surrounding the constructions, and often largely dictate the actions of the human beings who deal with them. In the way that a person who falls overboard has little option but to swim for his life, the navy which constructs a vulnerable battleship or the mathematician who constructs an inconsistent system has little option but to modify subsequent ships and new systems in fairly determinate ways. There is always some choice as to how to proceed, but the possible choices are usually relatively few in number and can be specified in an exact way. The politician may sometimes be left with relatively few choices but the alternative policies which he may adopt cannot be so exactly specified and the vagueness at least produces the illusion that he has much more freedom of action. Thus in naval or mathematical affairs the persons seem to be governed by the hard realities while in politics they seem to be creating the realities themselves and controlling the situation rather than vice versa. However, I will argue later that such a contrast is illusory and that the distinctions drawn between the different kinds of histories are hence superficial.

Oddly enough, it is difficult to say what this sort of technological history *lacks*. To name a few features, it displays counterfactuals, strategic evaluations, and preparatory reorientation. There is even a quasi-statistical reconstruction of the ideologies of different navies, based on their differing behavior, although this is most apparent in passages not quoted. Moreover, there is considerable reliance on various more general causal principles based on science and common sense. Indeed, the reader is invited to reconsider this passage once he has completed the others. What appeared at first to be a marginal example of historiography turns out to be one of the best examples of all.

5 General History

Earlier, I mentioned Collingwood's distinction between what he calls scissors-and-paste history and what he calls genuine or scientific history. The former consists in taking one's sources as authoritative, selecting from them, and then either copying them down or rewriting them without making important changes. It is characteristic of scientific history to take nothing as authoritative and treat the sources simply as evidence from which one can reason. One might come to the conclusion that what the sources say is true, but one can never assume this at the beginning. Further, Collingwood thinks that even critical history, where one subjects all one's sources to scientific criticism, is not really the best kind of history because it is still limited to the sources in the sense that it cannot tell one about something to which the sources do not refer. For Collingwood scientific history in its purest form allows us to make inferences about matters that the sources do not deal with at all; this is done, roughly, by starting with a statement which the historian formulates himself and then asking of a source, "Does the fact that this document was produced raise or lower the probability of this statement?" In this sense, it is possible to go beyond the sources.

The general distinction between scissors-and-paste history and scientific history is an important one, but when Collingwood made it he seems to have been thinking more of the history of remote periods than of the history of the contemporary world. As we saw with Granet on ancient China, when there are very few sources the historian's object is to wring as much information out of them as possible, yet to be critical of them and not accept them as literal truth. When we are dealing with, say, twentieth century Britain as opposed to ancient China the situation is far different. As an example of a general history of a society in recent times we will take Charles Loch Mowat's *Britain Between the Wars 1918–1940.*[9] Here Mowat has any quantity of reliable sources to work from: records of parliamentary debates, statistics compiled by government agencies, and all manner of "social book-keeping." There is little point in criticizing these sources in the way that Collingwood seems to recommend; they may be taken as perfectly authoritative and Mowat accepts them as such except, perhaps, when there is some special reason to suppose that a mistake has been made. One cannot find the kind of hidden meaning in birth-rate statistics that one might find in an ancient story about a Greek king, and it is pointless to approach them in the same way. However, most of Mowat's sources are not even public records; rather, they are the works of other historians, both professional and amateur. For instance, he cites such works as G. D. H. Cole, *History of the Labour Party*, H. V. Hodson, *Slump and Recovery*, Colin Clark's article, "Age at Marriage and Marital Fertility," and many others; further, he relies on them directly for the relevant facts. Thus he says concerning the Campbell case (where the editor of a Communist paper was arrested): "The re-opening of the matter may have been partly MacDonald's own fault. He had talked too freely to a journalist, seeming to protest too much about the case, and to blame it on the Attorney General" (p. 184). Mowat's only reference for this is J. Scanlon, *Decline and Fall of the Labour Party*. His procedure here can be classified as scissors-and-paste history since he simply takes statements from Scanlon, puts them in his own words, and gives suitable reference. However, this method of work is necessary for the kind of historical writing in which Mowat is engaged. The problem here is not to establish the facts; the number of relevant facts is so huge that there has to be a historical division of labor. Thus, some historians write concerning the history of the Labour Party, of the history of labor in the coal mines, or of the development of minimum wage legislation, and on a host of other specialized topics. Some of the specialized historians whom Mowat cites were themselves involved in the events they tell about, but they usually played relatively minor parts and may be objective despite their involvement—they are usually "historians writing with some first-hand experience" as opposed to "prominent figures writing their memoirs." A historian such as Mowat, writing a general history of the period, not only looks to the specialized histories for his facts but even depends upon them to organize his facts for him in a relevant way. Of course he chooses only historians he believes to be competent and objective, and exercises particular caution where they are not professional historians. He must at some point rely on them in a way of which Collingwood would seemingly disapprove; for without such reliance, the historian would find it altogether impossible to write a general history of a contemporary society over a period of years.

Bullock, like Mowat, is concerned with a large subject, but he asks different questions. The crux of his book consists in establishing the motives and intentions of key figures at particular times. Mowat, on the other hand, spends much less time talking about personalities, their motives, and intentions. Rather, he is trying to write a history of the sorts of pressures that would have affected any British politicians between wars. To trace the pressure placed by a certain segment of the community upon the rest of it, one has to chronicle individual events and bring together sets of facts. If during a certain period there was increased pressure from labor for increased wages and better working conditions, one has to collect together accounts of the important strikes which took place during the period, including threatened strikes, and one has to assess the likelihood of a general strike at various critical moments. Further, one has to find out about and record whatever conferences took place which were designed to reduce this pressure and what sorts of outcomes they had. The important thing is not to establish the truth of these individual relatively noncontroversial facts (which are too numerous for one person to collect and still be able to do anything else), but to group them into significant patterns. Ordinarily, a significant sequence of events is one such that all the events of a certain class are included and such that a certain factor varies continuously. That is, it either increases continuously or decreases continuously, or rises to a high point and then falls, or vice versa, or displays some cyclical pattern. One can always find some pattern or other in any set of events, but the simpler patterns tend to be more significant and the historian is still in the position of having to use his intuition to decide which patterns are significant and interesting. One may, for instance, take a set of strikes and find a general pattern among them; it may be that the first strikes are relatively local and easily settled but that they become increasingly serious as time goes on until some sort of crisis is reached, perhaps resulting in a general strike. There may then be a general falling off of labor unrest, or it may take a new form and a new pattern may be established with respect to some variable other than the generality of strikes. For instance, the energy which was previously put into strikes may be put into the establishment of a cooperative movement, and this change will give rise to new patterns which the historian such as Mowat can trace. The historian establishes a pattern legitimately if he includes all the strikes of the period in his account and not just those which fit into a pattern which he has antecedently imposed on the period. Having established a pattern, his next move is to establish important points within the pattern where any changes of direction take place. Often such patterns can be represented on graphs; the significant events to be isolated will be those represented by changes of direction in the graph. These significant events must then be explained either by reference to earlier events in the pattern or by reference to events entirely outside the pattern, or both.

In our example the particular pattern which Mowat is investigating is the rise of socialism in British society between the wars. His main thesis is that a move was made in this direction immediately after the First World War but that it did not come in the way that one would expect and that it did not come directly as a result of labor unrest:

> Thus harmlessly did the acute industrial unrest which followed the war die away, without bringing about either the reconstruction of society or the nation-

alization of industry. Yet two measures were enacted in
1919 and 1920 by parliament—the parliament in which
the Conservatives were by far the largest party—whose
effect, apparently quite unobserved by their authors and
the public, was tremendously to enlarge the functions of
the state in promoting the welfare of the people. The two
measures were the Housing and Town Planning Act of
1919 and the Unemployment Insurance Act of 1920. Both
aroused little or no opposition on points of principle in
parliament. Both provoked no comment in Conservative
periodicals such as the *Spectator* and the *Round Table,*
or in the Fabian *New Statesman,* which revealed any
understanding of their implications. [P. 43]

Mowat then gives the details of the Addison Act (as the
first act was generally known), which provided government support for housing, and describes its effects:

It carried the government into the business of housing.
Later acts carried it further. The building of houses with
the aid of government subsidies was one of the largest
enterprises—certainly the largest collective enterprise—
of the years between the wars. It meant that the new
Ministry of Health was in large part a ministry of housing and as such one of the most important departments of
state. It helped to cover the outskirts of towns with muni-
cipal housing estates and to embellish the villages with
the ubiquitous 'council houses' of the interwar years,
much criticized on aesthetic grounds, and insufficient in
numbers for the need, but in general far better planned
and equipped than the older houses for working-class
families which they supplemented or replaced. [Pp. 44–
45]

Mowat next discusses the Unemployment Insurance
Act of 1920, which had an equally easy passage, and
assesses its significance:

The Act had large consequences hardly to be fore-
seen. By providing aid for the unemployed from the
state in the form of something like 'outdoor relief', it
carried further the process of breaking-up and ending
the Poor Law recommended (though with variations of

emphasis) by the majority and minority reports of the great Royal Commission on the Poor Laws of 1905–9 and begun by the health and unemployment provisions of the National Insurance Act of 1911. It did not itself provide for family allowances, but they followed soon afterwards. It did not provide for non-contributory benefits; indeed, one reason why the bill was accepted so easily was that it was based on the beguiling principle of insurance. Yet the modest insurance scheme of 1911 was extended by it into a vast, uncharted area at a time when there had been no recent experience of large-scale unemployment and when the conditions of the boom seemed to promise that no such event would occur. Thus the Act owed as much to an accident of timing as to prewar precedent and war-born ideas of a new society. The onset of heavy and continuous unemployment in 1921 swamped the new scheme, and wrecked its solvency, piling an 'ever-changing mass of doles' on top of the system of insurance. (Reference to R. C. Davison, *Unemployed: old policies and new*). For once the principle of state aid to protect the unemployed workers from the consequences of industrial fluctuations was accepted, the state's aid could not be withdrawn just because it was irreconcilable with a system of insurance; payments which were not covered by previous contributions would be expected and would be granted. [P. 46]

As in his account of labor unrest, Mowat is faced with a great series of social legislation stretching out of his period in both directions. His first problem, the general pattern towards socialism being obvious, is what points in this general curve to talk about, to try to explain, and to use in explaining later events. We find that two of the events so selected are the two acts mentioned above. The choice he has made is not an obvious one since neither of these acts was very controversial and both passed almost unnoticed. First, he shows that even a conservative government managed to commit itself to a social welfare program during very unusual circumstances, the end of the war. When the program was proposed, the government did not expect to pay much if any of the cost; hence, the program did not appear to be a 'socialistic' one. As a matter of unforeseen hard fact, however, it turned out that the programs would not support themselves; and the Conservative party, having proposed the schemes, could not then very well cancel the program just because it needed to be refinanced. A further step in the argument is that the bills did not *seem* to be out of line with precedent and that it did not *seem* that they would have very great consequences; therefore, they did not stir up controversy. The final and most important step in his account is that these two acts set irreversible precedents and therefore led to the great government-sponsored social welfare programs of the future. Thus Mowat's conclusion is that these welfare programs are not traceable to labor unrest at the end of the war, which had died down without producing anything, but to a Conservative government's prior commitments and a number of actions which, while not unwitting or accidental, were taken relatively lightly and without the amount of thought and effort that one would expect.

Mowat's most important assertion is that of a causal connection between two pieces of legislation and later social and economic developments. Mowat does not say exactly what he thinks the causal connection is between the Addison Act and large scale public housing, but he clearly thinks there is one. Similarly with the Unemployment Compensation Act and the large scale dole of later times. I wish to give a more detailed analysis, and, since our paradigm cases of causal connection come from the physical sciences it will be necessary to compare briefly the causal connection that we have here with those found in science. Suppose that one heats a gas in a closed container so as to approximately double its temperature on the absolute scale. One will then find that the pressure of the gas is approximately doubled, and we have no hesitancy in saying that the cause of the increased pressure is the increased heat. This explanation is superficially similar to Mowat's explanation, or most historical explanations, in that we are considering the cause of a single event, or of a few specified events, as opposed to a general feature of the universe. There are three particularly important features of the physical explanation which are not altogther exemplified by Mowat's explanation, however. First, in the former explanation we appeal to a set of initial conditions, the initial temperature of the gas, its being heated, the constancy of the volume occupied, and so on. Secondly, we appeal to general laws—in this case the universal gas law and whatever auxiliary laws may be needed. Thirdly, it is possible to deduce from the law and the initial conditions the counterfactual, "If the gas had not been heated and its temperature and volume had been held constant, then its pressure would have remained constant." How much of this is then true of the relationship between the Addison Act and some later event characteristic of government housing, say, the building of council houses? First we have our initial conditions, or "causes"— the passage of the Addison Act, the general state of the British government, and so on, almost without end. Of course, even in our scientific case we cannot list all of the initial conditions since many will have to do with the instruments which tell us what the temperature of the gas was in the first place, how much it was heated, and so forth. Our historical case does not differ from the scientific case in that we can list all of the initial conditions in one while we cannot in the other; we obviously cannot do this in either case.

We come next to the laws and we must ask whether there is anything in Mowat's case which corresponds to the universal gas law. One might propose, for instance, a law which says that, under certain specified conditions, all acts of the British Parliament will be carried out. One might then try to deduce from the passage and the contents of the Act certain consequences in the field of public housing. The trouble, however, is that these consequences which one might be able to deduce are not the important ones. Mowat does not say that the Addison Act contains in itself directions for carrying out more than a very small part of the government housing program which he takes to be important; he says that it served as a precedent which could be easily extended. But it is the extensions of the act, both in terms of other acts and actual practices, which are important. Later parliaments and later governments were able to feel, because of the Addison Act, that in putting through their schemes they were not doing anything particularly radical or anything which would provoke violent opposition. Further, Conservative criticism was considerably muted by the circumstance that the Act had been passed by a Conservative government and parliament. Consequently, it will not be enough to have laws which say that all acts of the British parliament are carried out; we will also need laws which would say, roughly, that under certain specified circumstances the closer new legislation is to previously adopted legislation the easier it is to get it passed. Of course, as we bring in new laws we need to bring in new sets of initial conditions to go with them, and the situation soon gets out of hand.

But it is still not clear that our historical case (which may or may not be representative of other cases of historical explanation) is different from the scientific case in kind rather than in degree. In the scientific case we also need auxiliary hypotheses and laws; the universal gas law tells us that a gas whose volume is held constant and whose pressure is doubled on the absolute scale will be approximately doubled in temperature, but it does not tell us how to determine when the pressure or temperature is doubled. We need instruments to measure these phenomena and, wherever we have instruments, we need laws to describe their behavior. Moreover, since we have to know that the instruments are read correctly and used correctly we would ultimately need further laws governing human behavior as applied to instruments. This last stage would not be counted as part of the scientific explanation, but we must nevertheless resort to laws and initial conditions on this level if we are to give a *complete* explanation and compare it with a historically complete causal explanation. There is thus a certain tendency for a scientific explanation to look neater than a typical historical explanation because the messier part of the former is said to lie "outside the science concerned." Nevertheless the difference is that in our scientific case we have concepts, such as temperature and pressure, which specify their own standard conditions of observation and let us abstract from all the chance factors which may enter into any particular observation. It is then possible to state relatively general laws which have relatively few exceptions and which require relatively few auxiliary hypotheses as long as we stick to that level of explanation.

It has been pointed out by A. M. MacIver that there are levels of explanation in history as well as science and that what is relevant on one level of explanation need not be on another.[10] However, there is not such a sharp difference between levels in history as in science; the question is just how general or how specific are the events with which we are dealing. That is, are we just trying to explain a rise of two cents a bushel in the price of corn or the occurrence of the French Revolution? Given any two historical events at a different level of generality we can find one in between that straddles any borderline we may draw. But in science there are operationally defined concepts and we can talk about the causal relationships holding between any instances of these concepts without ever talking about the observations linking them to the familiar objects of everyday life; thus it is never necessary to depart from a previously chosen level of generality. The practical upshot is that in history we cannot distinguish between the main laws and the auxiliary hypotheses needed to apply the main laws; we have no set of conventions for deciding which are the most basic and which are involved only in the verification and application of our basic laws.

At this point C. G. Hempel suggests that the historian

does not really supply an explanation but only an explanation sketch.[11] In his words, such a sketch consists of a more or less vague indication of the laws and initial conditions considered relevant, and it needs filling out in order to turn into a full-fledged explanation. This filling out requires further empirical research for which the sketch supplies the direction. Thus we might interpret Mowat as saying that in order to explain the appearance of such things as council houses one would have to mention the Addison Act prominently; Mowat's explanation sketch would not say exactly *what* part this Act would play in the ultimate explanation, but it tells us in which directions to look. In this way the sketch suggested laws which relate the passing of acts to actual patterns of events in the world and laws which describe the way precedents operate. Further empirical research would then be necessary in order to discover in what sorts of conditions these laws hold; the conditions might then be incorporated into the laws themselves. Hempel talks as if an explanation sketch is something we could really fill out and make into an actual explanation, but, as we have seen, the historian cannot in practice complete the filling-out process because he does not have a sufficiently large conceptual framework, peculiar to history, which would enable him to distinguish basic hypotheses and laws from auxiliary hypotheses and laws.[12]

Not only does the historian typically give us an explanation sketch instead of an explanation, but what he gives us is usually, as in the present case, a partial list of the needed initial conditions rather than a partial list of the needed laws. One could give an explanation sketch of the opposite sort formulating some of the laws which connect the enactment of certain statutes with the appearance of certain sorts of public housing.[13] But since Mowat, like most historians, is more interested in particular events than in general laws, it is on events rather than generalizations that the center of gravity of the explanation sketch is to be found. Of course, for there to be a causal explanation at all there do have to be general laws, whether they are explicitly mentioned or not, and once there are laws there will be counterfactuals that can be derived from them. If we had here a general law which specified a connection between the passage or non-passage of an act such as the Addison Act and the appearance or non-appearance of housing such as the council houses at a certain later date, we could then deduce a counterfactual which might, for example, say that if the Addison Act or something similar had not been passed then there would have been no council houses or anything similar before a certain date, perhaps the beginning of the Second World War. Since we do not have this law we cannot derive the counterfactual statement. We know that some counterfactuals could be legitimately asserted since there must be some laws which are presupposed, but since we do not know exactly which laws are involved we cannot specify these counterfactuals with any precision. Thus it is that the historian does not really know what to do about counterfactual statements. When Mowat singles out the Addison Act as being of particular importance he commits himself only to saying that if it had not been passed the situation with respect to public housing would have been importantly different. He cannot make a specific counterfactual assertion and say how the situation would have differed without also making specific generalizations, and, of course, he does not attempt to. At this early stage we do not want to talk about history as such or make generalizations about historians, but we can review the principal features of this sort of history. First, there is the picking out of a pattern of events; secondly, there is the picking out of crucial events within the pattern; and thirdly, there is the attempt to relate these crucial events to one another in a causal way. In examining these causal connections it is characteristic to give explanation sketches rather than explanations. Among the examples chosen so far, Mowat is not, of course, the only one to be interested in causal connections; such an interest is also present in Parkes, Bullock, and Granet, and causal explanation of one sort or another is probably just as essential to the tasks which were undertaken by these authors. It is just that Mowat is more explicit about his causal inferences and, since his history is a more general one than the others, the causal patterns receive more emphasis than they did in the others.

This sample differs from most of those previously considered in that there is very little discussion of particular historical figures, at least in the parts of the book under scrutiny here. What sympathetic identification is present takes a peculiar form. Instead of being asked to identify with some person in the making of some decision, we are asked to identify with "the conservative politician who would have liked to have attacked public housing but did not want to attack his own party's role in initiating public housing." Again, there is strategic evaluation, but it is the Conservative Party, or, really, the whole parliament, that is characterized as not realizing what it was getting into. In this respect of dealing with sets of people as opposed to individual persons, this sample resembles Granet's social history despite the many other differences involved.

6 Textual Criticism and Historical Translation

To exemplify textual criticism and historical translation, we will look at the disagreement between two scholars, Waley and Duyvendak, about the proper translation and interpretation of an ancient text.[14] One might suppose that a question such as this belongs to the study of literature rather than to history, but in this case the question is historical both in its nature and in its consequences. The text is the *Tao-te-ching,* one of the most important books of old China, and the single most important source for Taoism. The difference between the translations and interpretations of Waley and Duyvendak is so great that, as we take one side or the other, we get a completely different point of view of ancient China's intellectual climate. Waley interprets the text as being basically political in outlook, and he sees the first portion of it as an attack on the Realists (Chinese Machiavellians). He then looks to this interpretation when he is confronted with difficult passages in his translation. Duyvendak, on the contrary, almost never mentions politics and interprets the text as a metaphysical treatise with mystical overtones. Thus, as we adopt one interpretation and translation or the other, we see the ancient Taoists either as a group of people passionately bound up with political affairs and partisan debate or as persons completely withdrawn from practical affairs and interested only in meditation and "the ultimate riddles of the universe."

Disputes over the best translation of a difficult passage in, say, a contemporary German text are not historical in nature. However, the situation is very different when we move to an ancient Chinese text; different translations of the same passage may, and often do, vary wildly from one to another, and there really is no single correct translation. It is more a matter of reconstructing the text than one of translating it. Both Waley and Duyvendak, as opposed to many of the other translators, say that they are trying to give a historical translation; that is, they are not trying to say what the text would mean to a modern Chinese, but are trying to recapture the original meaning that it would have had for persons living in the fifth century B.C. This being the case, there can be no such thing as a "pure" translation. One cannot simply look the characters up in a dictionary, write down the synonyms in English, and then adjust the syntax so that the sentences parse.

Rather, one has to have an interpretation before one can begin to translate at all. Of course, the translator has to have familiarity with the text before he can interpret it, but he also has to realize that his first view of the text may be very different from his final view. At the beginning the translator has only a rough view of the sorts of ideas that the book is concerned with; in the end he hopes to translate the text in such a way that it is coherent, makes sense, and presents a point of view with which we can sympathize, at least if we try hard enough. In order to get this much out of this little the translator must set the text in its historical perspective, reconstruct the biases and prejudices of the author or authors, reconstruct the intellectual tradition to which they belonged, and reconstruct the debates that they must have had with opposing schools of thought. When he has done all this he can go back and revise his original intuitive translation of the text; in fact, his own final translation may bear little or no resemblance to the intuitive translation he would have given before beginning his historical research.

As it happens, the translator can take all the historical knowledge he has of the period and apply it to the translation in some way or other. Moreover, the relevant historical knowledge may be of almost any kind. This knowledge may be of military or political events, or it may concern the usages that a certain Chinese character had in eras prior to the writing of the text under consideration. For instance, a method which Waley uses, but which is not typical of Duyvendak, is to take each of the key characters of the text and give etymologies which trace them back as far as possible. Thus, in translating the *Analects* of Confucius, Waley shows particular interest in the word "jen," which he eventually translates "good," as applied to men. In tracing the character he finds that it was first used to denote men as opposed to animals and later used to refer to a man belonging to the tribe as opposed to a stranger; still later, its use was further restricted so that one only applied it to men of whom one approved. Consequently, Waley is led historically to his translation of the character as it appears in the *Analects*. Waley also uses the etymological method in translating the *Tao-te-ching*, but here it is of secondary importance. Since he sees the beginning of the text as an attack upon the Realists, and since the Realists occupied a position of great political importance in China at the time, many further possibilities are opened up. Much of western China was then controlled by semi-barbarians with particularly ruthless ideas about military conquest and the consequent governing of the conquered peoples. We know quite a lot about them both from their actions and from the Realist (Legalist) political and philosophical texts which their wise men left behind. Waley can therefore operate from the premise that he knows the sort of thing that the *Tao-te-ching* is directed against; he thus treats many obscure passages in the text as containing veiled references to, and attacks upon, known Realist views. He thinks that in this way he can reconstruct passages in the text that would remain obscure otherwise, and it is in this way that his external historical knowledge makes possible his translation.

Duyvendak, on the other hand, sees the *Tao-te-ching* as representing one side of a dispute, not between the Taoists and Realists but between the Taoists and Confucianists. Where Waley refers to a Realist doctrine in order to clear up a passage in the text Duyvendak refers to a Confucian doctrine; one can easily see how this gives his translation an altogether different tone. Duyvendak also frequently compares passages in the *Tao-te-ching* with passages to be found in other Taoist texts; when he is doubtful about the correct translation of a phrase he looks to the appearances of the same phrase or construction in these other books and then tries to give a reading which will suit all the texts taken together. When he is able to do this he succeeds in broadening the base of his evidence and gives his translation greater authority. But, of course, the same sort of historical evidence that was relevant to the *Tao-te-ching* will be relevant to these other texts. The ideal of the translator would be to unify the whole body of ancient Chinese literature in the sense that one would give "consistent" translations of all the texts and then be able to support this unified system of translation with straight historical evidence. The ultimate situation, then, is that the translation of any one text really depends upon the establishment of a whole intellectual history of ancient China. Since the intellectual life of the time was much more dependent on the political and social developments of the time than is the intellectual life of our times, the intellectual history of the period presupposes a general history of the same period. On the other hand, one has to have some knowledge of the intellectual developments to write an adequate general history of the time, and one cannot write an intellectual history until one can translate and reconstruct the main texts. Hence the translation (reconstruction) of texts is part and parcel of the historical study of ancient China. It is not a matter of translating an ordinary book from one language to another for the convenience of some person or group of persons; it is a matter of taking a book which no one understands in its original form and translating it into some living language (even modern Chinese will do) so that it will be rendered intelligible. Then, and only then, can it be used as a historical source.

The most important chapter in the *Tao-te-ching* is usually thought to be the first one; the way in which this chapter is interpreted and translated goes far to commit the translator to a corresponding sort of interpretation and translation of the whole text. As much the same thing can be said for even the first couplet within that chapter, it is the translation and interpretation of that couplet that we will trace. Fortunately, even one who does not know Chinese can follow and compare translations of these passages. Since the expert Chinese linguist does not know what meanings the ancient Chinese attached to certain familiar characters, he does not have as great an advantage over the novice as one might suppose. Paul Carus transliterates the first two lines as follows:

tao	k'o	tao	fei	ch'ang	tao
(the reason)	(that can)	(be reasoned)	(is not)	(the eternal)	(reason)
ming	k'o	ming	fei	ch'ang	ming
(the name)	(that can)	(be named)	(is not)	(the eternal)	(name) [15]

To give some idea of the meaning we have set Carus's character-by-character translation in parentheses even though the translation is not a very good one. The great amount of variation from one translation to another can be seen by comparing the following randomly chosen translations of the same passage:

A way that can be described is not the Eternal Way: A name that can be named is not the Eternal Name.[16]

Tao that can be expressed is not Everlasting Tao. The Name that can be named is not the Everlasting Name.[17]

Existence is beyond the power of words To define: Terms may be used But are none of them absolute.[18]

There are ways but the Way is uncharted; There are names but not nature in words: [19]

Waley (p. 141) translates:

The Way that can be told is not an Unvarying Way; The names that can be named are not unvarying names.

He then paraphrases:

The Realists demand a ch'ang-tao, an 'unvarying way' of government, in which every act inimical and every act beneficial to the State is codified and 'mated'

to its appropriate punishment or reward. The Taoist replies that though there does exist a ch'ang-tao, 'an unvarying Way', it cannot be grasped by the ordinary sense
nor described in words. In dispassionate vision the Taoist
sees a world consisting of the things for which language
has no names. [Pp. 141–142]

(These secret essences are mentioned later in the chapter.)
Duyvendak translates:

> The Way that may truly be regarded as the Way is other
> than a permanent Way.
> The terms that may truly be regarded as terms are other
> than permanent terms. [P. 17]

He comments:

I. This first chapter is fundamental for the right understanding of the entire book.
The author starts by giving some definitions. What
is *Tao*(I)?
The word means "way". Now the characteristic feature of an ordinary way or road is the fact that it is unchangeable and permanent. However, the Way, which is
discussed here, is characterized by the very opposite:
this Way is never-ending change. Being and Non-being,
life and death, alternate constantly. Nothing is permanent
and unchangeable. The very concept of "way" therefore
acquires an opposite meaning. Of the many paradoxes in
the *Tao-te-ching* this one is the first and greatest.
Terms, *ming* (9) [see transliteration above]
"names", serve to define, in order to fix the meaning of a
concept once and for all. About the beginning of the
third century B.C. there were in China lively discussions
about the true relationship between name (or term) and
reality. Confucianists such as Hsün-tzǔ held that, in a
static world, the meaning of a certain concept was established for all time by the use of a certain term. The
Taoists opposed such a view: in a constantly changing
world the meaning of concepts are neither constant nor
permanent. Therefore true terms are such terms which
express this constant inconstancy, which is the very opposite of what Confucianists had in mind.
The majority of the translators understand the word

ch'ang (2) "constant, permanent" as "eternal", and, in connection with a different interpretation of the first part of the sentence, they arrive at some such translation as:

"The way that may be trodden (or: that may be expressed in words) is not the eternal Way.

"The Name which may be named is not the eternal Name."

The idea is supposed to be, that a distinction is made between an "eternal" Way and Name, i.e. a Noumenon, and a Way or Name of the world of phenomena, which is the only one that may be expressed in words. I consider this interpretation as erroneous. The words rendered by me as "may truly be regarded as the Way" and "may truly be regarded as terms" are *k'o tao*(3) and *k'o ming*(4). I believe that *tao* and *ming* are used as verbs with a factitive aspect: "to regard as *tao* and *ming*". *K'o* has the sense of: "to be capable of, to be fit for."

The word *tao* is frequently understood as "to say, to express in words." No doubt it has this meaning, but as such it does not occur elsewhere in the *Tao-te-ching*. There is a passage in *Chuang-tzu*, XXII, 7 (Legge, II, p. 69), sometimes quoted in support of this interpretation which runs: "The Way can not be expressed (lit. "said"; . . .). However, the verb used there is not *tao* but the ordinary *yen* (5) "to say".

I consider the translation of *k'o tao*(3) as "may be trodden" as unwarranted.

The negative *fei* (6) is not a simple negation. I take it in the same sense as in the famous saying of the sophist Kung-sun Lung: "a white horse is not a horse", that is, the special concept white horse is not identical with the general concept horse. In my translation I have tried to render the value of *fei* by: "other than," i.e. not identical with. The way which may truly be regarded as the Way, and which is the subject of this book, is very different from the usual concept of an unvarying permanent way. [Pp. 17–19]

It can now be seen that in the very first line there is a great difference between the two translations. According to Waley's version, the first line asserts that all the "ways" with which we are familiar, including ways of governing, are changing and lack permanence. But on his interpretation this couplet also asserts that there is a permanent way underlying all the apparent change; while we cannot use language to talk about this way, Waley thinks that the Taoist thinks that it can be apprehended with special techniques. The upshot is that familiar perceptible ways vary, but that the real way is unvarying. Duyvendak's translation and interpretation of the same line attributes to the Taoist the exactly opposed view; namely, the real way is not to be *confused* with any permanent way, such as a road, but actually consists in constant change. Duyvendak explicitly denies that there is any reference to any hidden permanent way, while that is exactly what Waley asserts.

The difference here can actually be narrowed down in large part to a difference in the translation of the words *"k'o tao."* Everyone agrees that *"k'o"* has some such meaning as, "to be capable of," but the question is whether the two words, taken together in this particular context, should be translated as "can be told" or as "can be truly regarded as the Way"; the former translation makes the ultimate Way unvarying while the latter makes it constantly changing. Duyvendak's translation is the more unconventional one; we will soon examine the sorts of justifications that can be given for it and which he leaves implicit. Still, even though he does not make explicit the general grounds on which one translation is to be preferred to another, he does make some explicit objections to the sort of translation that Waley gives. Here he points out that while *tao* does have the alternative meaning "to say," it does not occur in that sense elsewhere in the *Tao-te-ching*. He mentions the passage from *Chuang-tzu* because this is also a Taoist text and a sort of sister text. If *tao* were there used in the sense of "to say, to express in words," there would be some reason to translate it that way in the *Tao-te-ching*. But Duyvendak's point that the verb used there is not *tao* but a different one is decisive in rejecting this consideration.

In translating the second line much the same problems arise, but they now center on *ming* instead of on *tao*. Here Duyvendak supposes there to have been a dispute with Confucianists such as Hsün-tzŭ rather than with the Realists. He sees the authors of the *Tao-te-ching* not as denying the possibility of a permanent set of rules for government, but as denying the constancy of concepts and words. Thus, all sorts of important historical questions are intertwined with such things as the correct rendering of the second occurrences of *tao* and *ming* in the first and second lines respectively. We must now ask exactly what sort of a dispute we have and what sorts of reasons could be given for favoring one interpretation and translation over the other.

The first demand to be made of a translation has to do with the translator's necessary assumption that the text made clear sense to the men who wrote it. Such an assumption is not always a safe one. We know, for instance, that the Neo-Taoists of a much later period prided themselves on their ability to engage in what they called "pure-wit" conversation; since we also know that they prided themselves on getting drunk and staying drunk, it seems quite likely that they were talking pure nonsense. The attempt to make sense out of anything written under such conditions might then be a waste of time. However, in the case of the *Tao-te-ching*, the original assumption seems to be a reasonable one. For one thing, it seems that any book which has had as much influence as this one must have made some sense, at least to some people. Further, we do not have the sort of collateral information about the ancient Taoists that makes us view the work of some of the Neo-Taoists with some skepticism. Of course, when we are dealing with the writings of persons who were at least part-time mystics, even the best possible translation and interpretation will not give us perfect clarity. Still, that interpretation and translation which yields the greatest degree of intelligibility is certainly to be preferred, all else being equal.

75

The second demand is for what I will call external consistency of translation. That is, key terms in the *Tao-te-ching* must be translated in the same way that they are in the *Chuang-tzu* and other similar texts. At least, if this is not done, there must be independent evidence to the effect that a change of meaning has actually taken place.

The third demand is for internal consistency of translation in that a term or character appearing at different places in the text must be translated in the same way. There may be times when it is impossible to do this and still satisfy the demand for intelligibility; in those cases the translation which shifts the meaning of a term the least and which can best explain the shift naturally has the advantage.

The fourth demand might be called the demand for historical intelligibility. In general the text must be translated and interpreted in such a way that it could have played the historical role which we know that it did play. This would rule out an interpretation and translation which, for instance, made the *Tao-te-ching* echo very closely the thoughts of Confucius throughout. We know from other sources that it is one of the chief works of Taoism and we also know that the Taoists were in conflict with the Confucianists over matters of doctrine. Hence, we could not accept an interpretation which would remove all grounds for doctrinal conflict and which would make impossible a dispute which we know to have taken place.

The last demand has to do with the degree to which the translation is literal. In the extreme case the translator might satisfy all the other demands but produce a work twenty times the length of the original, containing everything which the translator thinks the authors should have said whether they said it or not. The translator would then be doing what Thucydides is often accused of doing. Hence, all other things being equal, we prefer the translation which preserves the closest possible correspondence between the Chinese characters and the English phrases used to translate them. In our case, however, the paraphrase which both authors give for the text does as much to reconstruct the text as the translation itself. The consequence of the demand for literalness, then, is that the assertions contained in the paraphrase be as closely rooted as possible in the text itself. In both cases the paraphrase turns out to be necessary to show that the other demands have been met. Here again, the translator should be able to complete his reconstruction of the text while attributing to the authors the minimum number of implicit assertions which cannot be found in the text proper.

We can now interpret both Waley and Duyvendak as putting forward hypotheses which can be judged according to these demands. Since both translations are major works of scholarship, they satisfy the demands to a relatively high degree, and it will not be possible to eliminate one completely in favor of the other. Nevertheless, it will still be possible to find some grounds for preference. The situation is really much like that in empirical science. There a hypothesis must explain certain phenomena, it must be internally consistent, and it must be consistent with the general body of accepted scientific belief. When we have two competing hypotheses which explain the phenomena and which are consistent both internally and externally we choose one according to the principle of economy. That is, we choose the one which involves the smaller number of *ad hoc* hypotheses. Applying these criteria to the two translations of the *Tao-te-ching*, we find that both translations render the text intelligible in itself and both render it intelligible in terms of controversies known to be taking place in China at the time; both translations therefore satisfy the first and fourth demands to a very high degree. Further, both translations are in accord with what is known of ancient Chinese usage. Consequently, we can say that both hypotheses explain most of the phenomena.

However, the demand for internal consistency,

which reflects another part of the set of phenomena to be explained, is not equally well satisfied by both hypotheses. On the one hand, Waley translates the character *tao* in two radically different ways in the same line; in its first occurrence in the first line it is translated "Way" while in its second occurrence it is made into a verb and given the meaning "to tell about." On the other hand, when Duyvendak translates *k'o tao* as "may truly be regarded as the way" he is able to repeat the English "way" where the Chinese repeats *tao* and give an internally consistent translation. In this respect even Carus's translation, "The Reason that can be reasoned," has an advantage over Waley's. Of course, Waley is not being *logically* inconsistent here; there are cases where the same term actually is used in two different ways in the same context as, for instance, in a play on words. Nevertheless, the hypothesis that there is a play on the word *tao* here is an *ad hoc* hypothesis. If the *ad hoc* hypothesis is necessary for explanation then it has to be made; but if there is an alternative theory which gets along without such an *ad hoc* hypothesis then the alternative theory is, all other things being equal, to be preferred. Here all other things are not equal and, quite apart from this demand, Duyvendak's hypothesis is more economical. One of the basic features of Waley's translation is that it construes large chunks of the *Tao-te-ching* as having a hidden political meaning which it does not seem to have. That is, even in Waley's translation the political references and terms do not appear in the text itself; in order to explain what the text means he has to attribute political symbolism to the nonpolitical terms appearing in it. Duyvendak does not need to import symbolism, and when he postulates disputes with other writers, such as Hsün-tzǔ, the disputes concern matters closely related to the text. Thus Duyvendak's hypothesis better satisfies our fifth demand in that his paraphrase is much more literal and is much more rooted in the text than is Waley's. To sum up, Duyvendak satisfies two demands better than Waley and does as well by the other three. This amounts to saying that the former explains everything with a greater degree of economy, and is to be preferred from a historical point of view. We have, of course, consistently ignored all aesthetic and stylistic factors since they have no historical relevance.

For our present purposes it does not really matter which translation is better since we are more interested in the structure of the dispute than in its outcome. Our judgment of preference was thrown in just to illustrate how one might come to prefer one hypothesis to the other. The important point, then, is that we can construe the dispute as being like a scientific one provided that we make our initial assumption that the text makes sense and can be translated so as to give an intelligible result. It is sometimes said that in science we have to begin by supposing that nature can be understood, but this is an entirely different sense of "understand." When we speak of understanding a text we mean it literally, but when we speak of understanding nature we mean it only metaphorically. What we mean is simply that we can formulate laws that hold true for nature. There is a basic difference between the historical dispute we have been considering and a dispute in one of the natural sciences. Nevertheless, despite the differences in subject matter, there is a strong analogy between the procedure used in the two cases: we find something to be explained, we formulate hypotheses to explain it, we have certain necessary conditions for the adequacy of a hypothesis, and finally we compare hypotheses for economy. It is instructive to see that in an area which seems far removed from science, and whose subject matter *is* far removed, there is still surprisingly little difference in the methodology used. It may still be that the historical method is irreducible to any sort of scientific method, but textual criticism is not the sort of case that one would choose to substantiate such a thesis.

The assumption which most distinguishes this sort

of reasoning from a scientific inquiry, the assumption of the intelligibility of the text, is again closely related to Collingwood's notion of imaginative reconstruction. One is in general supposed to form a hypothesis in such a way as to put oneself in the position of the historical figure in the sense of being able to imagine what he was trying to accomplish and what sorts of strategies appeared open to him in achieving these ends. As the historical figure here is a philosopher (or group of philosophers), we are required to formulate a position which we take him to be defending. Individual passages in the text will then be arguments and we must imagine an alternative position for them to be directed against just as we must postulate an opposing concentration of troops in order to understand a military outflanking movement of troops. The assumption of the intelligibility of an ancient text is hence a special case of a more general process described by Collingwood.

7 Statistical History

Our next example will be Charles Tilly's analysis of the Vendean counterrevolution of the 1790s.[20] A revolution or counterrevolution of large scale presents the historian with a peculiar problem in that he seems to be required to ask and answer certain questions about mass ideology that are not nearly so prominent in other sorts of historical studies. Bullock's assessment of von Papen, above, illustrates the historian's attempt to establish the intentions and motives behind the actions of an individual historical figure. Our last sample illustrated the historian's attempt to discover the ideology represented by a particular text, and presumed to be held by a group of persons living in the specific historical period. But even there the historian was not trying to discover the ideology of the Chinese masses, but was concerned only with the beliefs of one school of intellectuals. In fact, it is true generally of intellectual history that it is much easier to discover the basic beliefs of the intellectuals, who have left behind writings, than it is to penetrate the beliefs and feelings of the masses. For this reason it is relatively unusual for the writer of intellectual history to succeed in tracing accurately the downward spread of ideas in a society. Working from the other end, the social historian may succeed in describing the social structure and the social customs of a society during a given period, but, if no revolution occurred therein, he is not likely to tell us much about popular belief. He may tell us how people behaved, but he is not likely to tell us how they felt about the way they behaved. There are obvious difficulties in discovering the beliefs of the masses, and it is only within the last ten years or so that the art of polling has become something of a science. Furthermore, most polling has concerned political issues and has been largely limited to respondents in industrially developed societies. When dealing with a past age for which there are no such techniques, it is quite natural for the historian to write off popular belief as an imponderable.

When a revolution occurs, however, questions about popular actions and attitudes take on a new force and urgency. The historian is tempted to ask what made the people revolt and to look for the answer in ideology. Even if he should think that popular belief has little or nothing to do with the revolution, he still seems constrained to find out what the popular beliefs were in order to show that they were not significant. Some of the historians cited earlier, such as Mowat, have dealt with mass movements in non-revolutionary society, and could conceivably have asked similar questions. Mowat might have asked why the mass of the British people in the twenties wanted higher wages and better housing. Or, to draw an example from direct observation, we could ask why it is in postwar America that such a large number of persons have wanted a college education. The answers may seem obvious—that the British workers believed they would be happier if they had higher wages and better housing, and that Americans believe going to college is the best way of getting ahead in the world. If one is prepared to accept answers of this sort, then the questions have such obvious answers that they are not worth asking. If, on the other hand, one is not satisfied with answers of this sort, the question becomes very difficult indeed. A social psychologist might, for instance, attack the second question through an elaborate questionnaire in which he would try to isolate various motives for going to college. In this way he might find out which of the following sorts of factors are dominant: purely economic motives, social prestige, simple obedience to the desires of parents, intellectual curiosity, and so on. Since people will not respond honestly to direct questions of this sort, the questionnaire would have to be cleverly designed. This is the sort of technique needed to answer such a question in any very illuminating way, and, of course, it is exactly the sort of technique not ordinarily at the disposal of the historian. Hence, questions of this sort are ordinarily not asked, sometimes because they are too hard and sometimes because they are too easy. But when a revolution occurs these basically psychological or sociological questions become so important and interesting that historians are likely to try to answer them without having the necessary techniques. This practice, which leads to pure speculation and bad history, is the sort of thing that Tilly is particularly concerned to avoid.

When a revolution or large-scale counterrevolution such as the Vendean one occurs, the masses begin to act as they have not acted before. When they do not revolt but continue to act as before, it is relatively easy to avoid asking what makes them act as they do; but in a revolution, when everyone is acting in new ways, the question of what makes them act in these new ways cannot be pushed under the rug. One way of answering such a question is simply to introduce a new ideology in order to explain the new actions. In such a case the historian usually has independent evidence to the effect that the new ideology suddenly became more widespread at the time. This independent evidence usually does indeed show that the new ideology spread quickly among certain strata of the society, but it often does not show that the group rebelling most strongly was the one most strongly influenced by the ideology. The traditional historian's move here is simply to postulate that they were influenced by the ideology in order to explain their rebelling at all. The pattern here is quite different from that of Waley-Duyvendak. There we started with a source which constituted at least a large part of the evidence, and our authors tried to construct hypotheses as to the ideology of the Taoists that would fit the evidence and explain it as economically as possible. In accounts of the Vendean revolt we also have a hypothesis as to the ideology of, say, the petit bourgeois in 1789, but traditional historians are typically less interested in adducing evidence for the hypothesis than they are in using the hypothesis to explain mass action.

In terms of general scientific procedure there is nothing wrong in explaining new data on the basis of a hypothesis one has previously accepted; in fact, if the hypothesis can be used successfully in this way it is confirmed to some degree. Further, there are many hypotheses in science which have been introduced simply for their explanatory power and which are such that all the evidence for the hypothesis is indirect. This is true of most hypotheses involving such hypothetical constructs as electrons, quanta, and so on. The parallel in history would be to introduce an ideology which explains mass action during a revolution even if there is no direct evidence to the effect that the revolutionaries were attracted by that ideology, or even knew about it. Such a course, however, seems inappropriate for history because we are not dealing with subatomic phenomena which are not directly observable; it is a basic historical assumption that an important historical event in a reasonably well-documented period will not be felt solely through its consequences but will also leave direct traces of its own. For example, one might find that one could explain certain social and economic changes in America in the 1880s by hypothesizing a war with a large European power. But one does not conclude that the war occurred unless one can find reports of battles and other pertinent records. Tilly thinks that the traditional historians of the French revolution and the Vendean counterrevolution have brought in hypothetical ideologies in much the way that our hypothetical war might be posited. Tilly's problem, then, is to explain mass action, but to explain it in some more adequate way.

Most of the earlier historians of the Vendean counterrevolution had distinguished three important social classes: the priests, the nobles and the peasants. As they took the motivation of the priests and nobles to be self-evident, their main question was that of discovering the motivation of the peasants. Tilly points out that the historians favorable to the revolution tended to describe the Vendean peasant as rigidly religious in a primitive sort of way. Thus Savary says that for such a peasant, religion meant "lighting a candle for St. Michael, and one for his serpent" (p. 34). Tilly's quotation from a Catholic historian, Abbé Deniau, describes much the same set of facts, but with approval and with a different emphasis:

> Confined in their Bocage as a result of the difficulties of communication with the adjoining territories, the Vendeans lived a familial existence; people from the same neighborhood ordinarily met only on Sunday and the days of markets or fairs. . . . These sedentary habits had naturally preserved them from the pernicious influences of the so-called civilization of the time; so they were profoundly religious, full of lively and simple faith, always faithful to their Christian duties: celebration of all the holy days, prayers morning and evening, participation in the sacraments, fasts and abstinence, recita-

tion, at vespers, at Rosary, everything was accomplished
punctually and with the most edifying piety. [P. 37]

Tilly adds, "After a good deal more description in this
vein, the author goes on to portray the Vendean as the
spontaneous defender of wronged religion" (p. 37). Then
he quotes another such historian, Muret:

> When the news of the king's death resounded like
> a thunderbolt through the Bocage, it aroused a sentiment
> of horror and deep shock. . . . Everything that had hap-
> pened in the last three years must have accustomed
> men's minds to crime, and yet this one was beyond
> imagining. People could hardly believe that the scoun-
> drels had dared to stain their hands with the blood of
> the Lord's anointed, and they wondered what plague
> would strike the earth after such a transgression. No
> more than an occasion was needed to touch off the emo-
> tions that were boiling in everyone's heart. [P. 37]

This "occasion" turned out to be the imposition of military
conscription by the central revolutionary government.
Concerning Muret's method, Tilly remarks:

> With the greatest of ease, Muret swings among
> the levels of ideology (royalism), motives (righteous in-
> dignation) and causes (this state of mind plus the "occa-
> sion" offered by the imposition of conscription). These
> gymnastics are quite impressive, since they allow the
> author to judge the counter-revolution, assign the re-
> sponsibility for its occurrence, judge the intentions of the
> principal participants, and explain it, all at the same
> time. [P. 37]

Since Tilly is as interested here in the methods used to
explain the counterrevolution as in the explanation itself,
he takes the time to criticize those explanations of the
counterrevolution which center on establishing the intentions of some group or other. His most serious criticism of
this method is that it discourages comparative analysis:

> So long as one holds an individualistic, psychological
> view of the actors, he will find it hard to see the rele-

vance of systematic comparison with other actors; what seems to matter is the sympathetic understanding of those who did something, not of those who did not. Many writers have noted that the people of the larger cities, the Loire Valley and the plains surrounding the Vendee generally supported the Revolution. Then they have passed on to what they regarded as the business at hand, the description of the men who resisted the Revolution. They have not given serious attention to the most searching question of all: why the Vendee, and not somewhere else? In the rush away from this question, historians of the counter-revolution have also left behind the tasks of delineating accurately the territory whose inhabitants took active part in the fighting, as well as determining exactly what sorts of people participated most vigorously. Without these tasks accomplished, it is hard to see how a valid explanation could even begin. And until statements of the order of "The peasants were religious" are translated at least into others like "The peasants were *more* religious than those elsewhere, and religious peasants are more likely to resist revolution", it is even harder to see how any explanation could be verified. [P. 47]

Tilly then suggests that a sociological approach be substituted for the traditional questions about intentions. He would ask questions like these:

1) What were the real differences between the areas in which the counter-revolution sprang up in 1793 and those which remained calm, a) under the Old Regime, b) during the early Revolution? 2) What was distinctive about both the organization and the composition of the *groups* which actively supported the Revolution, and those which actively resisted it, over the period 1789–93? 3) What significant changes in the social situation occurred during the same period? 4) Is there any general knowledge available that helps to assemble coherently the answers to these three questions and the fact of counter-revolution? [P. 50]

To aid in such an analysis he presents some tables which can be compiled from available evidence. I will list them simply as I, II, and III.[21]

TABLE I
Percent Distribution by Major Social Category

Category	Estimated Occupational Distribution of Adult Males Rural Communes	Army Volunteers	Bearing Arms with Rebels (Revolutionary Sources)	Bearing Arms with Rebels (Counter-Rev. Sources)	Aiding Rebels (All Sources)
Noble	0.29	0.0	0.61	0.0	1.95
Priest	1.28	0.0	0.0	0.0	8.87
Bourgeois	8.03	28.96	14.72	1.62	21.00
Hired Hand	14.28	}	6.75	9.43	3.68
Other Peasant	44.77	} 4.52	20.86	53.91	37.88
Weaver	10.62	}	31.29	14.56	8.44
Other Artisan	20.73	} 66.51	25.77	20.48	18.18
Number Identified	—	221	1121	841	801

TABLE II
[Social and Political Activity in Two Districts Compared]

	Counter-Revolutionary District of Cholet	Revolutionary District of Saumur
Number of reported (counter) rebels per 1000 population	9.83	0.04
Emigrés reported per 1000 population	4.1	7.1
Percent of priests taking Civil Constitution oath	5.3	64.7
Army enlistments per 1000 population, 1791–92	2.3	7.0

TABLE III
Estimated Occupational Distribution of Adult Males:
Rural Communes (Per Cent)

	Revolutionary District [Saumur]	Counter-Rev. District [Cholet]
Noble	0.47	0.16
Priest	1.42	1.10
Bourgeois	1.69	8.43
Hired Hand	29.19	11.26
Other Peasant	51.11	41.13
Weaver	2.35	21.27
Other Artisan	13.77	16.64

Table I tends to indicate that the counterrevolution was not just a peasant rebellion and emphasizes the important role played by the artisans. Table II compares the most counterrevolutionary district of Southern Anjou, Cholet, and the most undividedly revolutionary district,

Saumur. The comparison indicates the counterrevolutionary district had dramatically fewer priests taking the civil constitution oath and many fewer army enlistments. The first important conclusion to be drawn from these tables is that it is wrong to identify the counterrevolution with any single social class or even with the priests and peasants in cahoots. For example, Table I shows us that artisans, as a class, were disproportionately involved in the counterrevolution, but also that they furnished most of the volunteers for the revolutionary army.

The fact that revolutionary and counterrevolutionary districts were clearly demarcated and existed side by side gives Tilly the clue which takes him to his suggested explanation. Instead of trying to pin the responsibility on a particular class or classes, who might be assumed to share an ideology, he tries to assess the degree of homogeneity within a district and connect this quality with its revolutionary or counterrevolutionary character. He therefore thinks that it makes sense to investigate further the differences in social organization between revolutionary and counterrevolutionary districts. For this we look to Table III. Tilly thinks here that the lower proportion of hired hands in the counterrevolutionary district indicates that the peasants were little involved in the money economy as compared to those in the revolutionary district. On the other hand, he notes a much higher proportion of artisians and bourgeois in the counterrevolutionary district. Thus, he concludes that the counterrevolutionary district shows more internal differences (between money-oriented town-dwelling artisans and rural barter-oriented peasants) than the revolutionary district:

> To put the matter all too baldly, such a social situation (that of the counter-revolutionary district) is much more favorable to violent local conflict between "old" and "new," "backward" and "progressive" than is a uniformly advanced, or a uniformly backward, social setting. In fact, it is not far off the mark to say that throughout the

West, the peaks of counter-revolutionary activity were
not in the backward sections so much as at the junctions
of rural and urban ways of life. [P. 55]

Tilly does not propose this as the sole explanation of
counterrevolution; and in this article, which is concerned
mainly with methodology, he does not attempt to give
such an explanation. He further qualifies his approach by
suggesting that there is still room for discussion of ideology
in explaining the counterrevolution and that talk of motives is not necessarily irrelevant. However, one can easily
see how Tilly's account might be elaborated into an explanation. For instance, if one asks why it is that areas
with greater internal differences supported the counterrevolution, the answer might be that an area transitional
between the new money economy of rational agriculture
and the old purely traditional agrarian economy might
not function effectively as a unit. It might then be that
while the standard of living has not yet approached that
of the modernized districts, and is still approximately that
of the archaic districts, many of the traditional satisfac-
tions have been lost, owing to change of customs and overthrow of institutions. Such factors as these might make
the residents of a district more dissatisfied generally and
more prone to rebellion against any sort of central government, royalist or revolutionary. The general dissatisfaction
might then combine with other factors to produce a
counterrevolution. Of course, this explanation is an unsupported hypothesis which would then have to be at
least partly verified by examining the economic conditions of the region. The next step, which Tilly does not
take and for which the evidence may be lacking, would
be an economic comparison between the two districts
which are compared socially and politically in Tables II
and III. By reasoning in some way similar to this there is
a possibility of constructing a hypothesis which would explain the counterrevolution and which could be supported

by statistical evidence of one sort or another. Thus, we could get an explanation of a historical event which would be entirely different from the sorts of explanations considered up to this point. The basic rationale is a simple one: many important historical events, perhaps most, have their origin in social movements of one sort or another. Contemporary social movements, such as the increasing tendency for Americans to send their children to college, can be explained by the methods of sociology and social psychology which resolve themselves ultimately into comparative statistics. There is nothing about the present world which makes these methods applicable to it in a way in which they would not be applicable to past times —provided, of course, that documentary evidence is plentiful enough to permit compilation of the relevant statistics. In short, if sociology of the present is possible there is no a priori reason why sociology of the past should be impossible, at least as long as it does not depend on questionnaires.

The crucial role of the sociological study lies at least as much in telling us what has to be explained as in explaining it. Collingwood's methods suffer from the defect that they do not tell us *which persons* in the historical situation we must identify with. In some cases the people who stayed in their houses and hoarded groceries may have played as important a role as those who conducted reigns of terror. The sociological study, to the extent that it is possible, tells us which groups of people were crucial, either for their actions or their non-actions, and these are the people that we must come to understand. In some cases one must not only identify with such figures as generals or politicians, but also put oneself in the position of a typical peasant who, perhaps, did little more than withhold his active support from a popular movement of the time.

It should now be clear that the use of comparative statistics does not in itself give an explanation, historical or sociological, of any event. However, in just the way that it may suggest to the historian whom he might want to identify with sympathetically, it may also suggest to him what needs to be explained and what facts might be used in giving that explanation.

8 Economic History

One of the peculiarities of economic history is its seeming indirectness. The economic historian may have to spend many years studying apparently uninteresting questions, such as the extent of the English sugar trade with Morocco in the sixteenth and seventeenth centuries, in order to finally build up a picture of the international trade at the time. This picture has obvious historical importance and value, but the pieces which go into the picture, while interesting to the historian who puts them together, seem more trivial to the non-specialist than the pieces out of which other sorts of history are put together. In order to answer his question a historian may have to trace each shipload of a given commodity arriving at a particular port during a given period; other economic historians will be simultaneously doing the same thing for other commodities at other ports and, when everyone is done, it may be possible to discover the patterns of world trade and trace the flow of money during the period. It is almost as if the military historian had to establish that a battle took place by studying diaries left by individual soldiers who took part in the battle; if he had to proceed in this way it might take him years of research to discover when and where the battle took place, and he might have to leave it to others to establish the significance of the battle. The difference is, of course, that people of past ages have always recognized the importance of battles and have always left us descriptions of whole battles rather than of tiny pieces of them. The descriptions may be inaccurate, biased, and distorted in any number of ways, but at least the historian has raw materials of the right sort to begin with. On the other hand, the opening up of a new trade or a rise in unemployment may have been more important than the outcome of any number of battles, but the reporting of it is likely to be far more sketchy. Although there may be a considerable body of documents relating to individual events (the sailing of a ship, or a person's not being able to find work), only the cumulative statistics matter, and the historian will probably have to compile these for himself. It has only been in relatively recent times that departments of Commerce and Labor have put out masses of economic information which is useful as it stands.

The basic problem behind the passage to be discussed, from E. G. Campbell's *Reorganization of the American Railroad System, 1893–1900*, is that of assessing the consequences of the panic and depression of 1893, one of the business cycles to which America has always been subject.[22] For the reasons given above, this question has to be studied piecemeal, and one of the most important pieces is the position of the railroads at the time. Actually, one cannot even study the effects of the panic on all railroads at once, and one might conceivably have to take each railroad in turn. It is obvious that the depression had an adverse effect on most railroads and many did fail within the next few years. However, one cannot assume that all the railroads that failed during those years did so as a result of the depression. To settle this question, Campbell attempts to categorize the railroads that did fail. The major failures included three great transcontinental systems: the Northern Pacific, Union Pacific, and the Santa Fe; four prominent eastern trunk lines: the Reading, the New York, Lake Erie and Western, the Baltimore and Ohio, and the Norfolk and Western; and one large southern system. These failures, taken together, were of great importance and had profound economic consequences. However, Campbell quickly decides that the important classification is not a regional one; different roads in the same regions failed for different reasons. His ultimate classification is three-fold: those failing because of overexpansion, such as the Norfolk and Western and the Northern Pacific; those whose failures were primarily attributable to known mistakes of past managements, which were publicly known long before receivership, such such as the Erie and Santa Fe; those whose bankruptcies were followed by sensational disclosures of poor, or even criminal, mismanagement, such as the B & O, the Reading, and others.

The importance of this classification is that it separates those failures which could be laid to the panic of 1893 from those which could not. That is, a railroad whose management had been consistently pirating it over a long period of time could be expected to fail sooner or later, and, if the panic had not occurred, something else would have thrown it into bankruptcy. Mere overexpansion, however, does not necessarily bring about the failure of a business; in other circumstances the same expansion might be beneficial to the railroad, to the economy in general, and might even be essential in an expanding economy. It is just that these particular expansions, while they may or may not have been reasonable in themselves, happened to come at a bad time. These, then, are the assumptions presupposed by Campbell's classification (and a large part of his book is based on this classification). If the historian admits them it enormously simplifies his task because it allows him to largely disregard railroads in the second two classifications as far as the depression is concerned, once he has established that they suffered from bad management. Eliminating them leaves only the Norfolk and Western and the Northern Pacific, which Campbell examines in detail. In the case of the latter he decides that overexpansion is only one factor and that the road would have failed in the end anyway because the expansion was frenzied rather than rational and was accompanied by all kinds of corruption. Ultimately, it is only the Norfolk and Western whose failure Campbell lays peculiarly to expansion and to the depression, and it is his account of the tribulations of that road that we will follow.

As we have seen, whenever there is causal explanation, counterfactual statements will also be involved. But here Campbell gives us a much more precise counterfactual than those implied by Mowat's account of public housing and the dole. Campbell tries to make a case for the counterfactual assertion that if the panic of '93 had not occurred and business conditions had been normal, the Norfolk and Western would have prospered instead of failing. He specifies the cause of failure thus: "a company which had been efficiently managed and had excellent prospects for the future, completed an expansion program just before the panic of 1893 swept the country, and in the weakened financial position which expansion had invoked the depression proved too much for it" (pp. 35–36). This causal explanation and the counterfactual mentioned above are inextricably linked, as an analysis of the explanation will show.

In the years just before 1893 the Norfolk and Western had extended its lines into Ohio, into the not yet exploited mineral regions of West Virginia, and into the surrounding territory to the south and west:

> These regions were being slowly developed and coal and iron were being mined, but as the tonnage carried by the Norfolk increased, its revenues were not proportionately enlarged. The chief items of freight, coal and iron in this region and cotton on the southeastern parts of the system, were all low class freight, paying very low rates, despite the long hauls to markets. As a result net revenue was not improving at all.
>
> By 1891 conditions had begun to be somewhat alarming. Nevertheless an authority on railroad investments still foresaw a prosperous future for the system:

Some people anticipate a serious diminution of the surplus available for dividends in 1892; but even if this forecast proves correct, there will be no cause for apprehension. There can be no doubt whatever that the system possesses such inherent strength and such brilliant prospects that it will resume its prosperous career as soon as it emerges from the state of suspense its affairs have been in since the commencement of work on the Ohio extension.[23]

However, in October 1892 the semiannual dividend was only 1 per cent instead of the usual 1½ percent, and it was paid in a scrip convertible into debentures. Thereafter dividends on the preferred stock ceased entirely:

The company's annual report for the year ending December 31, 1892, revealed the difficult position in which the Norfolk found itself when the panic of 1893 occurred. The gross revenue for the year was the largest in the history of the system. More passengers and more freight were carried one mile during the year than ever before; the tonnage of iron ore, pig iron, coal, coke, stone and zinc established new records. But the net income showed a decrease from that of the year before. A decline in the price of cotton had created an acute depression in that industry, resulting in a 54 per cent loss in the number of bales transported by the road. The rates for carrying pig iron fell lower than ever and at the same time the tonnage of high class freight declined. The average rate received for freight was only 0.537 cents per ton mile for the system as a whole; to this the 0.663 cent rate received by the other roads in the same region offers a revealing contrast. [P. 37]

However, the road was still solvent at this point and Campbell brings in a "historical accident" to help explain the eventual collapse. In June 1893, a receivership had been mistakenly declared in connection with a debt of $44,000 which was owed to a creditor in West Virginia. Although the Norfolk and Western was ready and able to pay the debt, the cash set aside for it had been tied up at the request of a creditor of the claimant, and the money could only be paid over to the railroad's creditor on a court order. When the situation was clarified, the receivership was quickly annulled, but, as Campbell says, "during the three-day receivership the credit of the road had been damaged; that a great system, capitalized at $103,500,000 apparently could not pay a debt of a few thousand dollars seemed inexplicable and roused various rumors of imminent total collapse." (p. 38). Another difficulty which the system faced was the maturity of $525,000 worth of 6 per cent debenture bonds early in 1894. To cover this, more bonds were issued which would mature in 1900, but the circumstances under which they were offered indicated the weakness of the system's credit and aroused more suspicions:

> A continued decline in freight rates, despite a further increase in the gross revenues, brought a still smaller net income in the year ending December 31, 1893, and for the first time in years there was a deficit, $99,742, under fixed charges. The net fell off to $2,833,157, having decreased more than $500,000 in three years. At the same time, because of the additional mileage that had been added to the system and other capital expenditures, the fixed charges were growing every year. Contrary to the expectations of the management, the net did not increase with the gross receipts because of the increased operating expenses of the greater mileage and the concurrent steady decline of rates. In 1894 the average rate per ton mile for freight had fallen to 0.451 cents, a loss of 10 per cent from the figure the year before. This decline in rates, in turn, was due to several cooperating factors: the road's proportion of low class freight was constantly rising and that of high class freight was constantly dropping; although the Norfolk had to carry its coal twice as far as rival roads to transport it from the mines to tidewater, it was forced to cut its rates sufficiently to meet the retail market price its competitors charged; finally, about 439 miles of the 1567 mile total length of the system, 28 per cent, lay in regions which were yet to be developed and, since the depression prevented the rapid exploitation which had

been expected there, rates had to be cut to get any trade. Had the depression been postponed until the Norfolk had had time to develop these regions, the system's strength would have been immeasureably increased, but instead the depression caught the system at the precise moment of its greatest weakness. [Pp. 38–39]

In the face of these difficulties the road failed in February 1896. Thus, Campbell's whole argument adds up to the conclusion that if the panic had not occurred, or even if it had been delayed a year or two, the road would have pulled through, a conclusion reinforced by the fact that the system later became one of the country's leading railroads. It seems even more plausible when we look at the general pattern of railway development. When a railroad expands, as the Norfolk and Western did, into new territory, the usual pattern is for the land to be settled by railway employees in railway towns. Later, persons not connected with the railroad greatly expand the towns and engage in farming and/or industry. This then creates much more business for the railroad and in the long run greatly strengthens its position. However, the system is at a weak point when it has just completed its expansion (and almost certainly gone into heavy debt for this purpose) but before the new businesses have had a chance to develop. It is just at this point that the depression caught the Norfolk and Western, as Campbell has shown. Using the same techniques he is able to say how great a factor the depression was in the other railroad failures of the time. In a similar way, someone else could do this for other industries and the consequences of the depression could then be established. One can view economic history as the history of business cycles and all that they include; Campbell's account would then be a part of such a history and would explain the relationship of a particular industry to one of these cycles.

Let us now look at the sorts of arguments used. It has often been pointed out that history does not usually formulate general laws but makes use of them. For most kinds of history, however, even the general laws used cannot be formulated precisely. We have already seen how difficult it was to state the general laws presupposed by Mowat even though there clearly were some such presuppositions. By contrast, in this case all sorts of general laws can be clearly formulated; as in science, there are some relatively technical concepts such as gross revenue, net revenue, operating ratio, bonded debt, and so on. These concepts represent variables, and relationships can be stated that hold between the variables. Thus, net revenue is a function of gross revenue, fixed expenses, and operating expenses; gross revenue, at least for freight, is a function of total ton-miles and freight rates. One can even state less precise but still fairly reliable generalizations concerning the total ton-milage in a year, the degree of industrialization and development of the region served, and the state of the local economy. Most of Campbell's inferences follow from laws such as these. Often the laws are so sufficiently well known that they do not need to be stated; thus, the explanation of the final failure rests on the fact that the causes Campbell enumerates brought about net deficits, and it is a trivially true law of finance that no business can arrive at yearly deficits indefinitely and still maintain solvency. Because of the relatively precise nature of these laws Campbell is able to produce counterfactuals which are much more specific than most counterfactuals asserted or implied by historians. This kind of economic history occupies a position somewhere between political history and the natural sciences in this respect, reflecting the fact that economics is a more exact science than politics but is less exact than the natural sciences.

Another dimension for comparison is the use of models in the sense of systems which can be deduced from axioms and which may or may not be applicable to an actual state of affairs (if it is applicable, the state of affairs is a model of the system although other terminology is sometimes used). This method characterizes not only the natural sciences, but economics as well, and one would expect it to have some uses in economic history. While Campbell does not use it explicitly, the sorts of principles we have just discussed could certainly be taken as the rules of a game. In Part II we will see that there is a close connection between games and models. Further, because of its relative preciseness, economic history may well serve as a sort of paradigm around which other sorts of history will congregate in the future.

9 The History of Ideas

Our next example of historiography is drawn from J. Huizinga's *The Waning of the Middle Ages,* specifically his chapter on the political and military value of chivalrous ideas.[24] Prior to this chapter he has already explained the nature of chivalry and established the fact that chivalrous ideas were common among the aristocracy of Europe in the fifteenth century; he is here trying to see what sorts of effects these ideas had both for the practical life of the time and for later times. Since chivalry amounted to an ideology, Huizinga attempts the difficult task of showing how an ideology affects practical action. After following his account, it will be interesting to compare his way of dealing with an ideology with Tilly's. In many ways Huizinga's book is a sort of second-order history. While he is sometimes directly concerned with the history of ideas, for the most part he does not try to establish historical facts, even about the existence and spread of ideologies, and his documentation is rather sparse. He takes for granted the standard historical facts of the time and tries to interpret those facts; to this extent he is like Mowat, but where Mowat attempted to fit the events into patterns, Huizinga is more interested in relating the events to ideas and ideologies.

The chapter has two main theses: first, that chivalrous ideas were often the direct cause of political and military actions which would otherwise be almost inexplicable; second, that the goals of chivalry had important intellectual consequences and that traces of them can be found even in modern ideas of international law and world government. On the first score Huizinga is, of course, practicing scientific history (in Collingwood's sense) in not assuming that all actions attributed to chivalrous motives by the actors themselves or their contemporaries were in fact chivalrous:

> Chivalry during the Middle Ages was, on the one hand, the great source of tragic political errors, exactly as are nationalism and racial pride at the present day. On the other, it tended to disguise well-adjusted calculations under the appearance of generous aspirations. . . . The gravest political error which France could commit was the creation of a quasi-independent Burgundy, and it had a chivalrous reason for its avowed motive: King John, that knightly muddle-head, wished to reward the courage shown by his son at Poitiers by an extraordinary liberality. . . . The stubborn anti-French policy of the dukes of Burgundy after 1419, although dictated by the interests of their house, was justified in the eyes of contemporaries by the duty of exacting an exemplary vengeance for the murder of Montereau. [P. 94]

The key to Huizinga's distinction between an act which was really motivated by chivalry and one which he believes not to have been so motivated is his statement that the policy of the dukes of Burgundy was actually in accordance with the interests of their house. If an action could have been motivated both by practical interests or by chivalry Huizinga assumes the real motive to be the former and concludes that chivalry came into play only in explaining a policy adopted for other reasons. Of course,

Huizinga may be doing this just to be on the safe side. That is, his thesis is that chivalry influenced actual behavior significantly, and it may be that in arguing for this thesis he discards doubtful cases and assumes an action not to be motivated by chivalry when there is another possibility. However, he may be doing more than this, and many historians would subscribe to the rule: when there are two possible motives, one material and one ideological, give preference to the material motive. If the historian does this, it is because of his experience with people; such a rule is, in effect, a psychological generalization that people are more touched by their material needs and wants than by ideological considerations. Although it is the sort of psychological principle that psychologists do not actually discuss, it appeals to common sense. The historian cannot wait for science to answer all the questions which he would like to ask of it, and he has no alternative but to rely on his common sense in such cases. Thus it is that Huizinga does not attribute the policy of the dukes of Burgundy to chivalry. On the other hand, he is on safer ground when he *does* attribute King John's action to chivalry. It was approximately the worst policy for France that the king could have followed, and we can imagine no other motive for the creation of a quasi-independent Burgundy than John's desire to reward his son. Huizinga quite rightly puts it down to chivalry.

Huizinga next makes a much larger claim for the influence of chivalry on politics:

> Now there was one among the political aspirations of the epoch where the chivalrous ideal was implied in the nature of the enterprise itself, namely, the recovery of the Holy Sepulchre. The highest political ideal which all the kings of Europe were obliged to profess was still symbolized by Jerusalem. [P. 95]

One could certainly imagine practical motives for the later crusades such as the conquering of new territory or

101

the gaining of an economic advantage. It could be another case where chivalry was used as propaganda to cover up the real motives. However, Huizinga here argues not just from the existence of a desire to go crusading, but from the particular direction which this desire took:

> Here the contrast between the real interest of Christendom and the form the idea took is most striking. The Europe of 1400 was confronted by an Eastern question of supreme urgency: that of repulsing the Turks who had just taken Adrianople and wiped out the Serbian kingdom. The imminent danger ought to have concentrated all efforts in the Balkans. Yet the imperative task of European politics does not disengage itself from the old idea of the crusades. People only succeeded in seeing the Turkish question as a secondary part of the sacred duty in which their ancestors had failed: the conquest of Jerusalem.
>
> The conquest of Jerusalem could not but present itself to the mind as a work of piety and of heroism— that is to say, of chivalry. In the councils on Eastern politics the heroic ideal preponderated more than in ordinary politics, and this it is which explains the very meagre success of the war against the Turks. Expeditions which, before all else, required patient preparation and minute inquiry, tended, more than once, to be romanticized, so to speak, from the very outset. The catastrophe of Nicopolis had proved the fatal folly of undertaking, against a very warlike enemy, an expedition of great importance as light-heartedly as if it were a question of going to kill a handful of heathen peasants in Prussia or in Lithuania.
>
> In the fifteenth century each king still felt virtually bound to set out and recapture Jerusalem. When Henry V of England, dying at Paris in 1422, in the midst of his career of conquest, was listening to the reading of the seven penitential psalms, he interrupted the officiating priest at the words *Benigne fac, domine, in bona voluntate tua Sion, ut aedificentur muri Jerusalem,* and declared that he had intended to go and conquer Jerusalem, after having re-established peace in France. . . .
> [Pp. 95–96]

102

There is a great difference between explaining an individual action, like that of King John, and a mass action such as a crusade. However, Huizinga is not necessarily saying that everyone who went on a crusade did so out of chivalry, and he can admit that many individuals went for many different reasons. Rather, he is saying that chivalry was enough of a factor among the influential persons of the time to divert them from the real enemy and what should have been their primary objectives to less important objectives. Again, the principle is that if a person or group of persons act in what can be seen to be an irrational way in terms of their actual interests we then look for ideological motives. Here there is a handy ideological motive, well reflected in the literature of the time, which we can bring in to explain the diversion from the primary objective. Of course, there are always other possible explanations for a diversion, such as stupidity or misinformation. Here the explanation in terms of misinformation is inadequate because the Turkish military conquests were no secret, and we cannot reasonably suppose all the statesmen of the time to be too stupid to recognize a plain threat. Further, no historian who uses a method similar to Huizinga's can regard historical personages as wildly irrational or hopelessly stupid except in certain special cases where there is evidence to this effect. It is central to Huizinga's approach to attribute to persons or groups of persons motives for actions which they are known to have taken. He first imagines himself in the material position of the historical figure and then asks himself whether he would have taken the action which that person took. If he cannot imagine himself taking such an action then he imagines himself in the ideological position of chivalry and tries again; if he can then imagine himself taking the required action he considers that the action is explained by chivalry. This method works as long as the historical personalities do not trespass certain limits. Some attempts have been made to understand important historical figures

103

who were psychotic (by F. Wyatt, for instance), but the chances are that if the actions of a medieval king were mostly prompted by his momentary hallucinations, the historian could never understand his motivation; explanations in such a case would probably not be possible at all. This being the case, the historical method itself makes certain presuppositions about the figures studied, and we can at least say that Huizinga applies the method in a straightforward way, and draws the conclusion one would expect. It may not be a correct one, but, so long as we have no alternative way of dealing with this sort of problem, we can arrive at no more plausible one. The economic historian may be able to get along largely without sympathetic identification, but it is essential to what Huizinga is trying to do.

Another instance of the influence of chivalry was the institution of the duel between princes with a view to settling some political issue. These duels were elaborately prepared but seldom took place:

> In reading the summary of the carefully arranged preparations for these princely duels, we ask ourselves, if they were not a conscious feint, either to impose upon one's enemy, or to appease the grievances of one's own subjects. Are we not rather to regard them as an inextricable mixture of humbug and of a chimerical, but, after all, sincere, craving to conform to the life heroic, by posing before all the world as the champion of right, who does not hesitate to sacrifice himself for his people?
>
> How, otherwise, are we to explain the surprising persistence of those plans for princely duels? Richard II of England offers to fight, together with his uncles, the dukes of Lancaster, York, and Gloucester, against the king of France, Charles VI, and his uncles, the dukes of Anjou, Burgundy, and Berry. Louis of Orleans defies the king of England, Henry IV. Henry V of England challenges the dauphin before marching upon Agincourt. Above all, the duke of Burgundy displayed an almost frenzied attachment to this mode of settling a question.

In 1425 he challenged Humphrey, duke of Gloucester, in connection with the question of Holland. The motive, as always, is expressly formulated in these terms: "To prevent Christian bloodshed and destruction of the people, on whom my heart has compassion", I wish "that by my own body, this quarrel may be settled, without proceeding by means of wars, which would entail that many noblemen and others, both of your army and of mine, would end their days pitifully".

All was ready for the combat: the magnificent armour and the state dresses, the pavilions, the standards, the banners, the armorial tabards for the heralds, everything richly adorned with the duke's blazons and with his emblems, the flint-and-steel and the Saint Andrew's cross. The duke had gone in for a course of training "both by abstinence in the matter of food and by taking exercise to keep him in breath". He practised fencing every day in his park of Hesdin with the most expert masters. The detailed expenses entailed by this affair are found in the accounts published by de la Borde, but the combat did not take place.

This did not prevent the duke, twenty years later, from again wishing to decide a question touching Luxembourg by a single combat with the duke of Saxony. Towards the close of his life he is still vowing to engage in a hand-to-hand combat with the Grand Turk. [Pp. 96–97]

Here Huizinga's case is less convincing because it is too obvious. According to the chivalrous outlook which he has described, these duels are not really the *result* of chivalry but are a *part* of chivalry. That is, the proposing of duels might be looked upon simply as a part of that pattern of behavior which *constitutes* chivalry. If we take this view of the matter, the important question would then be whether such proposed duels had any important historical effects. It is not obvious that they did, and Huizinga does not even attempt to list any important consequences of these abortive duels. Thus we might conclude that these episodes tend to show that the princes of the time were in fact chivalrous, but we have to look further to see whether their chivalry was of historical importance.

Huizinga now cites cases where chivalry adversely affected military strategy and tactics:

> Froissart asserts that the knights of the Star had to swear never to fly more than four acres from the battlefield, through which rule soon afterwards more than ninety of them lost their lives. The article is not found in the statutes of the order, as published by Luc d'Achery; nevertheless, such formalism tallies well with the ideas of that epoch. Some days before the battle of Agincourt, the king of England, on his way to meet the French army, one evening passed by mistake the village which the foragers of his army had fixed upon as night-quarters. He would have had time to return, and he would have done it, if a point of honour had not prevented him. The king, "as chief guardian of the very laudable ceremonies of honour," had just published an order, according to which knights, while reconnoitring, had to take off their coat-armour, because their honor would not suffer knights to retreat, when accoutred for battle. Now, the king himself had put on his coat-armour, and so, having passed it by, he could not return to the village mentioned. He therefore passed the night in the place he had reached and also made the vanguard advance accordingly, in spite of the dangers that might have been incurred. [Pp. 98–99]

One could easily speculate forever about the king's real motives in this situation. For instance, he might have decided on practical grounds to extend his advance slightly but have given a chivalrous reason to sustain morale and to avoid explaining his decision. Such dual motivation is not uncommon. Captain Bernhard Rogge, of the German raider *Atlantis* in the Second World War, one day sighted a ship he took to be the liner *Queen Mary* in the Indian Ocean and steered away to avoid combat; he told his crew that such a valuable ship would certainly be escorted by a cruiser but admits that his real reason was that he did

not think that he could handle the *Queen Mary* alone.[25]
By this time chivalry was sufficiently diluted so that one
could admit running from a superior enemy, but the
enemy still had to be *greatly* superior. However, there is
no evidence that any such practical factor was present in
Henry V's mind, and such speculations really do not belong to history. It is often said in philosophy that one can
square *any* course of action with a number of different intentions and motives without being reduced to logical inconsistency. For instance, when one sees a man betting on
a horse at a race track it does not necessarily follow that
he believes that the horse will win; he may be a part
owner of the horse and bet on him for sentimental reasons
even though he thinks that the horse will lose. This being
the case, one could speculate endlessly on the real motive
for any historical action and keep inventing new motives
as long as one wants to. But it is clearly not the business
of the historian to do this. Generally, in explaining an action such as the king's further advance, the historian looks
to his evidence for motives as opposed to thinking them
up. Of course, there is ultimately no sharp line between
finding motives in the evidence and imagining them. It
always takes a certain amount of imagination and sympathetic identification to conceive of any motive at all and
there always has to be some evidence before one can im-
pute the motive to the character. At some point the historian has to use his own intuitive judgment and draw the
line as to which conceivable motives he is going to consider seriously; at some point the historian must stop and
rest his case in the same way that a jury must at some
point stop imagining possible avenues of innocence and
convict accused criminals of crimes. In this case Huizinga
convicts the king of chivalry, and it is probably true that
in at least some cases chivalry did influence what today
would be purely military decisions.

In the last part of his chapter Huizinga turns to
pure intellectual history and tries to show the effect of one

ideology upon another. In particular, he thinks that ideas
of international law and world government developed out
of the ideals of chivalry and implies that such international law as we have today is dependent on there having
once been a society with a chivalrous ideology. Of chivalrous ideas he says:

> In so far as they formed a system of rules of honour and
> precepts of virtue, they exercised a certain influence on
> the evolution of the laws of war. The law of nations
> originated in antiquity and in canon law, but it was
> chivalry which caused it to flower. The aspiration after
> universal peace is linked with the idea of crusades and
> with that of the orders of chivalry. Philippe de Mezieres
> planned his "Order of the Passion" to insure the good of
> the world. The young king of France—(this was written
> about 1388, when such great hopes were still entertained
> of the unhappy Charles VI)—will be easily able to con-
> clude peace with Richard of England, young like him-
> self and also innocent of bloodshed in the past. Let them
> discuss the peace personally; let them tell each other of
> the marvelous revelations which have already heralded
> it. Let them ignore all the futile differences which might
> prevent peace, if negotiations were left to the ecclesias-
> tics, to lawyers, and to soldiers. The king of France may
> fearlessly cede a few frontier towns and castles. Directly
> after the conclusion of peace the crusade will be pre-
> pared. Quarrels and hostilities will cease everywhere; the
> tyrannical governments of countries will be reformed; a
> general council will summon the princes of Christendom
> to undertake a crusade, in case sermons do not suffice to
> convert the Tartars, Turks, Jews, and Saracens. [P. 104]

In this passage Huizinga is really trying to establish no
more than that, for some medieval people, there was a
connection between the ideas of chivalry, the crusades,
and the hope of a universal peace; he asserts no connection with international law. However, he notes that in
1352 Sir Geoffroi de Charny addressed to the king a list of
"demandes," or questions of casuistry concerning jousts,
tournaments and war. Sir Geffroi is most interested in

jousts and tournaments, but questions concerning rules to be observed on the battlefield also appear in large numbers on his list of queries. Since Sir Geoffroi was also the founder of the order of the Star and made something of a profession of chivalry, this evidence establishes the connection between international law, in the sense of international rules of military conduct, and the other ideas of chivalry. Huizinga also mentions Honoré Bonet, a late-fourteenth-century ecclesiastical exponent of chivalry, who raises such questions as:

> May the king of France, waging war with England, take prisoner "the poor English, merchants, labourers of the soil and shepherds who tend their flocks in the fields"? The author answers in the negative; not only do Christian morals forbid it, but also "the honour of the age". He even goes so far as to extend the privilege of safe conduct in the enemy's country to the case of the father of an English student wishing to visit his sick son in Paris. [P. 105]

Huizinga does not pretend that any of these rules were observed in the barbaric warfare of the time, but he has gathered together enough sources to indicate that the connection between chivalry and rules which govern more than one nation existed in the thinking of the time. However, he argues that such few clemencies as were introduced at the time can be more plausibly attributed to the sentiment of honor and chivalry than to any fixed set of rules. We know that chivalry was prevalent and that there was some connection in the minds of some medieval people between the concept of honor and the observance of certain clemencies on the battlefield; we also know that there was no established international law at the time. The conclusion would be that any rules of combat which did arise only reflected actual practices, and the practices were the result of the chivalrous outlook. Thus the law comes last rather than first and is the effect rather than the cause. Actually, this seems to be no more than a historical hypothesis on Huizinga's part; to confirm or disconfirm it one would have to take presently existing international law, represented by such things as the rules for treating prisoners, and trace it back to the fourteenth century. One might then be able to trace it to chivalry or one might find along the way somewhere that quite different influences are mainly responsible for present-day international law.

In the following passage Huizinga tries to establish a similar connection between chivalry and patriotism:

> Taine said: "In the middle and lower classes the chief motive of conduct is self-interest. With an aristocracy the mainspring is pride. Now among the profound sentiments of man there is none more apt to be transformed into probity, patriotism and conscience, for a proud man feels the need of self-respect, and, to obtain it, he is led to deserve it." Is not this the point of view whence we must consider the importance of chivalry in the history of civilization? Pride assuming the features of a high ethical value, knightly self-respect preparing the way for clemency and right. These transitions in the domain of thought are real. In the passage quoted above from *Le Jouvencel* we noticed how chivalric sentiment passes into patriotism. All the best elements of patriotism —the spirit of sacrifice, the desire for justice and protection for the oppressed—sprouted in the soil of chivalry. It is in the classic country of chivalry, in France, that are heard, for the first time, the touching accents of love of the fatherland, irradiated by the sentiment of justice. [P. 106]

Here the basis of the argument is the supposed connection between both patriotism and chivalry and the sentiment of pride. Again, this is another historical hypothesis, suggested perhaps by psychological considerations, and it could be substantiated only by tracing patriotism and nationalism, as we now know these sentiments, to their sources. We might then discover, or not discover, a strong connection between patriotism and chivalry; this would obviously be a monumental task, and Huizinga does not attempt it. He points out that both patriotism and chivalry were at their strongest in France, but this fact is hardly sufficient to establish his conclusion; they might have existed primarily among different social or regional groups, and there might be other more important factors which were responsible for both. Consequently, much more work would have to be done on both hypotheses before we could reliably assert a strong connection between chivalry and either patriotism or international law as we know them.

The chapter concludes:

> Chivalry would never have been the ideal of life during several centuries if it had not contained high social values. Its strength lay in the very exaggeration of its generous and fantastic views. The soul of the Middle Ages, ferocious and passionate, could only be led by placing far too high the ideal towards which its aspirations should tend. [P. 106]

Here Huizinga has hit on an interesting fact: that one of the most barbarous of ages in practice also had some of the highest and least attainable ideals. However, his attempt to explain this anomaly seems to suggest that somehow the age is an independent entity which knows what is good for itself and how to treat itself; the age would then give itself an appropriate ideology. This, of course, is nonsense and cannot really be intended seriously; if Huizinga was not prepared to give a serious explanation he might better have contented himself with merely taking note of the anomaly. If an explanation of it were to be historical it would again have to be piecemeal. One would have to trace the ferocity peculiar to the age to see where it came from, and one would also have to trace the ideals to see where they came from: having done this one might be able to establish a common origin and specify the connection between them. If, on the other hand, one supposes, as Huizinga seems to, that there is some principle which always causes extreme ferocity to be accompanied

by extremely high ideals, the justification for such a principle could not be provided by history in the traditional
sense, but only by systematic psychology or sociology.
That is, to show that such a thing always has to happen
it is not sufficient to generalize over just the societies of
medieval Europe; rather, it would be necessary to have a
systematic theory whose applicability is not limited to any
particular places or times.

Huizinga starts by asserting that chivalry, thought
of as a system of ideas, influenced action in the political
and military spheres. He makes a good case for his assertion and suggests hypotheses connecting chivalry with
international law and patriotism. Here he does not really
substantiate the hypotheses, but they are intelligible and
might be substantiated. He ends by noting a phenomenon
and asking how it came to appear; but he does not even
succeed in producing an intelligible hypothesis, much less
evidence for it. One of the reasons that this sort of history
is so difficult is that while one begins by considering questions with which one has the equipment to deal, one is
likely to be led by degrees to more and more abstruse
questions. It seems that when dealing with ideologies,
their relation to one another, and their effect upon the
world, the historians using traditional methods can sometimes give arguments, sometimes make queries, and at
other times just note oddities. Perhaps one of the secrets
of success in this sort of enterprise is for the historian to
be conscious at all times as to which of these three things
he is and ought to be doing.

Since both Huizinga and Tilly deal with ideology
and its effect upon history, we must now ask if there is
any basic methodological conflict between them. We must
remember that Tilly did not seek to rule out all discussion
of ideology and intention in history, but merely objected
to the invention of ideologies to explain mass action. One
of the things which Huizinga is trying to do would hardly
be questioned seriously by anyone; when, for example, he

tries to explain the connection between chivalry and patriotism he is operating purely within the area of ideas and
trying to show how one set of ideas is connected with another set. At this point we objected to his account as not
being thorough enough, but there can be no objection to
the *sort* of thing he is trying to do here. In pure intellectual history both the causes and the effects are ideas or
systems of ideas; Tilly becomes concerned only when we
cross the line between ideas and acts, in our causal explanations, and postulate ideologies as causes of mass actions.
Of course, we have seen that Huizinga does not restrict
himself to pure intellectual history, and sometimes he does
explain actions by referring to thoughts as in the case of
the English king's refusal to return to the predesignated
village. However, even this is not the sort of linking that
really bothers Tilly; the action in question is not a mass
action, such as a revolution, but an individual action, and
we have good evidence linking the thoughts of the individual to the actions that he subsequently took. This sort
of explanation may not be fully scientific and it would not
satisfy a behaviorist, but it is the sort of explanation
which we constantly give in our ordinary conversation,
and it does not seem out of place in history, at least as it
now exists.

Huizinga does, however, want to do more than explain the actions of a few isolated individuals and he gives
these instances only as examples of a sort of behavior
which he takes to have been typical of the time. Of course,
one could always wonder how typical this sort of behavior
really was, and the answer would have to be just that this
is the sort of thing one constantly runs across in medieval
chronicles and literature. At some point we have to rely on
the judgment of a specialist, such as Huizinga, as to what
was typical and what was not, and it seems that we can
have reasonable doubts on this point only if some other
specialist disagrees. However, when Huizinga treats certain aspects of the crusades as consequences of chivalry he

goes farther, and he comes close to explaining mass action, as opposed to habitual individual actions, in terms of an ideology. It is at this point that one could substitute another methodology for the one Huizinga uses. One could first set up a measure of chivalry, say the number of arranged duels and jousts per year in a given district divided by the number of resident nobles, and one could then set out to discover independently the degree to which the varying districts supported the crusades (the index might here be the number of recruits as compared to total population). One might then find either a positive or a negative correlation between chivalric behavior and participation in the crusades, and one could thereby confirm or disconfirm the hypothesis that there was an important connection between chivalry and the crusades. This is presumably the sort of thing Tilly would want to do in such a case and, in view of the fact that Huizinga never seems to have thought of any such procedure, there does seem to be a conflict of methodology here. At least, a sociologically inclined historian in Huizinga's place might be inclined to push his inquiry further and give us hypotheses based on more solid evidence. Again, Huizinga is basically relying on the method of sympathetic identification. If one imagines oneself to be a noble of the late Middle Ages, one cannot imagine himself going on a crusade for reasons other than chivalry. The sociological historian is not really disputing the value of such a method; in fact he might admit it as a very fruitful way of thinking up hypotheses, but he then says that the hypothesis ought to be tested according to the methods indicated above. In this sense, then, Huizinga's approach seems to be incomplete and we can see how it might be completed using methods similar to Tilly's.

We should not pay too much attention to this one instance, however, because it is really the only case where Huizinga tries to explain a mass action by looking to an ideology. For the most part, he is concerned just to show that chivalry was prevalent at the time and that it often influenced the political and military decisions of individual kings and commanders. One could not use statistical methods to follow up his hypotheses since those methods can be used only where large masses of persons are involved and the decisions in which Huizinga is most interested are decisions of individuals. In such cases sympathetic identification seems to provide the best sort of evidence that we can get. Further, even when Huizinga is talking about the behavior of fairly large numbers of persons, he is usually not trying to explain some single mass action and does not really run foul of Tilly's objections. Rather, at such points he often gives no explanation at all. He identifies several patterns of behavior which he will count as chivalrous, and he wants to show that these patterns of behavior all interrelate. He is not really trying to correlate chivalry with some entirely distinct phenomenon, but is instead trying to explain what chivalry itself consisted in. In this way he wants to show that it involved a certain pattern of action in politics, a certain pattern of action in war, certain kinds of dueling and jousting, and a particular pattern of relations between men and women. One could imagine establishing a systematic correlation between these different patterns of behavior, but it would be difficult to do since we would have to have more complete information about the behavior of particular persons than we are likely to get. Huizinga, on the contrary, tries to show that all these different patterns of behavior amount just to different applications of the same values and the same code of honor. Thus, one can see that the same motives that might make an otherwise sane man propose a duel might also inhibit him from running away in the middle of a battle. Understanding how these different patterns of behavior interrelate is again a matter of sympathetic identification, but, again, it seems to be the best method available. Once before, in connection with the abortive duels, we criticized Huizinga for making it sound as if he were explaining the duels when he was in fact only explaining the nature of chivalry itself. However, if we do construe much of Huizinga's account as the explication of the nature of a phenomenon rather than an explanation of its appearance, many of the difficulties are resolved. Thus, we can conclude that, while Huizinga and Tilly use very different methods, they also, for the most part, deal with different sorts of problems. Only seldom does Huizinga use his methods to deal with problems which could be better approached in a statistical way.

10 Piecemeal History

Up to this point our examples have been taken from major works of history, and the passages chosen from these works have usually been crucial and controversial ones. It is also a feature of these and other major works of history that they have been intended not only for other historians but for the general educated public. In this respect history is unlike most of the sciences and even such disciplines as philosophy. It is fairly safe to say that any important issue in the physical sciences, concerning which scientists themselves disagree, will be stated in a highly technical way and will be unintelligible to a non-scientist. Even in such fields as economics and psychology, an issue under debate in the current journals is likely to involve technical concepts and be far enough removed from everyday experience so that it will not make much sense to the layman. Even in contemporary philosophy one finds such technical concepts as that of an analytic statement and that of a logically opaque context; a glance at the current journals should convince anyone that it is the relationships between concepts such as these that are of real interest to practicing philosophers. It stands out as a peculiarity of history to be so organized that its ultimate product is not simply intended for other members of the same profession. Later on, we will have to see whether this is an accidental or essential feature of history, and see why it is that history has this peculiarity. While historians may write books intended for "the general educated public," they are also interested in uncovering obscure facts which the ordinary citizen would regard as being too trivial to be interesting. Since these smaller points are usually of interest only to other historians, they typically appear in articles and notes in the historical journals; thus, even in history, there is an area of discussion from which the average citizen is excluded, not because he would not understand the articles, but because he is not interested in their content. Nevertheless, history still differs in an important way from the other fields we have mentioned because these articles establishing smaller points are not ends in themselves, but are intended to enable other historians to arrive at soundly based conclusions about matters which are of intuitive interest to a much wider audience. No matter how small the point, one usually finds the author suggesting or hinting at its significance and its possible use in establishing a more general point.

One such paper that makes a small but significant point is Solomon Wank's "The Appointment of Count Berchtold as Austro-Hungarian Foreign Minister" (*Journal of European Affairs*, 33 [1963], 143–151). Since Count Berchtold was the Austro-Hungarian foreign minister at the outbreak of the First World War he is of interest to historians. There is also some controversy about his ability and effectiveness; however, Wank is not concerned to evaluate him as a foreign minister but is just trying to clear up certain questions about his appointment. His principal sources are the unpublished notebook of Baron Francis von Schiessl, Emperor Francis Joseph's chef de cabinet, and an unpublished letter of Cajetan von Merey, the Austro-Hungarian ambassador to Italy from 1910 to

1914, to his father. The situation was that Aerenthal, Berchtold's predecessor, was dying of leukemia and had considerable say in appointing his successor. According to Schiessl he recommended Burian, the then minister of finance; Pallavicini, ambassador to Turkey; and Berchtold, a former ambassador to Russia. Aerenthal also says something about the strengths and weaknesses of each candidate, but his reservations about Berchtold seem to be the most serious; in particular, he says that he did not think Berchtold's nerves would stand the position, and that he also thought Berchtold would seek too rapid a rapprochement with Russia. According to Merey's letter, Aerenthal recommended candidates in the following order: Burian, Seczen (the ambassador to France), and, lastly, Berchtold. Merey adds that Berchtold's policy is odious to him personally, and also to the Italians, implying that it was indeed different from the policy of Aerenthal.

Thus Wank has two sources which agree in some respects but disagree in that one mentions Pallavicini, the other, Seczen for second choice. Wank does not try to adjudicate this conflict; he concludes simply that Berchtold was not Aerenthal's first choice, but was appointed by default. The others may have been eliminated because they were Magyars and the Archduke Francis Ferdinand (of Sarajevo fame) did not want a Magyar foreign minister, or it may have been because they were not sufficiently pro-Russian to suit the emperor. Wank is not concerned to settle this issue either. Secondly, he argues that Berchtold was not merely carrying on Aerenthal's policy. Aerenthal himself suggests that Berchtold, who had been an ambassador to Russia, would make changes in his Russian policy, and Merey says that Berchtold had in fact made policy changes, although his letter does not say what they were. What Wank has done is very simple; where his sources contradict one another, he abstains from judgment, and where his sources agree, he accepts their joint import. One can imagine that another historian, using Wank's result, might want to argue that Berchtold's policies cannot really be laid against the Austro-Hungarian government on the grounds that he was not really the man they would have preferred to have. Wank himself suggests that his conclusion tends to discredit the view that Berchtold merely carried out Aerenthal's policies and that it was these policies which led to disaster in the end. Even though Wank's points are small ones, it is clear that his article is not what Collingwood would call scissors-and-paste history, and that it involves a critical look at the sources instead of blind acceptance of them. Still, Wank's method consists simply in finding as many sources as possible bearing on the issue, comparing them, and accepting them when they agree. The value in such work is not to be found in any complex chains of argumentation, but is represented by the effort needed to dig out some obscure unpublished material and set forth what is important in it in a readily accessible form.

Another even briefer note which sets out to make a small point is P. D. G. Thomas's "Check-List of M. P.s Speaking in the House of Commons 1768–1774" (*Bulletin of the Institute of Historical Research*, 35 [1962], 220–226). The crux of this note is a list of the M.P.s who made speeches during that time and the number of speeches attributed to each. The source is the diary of Henry Cavendish, M.P. for Lost Withiel, who attempted to take shorthand notes of all the debates. He kept at this task with amazing persistence although he did miss a few debates and speeches. Again, Thomas does not merely count speeches and names and put down the numbers; some critical work is also involved. Although nine speeches have been attributed to a Mr. Roberts, Thomas finds that four of the speeches can be checked in other sources and were, according to them, made by Henry Herbert; since the other five speeches cannot be checked he concludes that Roberts may never have spoken at all. Similarly there were in some cases two or more members of the same name who may have made speeches. In such cases Thomas takes the speeches in question and compares the views which are expressed in them and the subjects that they deal with; in this way he is able to infer whether or not all the speeches were made by the same man. Suitable qualifications are then put into the checklist.

While Thomas's point is a small one, one can again see why it would be of interest to the historian of the period. Obviously the influence of a given M.P. has a good deal to do with how often he spoke; thus, another historian might be able to revise his estimate of the importance of a politician upwards or downwards by looking at Thomas's data. Like Wank's paper, the chief value of Thomas's list is in his digging out something obscure and putting it in readily available form. Like Wank, Thomas also uses other contemporary sources, checking them against one another. However, his analysis of the content of speeches whose authorship is not clear involves a critical technique which goes beyond the more obvious historical methods and is more typical of the history of literature.

Another similar historical note is "Health and Sickness in the Slave Trade," by Professor J. A. Nixon, which appears as an appendix to Chapter 11 in *The Trade Winds,* edited by C. Northcote Parkinson. Nixon's chief source is the record of the parliamentary investigation: "Report of the Lords of Committee of Council concerning the present state of trade to Africa and particularly the trade in slaves" (1789). Here Nixon reproduces the relevant evidence concerning the sickness of slaves, but he is more interested in sickness among the crews of slavers. From one of the witnesses he takes the following statistics concerning the crews of Liverpool and Bristol slavers for the period September 1784–January 1790: [26]

Number of vessels	350
Original number of crews	12263
Died	2643
Brought home of original crews	5760

He then notes the high death rate among seamen, 21.5 per cent, and also points out that we are not told what happened to the almost 4000 seamen who neither died nor were brought home. He cites also the statement made by the same witness that the seamen were "cruelly treated, whipped for very little cause, often without any." Nixon also refers to a rare pamphlet entitled "The Unfortunate Shipwright or Cruel Captain" by a Robert Barker, carpenter on board a slaver, who says that he was rendered blind "Through the violent and wilful actions of Captain Robert Wabshutt and Doctor John Roberts, both of the city of Bristol." Nixon then concludes that the 4000 seamen not otherwise mentioned deserted in the West Indies without pay because of their high death rate and cruel treatment. The owners could then ship another crew in the West Indies and had only to pay them for the homeward leg of the voyage from the West Indies to Britain. Thus the crews which took the ships out to Africa and from Africa to the West Indies served free, in effect, and were beaten for their trouble. Nixon then surmises that the unfortunate experiences of British seamen in the trade, along with their repugnance for slavery, may have had something to do with its being outlawed later. Once more, much of the value of this note consists in the discovery of obscure sources and the introduction of them into historical knowledge. This time there is relatively little comparison of sources; the crux of the piece is a hypothesis, the conclusion of which tells us what happened to the missing four thousand seamen. This time the conclusion, though a small one, is a surprising one: that seamen on slavers fared at least as badly as the slaves themselves. Again, the point is important almost entirely because it is relevant to a larger issue—the slave trade in general and its abolition. Examples of this sort of historical writing could be multiplied indefinitely; many of them come from economic history, where it is necessary to piece together trade patterns of another age by following the imports and exports of specific commodities, perhaps even shipload by shipload. None of these articles in itself is likely to be particularly gripping, but, taking them all together, it may be possible to reconstruct the trade relationships between nations at a past date. Armed with this information, the historian may be able to explain some of the more dramatic events of the time.

11 Evaluative History

It would be hard to find a serious work of history with more ethical judgments per page than L. B. Namier's *Diplomatic Prelude 1938–1939*.[27] Even though the book is not typical of Namier, and his fame as a historian is not founded on his use of ethical judgments, it affords an excellent example of ethical evaluation as made by historians. Our analysis is directed particularly to the fifth chapter, which treats the Anglo-Russian negotiations of the spring of 1939 and which amounts to a condemnation of the Chamberlain government for its hesitation and general lack of statesmanship.

It is obvious that wherever there is ethical evaluation there must also be counterfactual statements. If one condemns policy *A* because it led to disaster *B*, one must be prepared to say that another policy would have led to something other than *B*. Further, one implies that at least some of the alternatives to *A* would have had consequences which would not only be distinct from *B* but which would also be preferable to *B*. Thus, when the historian condemns *A*, he has to say not only that another policy would have had different consequences, but he has to specify those other consequences enough so that they can be seen to be preferable to what actually took place. It can then be seen that the historian will have committed himself to quite a lot in the way of counterfactuals. While Namier does not spell out counterfactuals precisely, he is bound to commit himself to some, as indicated above, and, in fact, he makes it pretty clear in the chapter's opening paragraph that he thinks that an abler British government could have concluded some sort of alliance with Russia which would have limited the rise of Germany:

> The tragic core of diplomatic history during the half-year preceding the outbreak of war is in the Anglo-Russian negotiations. It is difficult to write about them without the painful consciousness that here was perhaps the one chance of preventing the Second World War, or of ensuring Hitler's early defeat. But such were the prejudices, miscalculations, and suspicions on both sides that only on June 22nd, 1941, through Hitler's supreme blunder and Churchill's instantaneous action, was that unity established which foresight should have built up two years earlier. [P. 143]

One of the defects of this book is that it was begun in 1940 very soon after the occurrence of the events which it chronicles and published in 1948 before many of the documents became available. In these circumstances Namier had to look to newspaper accounts for many of his facts, and was not able to substantiate them in the usual way. His motivation in writing the book seems to have been to get his interpretation of the events across while leaving it to later writers to verify facts and provide documentation. We will thus concern ourselves entirely with his interpretation and not query the accuracy of his detailed factual statements.

The basic situation was that since Britain, France, and Russia all had much to fear from Germany in 1938/39 they entered into negotiations in order to coordinate their policies. Further, the British had already guaranteed Poland and wanted Russia to back them up in some way. On April 15, 1939 the British ambassador in Moscow made an approach which Chamberlain summarized as follows in the House of Commons:

> His Majesty's Government accordingly suggested to the Soviet Government that they should make, on their own behalf, a declaration of similar effect to that already made by His Majesty's Government, in the sense that, in the event of Great Britain and France being involved in hostilities in discharge of their own obligations thus accepted, the Soviet Government, on their side, would express their readiness also to lend assistance, if desired. [P. 151]

Namier has doubts about what this means, but his point is that throughout the whole period the British did not want actually to enter into an alliance with Russia; instead, they wanted an exchange of resolutions which would have the same net upshot in case of war but which would not be so embarrassing politically. On April 17 the Russians proposed the following, according to the London *Times:*

> The Soviet Government have put forward their plan for a triple alliance between Great Britain, France, and the Soviet Union, covering in the first place an attack against one of them, and in the second place an attack on any country in Eastern Europe from Finland to the Black Sea. They leave open for the present the question of mutual action in case of an attack against one of the smaller Western countries which Great Britain and France number among their vital interests. [P. 154]

They also suggested consultations among the general staffs. According to the *Times* on May 3, the British government, before considering any alliance of the sort proposed by the Russians, would have to take into account the views of many governments that were suspicious of Soviet intervention. Here Namier quotes a memorandum from Sir Eric Phipps to the French which appears in the writings of the Roumanian diplomat Gafenco. This document is taken to define the aims of the British government in its negotiations with Russia:

(a) to neglect no chance of obtaining Soviet help in case of war;

(b) not to compromise the common front by offending the susceptibilities of Poland and Roumania;

(c) not to alienate world opinion by lending colour to the German anti-Comintern propaganda;

(d) not to compromise the cause of world peace by provoking violent action on the part of Germany. [P. 157]

Namier argues throughout that the British govenment tended to neglect the important thing, getting Russian intervention in case of war, and to let themselves be sidetracked by a number of minor aims, such as the maintenance of the best possible relations with such countries as Poland and Roumania. This memorandum is a legitimate document which lends support to the case. However, in a footnote Namier quotes the report of the London correspondent of the *New York Times* on May 1:

> To-day the Cabinet's sinking spell came from the fear that Spain, Portugal, Japan, and—vitally important to Britain on moral grounds—the Vatican might be displeased if Britain were to enter an outright military alliance with the Communist colossus. . . . As far as is known, there has been no hint of warning from the Vatican, but there have been indications that English Catholics are disturbed by the implications of an alliance with Communist Russia. [P. 156n.]

Here Namier seems to choose sources which say what he is not quite prepared to say himself, and to quote them with no qualification. To suggest that the British government was seriously worried by what the Vatican and Portugal might think when confronted with a crisis of this magnitude is to suggest that it was totally incompetent. Namier does not produce any evidence for this report and the correspondent may not have been entirely serious when he wrote it; it seems that Namier's only reason for quoting it must be that he cannot bear to leave out anything which tends to make the Chamberlain government appear ridiculous.

The French, on the other hand, were much more willing to conclude an alliance with the Russians, and Namier seems to conclude that the success or failure of the negotiations depended mainly on the British. However, the British did not accept any of the Russian plans and, in the meantime, Litvinov was replaced by Molotov as Foreign Minister. This caused those in England who wanted an alliance and who had been negotiating with Litvinov a great deal of anxiety. As Namier says:

> In Parliament a fresh crop of questions about Russia was addressed to the Prime Minister who, obviously rattled, vented a peevish displeasure on the Opposition. To Attlee's remark that the delays were causing uncertainty, he snapped back: "I do realise that uncertainty is being created by a number of people who are all the time suggesting that if there is any fault it must be the fault of the British Government"—their "purely partisan attitude" is not "conducive to the interests of this country, but I cannot be held responsible for that". When urged "that the nation should be informed what the proposals made really are", he quoted *The Times* for the state of ignorance in which the U. S. S. R. kept its own people; and when Gallacher suggested his "making personal contact in order to get Stalin's own view", he replied: "Perhaps the hon. Member would suggest with whom I should make personal contact, because personalities change rather rapidly"—a partisan retort, conducive to no good and hardly befitting a responsible statesman in the middle of negotiations on which the peace of Europe most truly depended, and which his Government professed to treat seriously.[28]

After this point Russia began looking towards Germany rather than England and negotiations gradually went downhill until they finally failed altogether. Namier concludes:

> . . . the change is more likely to have been a gradual shifting of interest and emphasis than a sudden *volte-*

face. The shelving of the Jew Litvinov removed a personal obstacle to Russian-German conversations; it should have been a warning to this country, but was hardly taken as such; too little was read into it at the time, and too much in the light of subsequent events. As yet Russia merely resumed full freedom of movement; but the trend was away from the Allies, and the layout of the field would have made the game perplexing even for skilled, far-sighted, and alert players on the British side, and rendered it well-nigh hopeless for men who had tied themselves up in useless combinations and failed to perceive the danger ahead. [Pp. 159–160]

In order to show that, even at the time, some persons understood the situation better than the British government Namier quotes a report from John Owens, editor of the *Baltimore Sun,* cabled from London on May 10:

> Con-summate the alliance, say the Russians, and Mussolini would be negotiating in London and Paris within twenty-four hours. There would be peace. Fail to con-summate the alliance, or water it down, or even parley too long—again stating the policy when Litvinov was in office—and there will be war this year . . . .
>
> Are the Russians altruistic? They say not. Any major war, they reason, will retard their development. And no one knows where Hitler will strike. It may be in the East, and in a manner that will . . . compel the Russians to war even though they are not bound by the alliance. They claim that they are not so vulnerable . . . as Britain and France, but still they are vulnerable. Hence they serve themselves when proposing an alliance that in their opinion will bring Hitler to a halt. [Pp. 160–161]

To see what Namier has done here let us compare his account with what would be a complete historical account of the negotiations. This would in the first place contain all the proposals concerning the matter which were made by the British, French, and Russian governments toward one another. The historian would then consider each proposal, trying to explain why it was made as opposed to some conceivable alternatives; finally, he would trace each proposal to see what happened to it after it was passed to another government. After Parliament took a hand Namier covers the negotiations in more detail, but he himself regards the early stages as the crucial ones, and here he gives us much less than a complete account (probably because of the scarcity of available sources when he was writing). Nevertheless, he still manages to make a fairly plausible case for his two main points: 1) the British government did not want to enter into an outright alliance with Russia; 2) because of this they failed to get any sort of Russian support at all.

In passing, Namier mentions (p. 161) some possible motives for the British government's reluctance to enter an alliance: "weakness, ignorance . . . a dislike of the U. S. S. R., . . . an obstinate hope of reforming Hitler or of converting Mussolini and Franco, . . . regard for Poland, Rumania and the Baltic States. . . ." Namier thinks that the Russians may have attributed some of these motives to the British, but he does not attempt to say which if any of them actually operated, or which ones were the most important. However, there is a good deal of difference between them, and some are much more respectable than others. One of the historical methods which we have seen used on various occasions is the imaginative reenactment of the position of the historical personage and his sympathetic understanding of the person involved. But, in order to do this one must come to some conclusion about the motives from which the character, in this case Chamberlain, acted. We have also seen that the method of sympathetic identification is not the only way of doing history and that such historians as Tilly get along without using it at all. On the other hand, it seems, at least on the surface, to be of crucial importance to the sort of history that involves ethical evaluation. One cannot make ethical judgments about people generally, or about historical figures such as Chamberlain, by looking at a few isolated actions. If, for instance, a Negro leader institutes a violent insurrection against constituted authority, it makes a difference whether his intention is ultimately to get certain rights for his people or to loot the local stores whatever the outcome of the insurrection may be. Now it is sometimes possible to establish with reasonable reliability the motives from which a person acts simply by looking at a large number of his actions taken together and without trying to imagine oneself in his place. Thus, it is conceivable that even a biographer who collected a large enough mass of facts might substitute some sort of statistical method for sympathetic identification. However, it is clear that Namier is not trying to do this for Chamberlain or his colleagues, and he does not produce nearly enough information about them to throw any light on the motives that they might have had. To understand Chamberlain as a person we have to understand his motives and intentions, and the only method left would be that of sympathetic identification. Since Namier makes no attempt to put himself in Chamberlain's position and imagine justifications for what Chamberlain did he is clearly not using this method and is not really trying to understand the man in any way at all. Rather he is trying to build a case against Chamberlain and is acting almost solely in the role of prosecuting attorney. This leads us to the conclusion that, while Namier *is* making ethical judgments about the British government of the time and about Chamberlain in his role as Prime Minister, this sort of ethical evaluation is different from the kind that we ordinarily make of individuals.

It will be argued later that the historian has implicit standards for the evaluation of such persons as prime ministers, presidents, and kings, and the standards are such that one can evaluate the performance of a person in one of those positions without knowing his exact intentions and motives and without making a moral judgment about the man qua man. Such an ethical evaluation will be seen to be a genuine one which is irreducible to any set of purely factual statements, but it is also different from the ethical evaluations which we make in our day-to-day conversation. The establishment of a historical evaluation of a public figure is somewhat simpler in that we can abstract from a certain range of motives and intentions, but it is still a very complex business. An outline of a method of evaluation will be provided in Part II, but in the meantime we can say that the logic of Namier's argument is as follows:

First premise: The occurrence of the Second World War and the near-victory of Germany was almost (apart from such a victory) the worst thing that could have happened.

Second premise: If an alliance between Britain, France, and Russia had been concluded quickly at this time, the war would either not have occurred or Germany would have been defeated quickly. (Note that this premise is counterfactual in form.)

Third premise: If the British government had been willing to conclude an outright alliance at this time, there would have been such an alliance. (This premise is also a counterfactual conditional statement.)

Fourth premise: The Chamberlain government was largely responsible for Britain's unwillingness to enter such an alliance.

Conclusion: The Chamberlain government was in large part responsible for the catastrophe that followed and can be given a large share of the blame for it.

This is an argument which draws an ethical conclusion from premises which do not say anything about motives or intentions; but, as noted above, such arguments may be valid if we treat the evaluation represented by the conclusion in a special way. One peculiarity of the argument is that we can be assured of the truth of the conclusion, not just if the premises are true, but only if the premises are such that they could have been seen to be true by reasonable persons at the time, and not just after the fact; i.e., the truth of the premises is not sufficient reason for accepting the conclusion. Even if all the premises are true, the government could not be blamed if, say, the second premise could not have been seen to be true at the time. The dispatch from Owens is important since it indicates that some persons did recognize the truth of the second premise at the time.

Still, there are many ways in which one could question the premises. One might wonder whether a Europe totally controlled by Stalin, which would be a possible outcome of the alliance, would have been better than the actual postwar situation. Even if there had been no war, which Namier takes as the most desirable outcome, would that have led to a situation where we would still be confronted by a Nazi Germany armed with nuclear weapons? Similarly, one could wonder: suppose an alliance had been made and Germany had attacked Russia first; could Germany then have conquered Russia, and could a French army based on the Maginot Line have prevented it? All sorts of questions can arise. In his evaluation of the Chamberlain government Namier is implicitly committed to answering all sorts of obscure and seemingly unanswerable counterfactual questions. We will see later that counterfactual statements, such as the second and third premises (and implicitly the fourth premise), involve many problems and are not to be assumed lightly. The real paradox here is that however shaky the foundations of the argument, it is one that most of us accept without serious reservations. That almost everyone blames the Chamberlain government for a good deal of what happened later is reflected by the connotation and use of the word "appeasement" today. It is thus not just a question of supporting Namier's argument; we will in the end have to formulate a historical methodology which allows us to make some of the same moves in a great range of cases.

Whatever our final conclusion, it is instructive to see a historian of Namier's reputation explicitly committing himself both to counterfactual statements and to ethical evaluations. Namier is certainly not unique in this, and it may be that many historians would like to draw the same sorts of conclusions, but are too cautious to venture so far. As an ideal in the writing of history, some people would insist upon a complete objectivity which would preclude the historian's making any ethical judgments as a part of his history, although he might still make them outside his official capacity, and he might still think that the point of history is to give the reader better grounds on which to make his own ethical judgments. We noticed earlier that it is characteristic of historical writing to make its way ultimately to the general public. That the general public has an inveterate tendency to rate historical figures evaluatively seems quite clear. It classifies some as great men; others, such as Caligula, as great villains; others as well-meaning but weak, and so on. In fact the main interest of even the educated public in history is probably mainly evaluative. It thus seems likely that even the completely objective historian is still committed to presenting his history in such a way that others can conveniently evaluate the men and policies of whom he writes. Hence, the most important kinds of historical writing must be capable of supporting counterfactual statements and ethical judgments.

12 Systematic History

Crane Brinton's *Anatomy of Revolution,* from which our last example comes, is largely an attempt to establish within history the sorts of uniformities that are basic to the natural sciences and to the social sciences generally.[29] Of course, we could have chosen a passage from Toynbee or Spengler instead, but Brinton is preferable because he is much more careful in establishing these uniformities and there is therefore a closer parallel between his work and the other social sciences. Further, Brinton probably enjoys a much higher reputation among historians than either Toynbee or Spengler, and there are a number of reasons for this. First, he has chosen a much more limited topic and is trying to establish uniformities over revolutions only and not over the rise and fall of civilizations or over human history in general. In fact, he limits his subject matter still further and considers only four revolutions: the seventeenth-century English revolution, the American revolution, the French revolution, and the Russian revolution. He asserts his uniformities to hold only for these revolutions and does not generalize his results indiscriminately over all the others.

If Brinton's conclusions could not be applied to any social or political movements other than these four revolutions they would be of somewhat limited interest. Despite his self-imposed limitations, there is no reason to prevent our generalizing about all revolutions of a particular *kind* which would have to be carefully specified. Brinton's main reason for making such a strong qualification seems to be to exclude from consideration the sorts of banana-republic revolutions where one clique of officers replaces another in the center of authority without the mass of the people being involved at all. The reader may then take these four revolutions as paradigms which roughly mark out a class of revolutions to any member of which Brinton's conclusions could be legitimately applied. Brinton differs from Toynbee in that Brinton does not attempt to predict the future in anything like the same way. We will later see that if Brinton's account is adequate and can be generalized even to this limited extent, then, given a revolution in midstream, one should be able to use the uniformities he establishes to predict future developments. Since no revolution of the right sort is occurring in the world at the present time we do not have occasion to make these predictions.[30] Brinton attempts to explain much less than Toynbee and, even if we can wring a few highly qualified predictions out of what Brinton says, he would never commit himself to anything like the vast array of predictions that Toynbee offers us. Thus, Brinton does not differ from Toynbee so much in what he is trying to do; rather, it is that he attempts much less and is much more careful in gathering evidence for the uniformities which he does believe to hold.

Brinton begins by comparing a revolution to a fever with its early symptoms, its crisis stage, and the gradual recuperation of the patient. He draws this analogy not to make any ethical evaluations, but because he regards himself as being in the situation of the physician who tries to make out the earliest stages of the disease and then predict its course at each further stage. The point of his analogy seems to be to distinguish what he is doing from what someone working in a highly developed natural or social science is doing. The physician does not doubt that there are natural laws governing every stage of the disease he is dealing with, but he also knows that he does not have access to these laws. The symptoms of which he takes note in order to make his diagnosis involve such things as pains in the stomach and flushed faces, and cannot usually be exactly described or numerically measured. Further, there is no hard and fast connection between the

134

symptoms and the disease; the disease may occur without any one of its characteristic symptoms, and there will even be cases where all, or almost all, the symptoms occur in a person who is not diseased (we can here count false pregnancy if we consider pregnancy to be a disease). Nevertheless, there is still a strong connection between the presence of the symptoms and the presence of the disease, and this is all that the physician has to go on. As Brinton sees it, the historian studying revolution in a systematic way is in a similar position.

At times Brinton refers back to the analogy, but most of his references to it come at the beginning and the end of the book, and in practice he uses a different model. His primary search is for uniformities and whenever he finds a uniformity he believes himself to have given an explanation of some of the phenomena involved. That is, he is trying to give an approximation of the causal laws governing the course of revolutions. Further, he recognizes quite clearly that these causal laws imply counterfactual statements and, as we will soon see, he has no hesitation in making such assertions. So far the situation is just what it would be in the natural sciences; the difference lies in the nature of the laws put forward. Even in the natural sciences one never discovers qualitative uniformities of the form: whenever an event of type A occurs an event of type B occurs. One is typically confronted with a number of factors such as heat, temperature, and pressure, which can occur in various degrees and which are always present in some degree or other. Ways are then found of measuring these factors numerically and they are put down as variables; in any particular situation one knows how to go about substituting a number for the variable. One then tries to find correlations between the variables, and the ideal would be the discovery that one variable is a function of the other(s) in the way that x^2 is a function of x. That is, it would be ideal from an explanatory point of view if, given the occurrence of one phenomenon, one could measure it and then by using some specified mechanical procedure one could calculate the value for the second variable (the function) and predict the corresponding phenomenon to occur with a particular intensity or degree. It is, of course, not quite that simple. The universal gas law, mentioned before, comes about as close as anything to the ideal; here we have three closely connected variables such that if we specify the initial states for all three and the final states for two, we can then come very close to specifying mechanically (using purely arithmetical operations) the final value of the third variable. Even here, however, we get a close approximation rather than a function in the strict sense. If the prediction were always exact we would have a function on a set of variables as opposed to a function on one variable, and this would be a perfectly legitimate function according to the definition of that concept. This turns out to be the ideal which Brinton also has in mind. In the body of the book he largely substitutes talk of variables for talk of symptoms, and at every point he is trying to find uniformities between them. Two important differences remain between Brinton's account and what one would find in the natural sciences (or the advanced social sciences). First, he has no way of measuring his factors numerically and hence no way of substituting constants for the variables. Secondly, in the end he always has to say that such-and-such a variable is a function of such-and-such other variables and perhaps other unspecified ones, but he cannot say exactly which variables are involved in the function, and he consequently does not attempt to give any way of calculating the value of one variable given the values of the other variables. Hence his account is a clear application of the scientific method to history, and it is the same scientific method that is used elsewhere. It is just that there are certain gaps which would have to be bridged, and which may eventually be bridged in order to make history into a fully developed science. Brinton himself is quite conscious of all this and compares the uniformities he finds with those to be found in biology or zoology (p. 179).

Brinton unashamedly commits himself to all kinds of counterfactual statements. Two quotations will suffice:

One might start with a characteristic American assumption, and say that in this country at least we have full freedom of opportunity. Very well, let us take at random some self-made twentieth-century Americans—Ted Williams, Henry Ford, Bob Hope, Theodore Dreiser. It would be comforting to be able to say confidently that in the societies of the old regimes these able men would have been kept down by hard-and-fast caste lines, condemned to obscurity or to revolt. Unfortunately, it would not be true. We must not, indeed, be indecently sure about such hypothetical matters. The professional athlete as such could probably not have attained in any other society than our own the wealth Mr. Williams has or as much honor—public attention, if you prefer—save perhaps in the Rome of the gladiators. Yet in early feudal society sheer physical strength and skill might have won him knighthood, and even in later societies noble patronage might have carried him far. Ford may be taken as the entrepreneur-inventor, and though one doubts whether any other society than our own would have made him a national hero, it is likely that in eighteenth-century France or in early twentieth-century Czarist Russia he could have secured substantial financial success. Mr. Hope is the man who amuses, and Western society has usually rewarded adequately, and sometimes highly, those who could amuse it. Perhaps aristocracies have never quite concealed their contempt and democracies have made no attempt to conceal their admiration for those who amused them. Yet actors, musicians, jesters and their like seem not, in spite of the example of Beaumarchais' Figaro, to have been greatly irked by their social status in the past. Certainly the French eighteenth century was kind enough to them, and paid them well in money and attention. As for Dreiser, he would presumably have been in his element among the *philosophes,* and with proper national and racial adjustments, among the Gorkis and the Chekhovs. He would have made proportionately quite as much money, and have been even more honored. [Pp. 64–65]

In speaking of the difficulties which Kerensky, a moderate who presided over a certain phase of the Russian revolution, had in using force to put down rebellions, Brinton remarks: "In 1917, however, even had Kerensky been the sort of man who could successfully organize repressive measures—and he plainly was not that sort of man—what we are bound to call public opinion would not in those days have permitted the execution of such measures" (p. 145).

There are any number of other passages which contain counterfactual assertions, and, of course, there is nothing surprising about this. Brinton has already committed himself to finding the sorts of uniformities that the scientist finds and we have already seen that these uniformities generate counterfactual statements in a perfectly legitimate way. I emphasize the presence of counterfactuals in the work of Brinton, Namier, and other writers since historians have not always recognized that they do make or imply counterfactual assertions; and, in order to arrive at an adequate interpretation of historiography, it is essential to see this fact.

It might be argued that Brinton is not really doing history at all, but is generalizing or philosophizing about history. Someone who argues in this way might also say that Namier was not so much doing history as moralizing about history, that Huizinga was not doing history but speculating about history, that Tilly was substituting sociology for history, and so on. If one is really going to be a purist about history, one might count only our first example, where Granet investigates the ancient Chinese chronologies, as a case of genuine history. However, even Granet had to presuppose certain general laws about persons, in that case the ancient Chinese annalists, and such laws involve counterfactuals. Thus, one cannot escape counterfactuals in history just by being a purist, and to exclude the other examples from the range of things that we are willing to call history accomplishes nothing anyway. Further, we have seen that history in its most highly developed form reaches the general public and that it interests people who are not interested just in knowing that such-and-such an event took place at such-and-such a time and at such-and-such a place. In particular, it seems to me that a work is made interesting to the non-specialist public either because it draws or allows people to draw the sorts of ethical conclusions typified by Namier's work or because it displays or allows the reader to see the sorts of uniformities of which Brinton speaks. Hence, our last two examples are of particular interest because they represent most clearly the sort of end product that all historical writing ultimately serves.

Brinton begins by discussing signs of the coming revolution under the old regime. He does not claim to discover the cause of the revolution but he does discuss a number of factors which he thinks are relevant to it. Not all of them need be present for there to be a revolution; some may be present in very high degree without there being a revolution (many of these factors prevail in present-day America) and he admits that there may be others which he has not discussed at all. Nevertheless, his suggestion is that, given any society in which all or almost all these factors are present in high degree, there is likely to be a large-scale revolution in a short time. Thus we have a list of variables which are largely independent of each other, and such that each variable is individually largely independent of the variable representing the likelihood of a revolution, but such that there is still a strong connection between the variables, taken together, and the revolution factor. Let us now look at some of the factors which represent uniformities Brinton has found in his four revolutions. First, the sort of revolution he is talking about occurs in a society which is basically quite prosperous but whose government is nearly bankrupt. Thus the picture is not that of a retrograde or chronically poor society, but of an economically rising society whose government has nevertheless encountered severe financial difficulties. Brinton thinks that a much more important factor is what he calls "cramp," the feeling of a certain class, which we might now refer to as the upper-middle or lower-upper, which is actually doing very well financially, that it is being unduly and arbitrarily hindered by the government and ruling class in reaching the top levels of the society. Brinton's picture of a key revolutionist is not the starving peasant but the prosperous merchant or banker who has already made a fortune but who is still allowed no voice in making laws and regulations governing trade and whose efforts to be admitted to the highest social circles are frustrated at all points. Some of the other factors which Brinton mentions are the incompetence of the government both in handling its finances and in knowing how to use force repressively, the desertion of the intellectuals from the ruling classes, and certain sorts of intensified class conflicts. The explanation stops short of a scientific hypothesis mainly because there is no numerical index for each factor and even given numerical values for the variables, there might still be no procedure for computing when a revolution will occur (and no algorithm for computing the probability of a revolution at any given time). Armed with these indices and, say, an algorithm telling us how to weight the various factors and arrive at a probability for the occurrence of a revolution within a specified time, we would then have a complete scientific hypothesis which we could test by applying it to other revolutions of the required sort. The algorithm itself might not be as hard to find as one would suppose. That some factors are more important than others could be provided for, as Brinton says, by awarding a maximum of one hundred points split up among the various factors according to their apparent importance. In arriving at the division one would have to approximate and sometimes guess, but there might be a way of improving these approximations later on. One might then initially hypothesize that if a society scores, say, 90 points there is a .9 probability that it will soon revolt. By looking at actual cases from the past and seeing how quickly they revolted if they did, or how near they came to revolt if they did not, one could then adjust these probabilities upwards or downwards. The real difficulties come when we try to find numerical indices in the first place. It seems possible to define a numerical index which would compare the solvency of the central government with the prosperity of the society as a whole, and another which would measure the prosperity of a society as compared to that of contemporary societies, but it would be much more difficult to define a numerical index for such things as the degree of alienation of the intellectuals. It is just this sort of difficulty that stymies the historian who wants to be as scientific as possible, and the reason that he is stymied is, as we noted before, that he has no system of concepts appropriate for the analysis and measurement of these phenomena.

Brinton sees a pattern common to all four revolutions under his consideration. Once the revolution breaks out the moderates take control first. These moderates tend to come from higher social classes than the radicals; one assumes them to be the men who felt cramp during the old regime. However, Brinton argues that at this stage there are actually two governments, the legal one of the moderates and the unofficial but real one which may be controlled through revolutionary clubs, labor unions, soviets, independent churches, town meetings, and the like. For reasons which Brinton discusses in detail the moderates are never able to hold on for very long, and they eventually give way to the radicals, who institute a reign of terror, which is at the same time a reign of virtue. Eventually an overburdened society throws out the radicals, and the process of reaction or thermidor sets in. This is the general pattern of revolution which Brinton delineates and, for each stage or substage he finds uniformities which are, in effect, causal laws. The following example of such a uniformity is taken from his chapter on the rule of the moderates:

There is, indeed, an almost organic weakness in the position of the moderates. They are placed between two groups, the disgruntled but not yet silenced conservatives and the confident, aggressive extremists. There are still freedom of speech and the other political rights, so that even conservatives have a voice. Now the moderates seem in all these revolutions to be following the slogan used so conspicuously for French politics of the *Cartel des Gauches* in 1924, a slogan that still gives difficulties to the noncommunist Left throughout the Western world today: "no enemies to the Left". They distrust the conservatives, against whom they have so recently risen; and they are reluctant to admit that the extremists, with whom they so recently stood united, can actually be their enemies. All the force of the ideas and sentiments with which the moderates entered the revolution give them a sort of twist toward the Left. Emotionally they cannot bear to think of themselves as falling behind in the revolutionary process. Moreover, many of them hope to outbid the extremists for popular support, to beat them at their own game. But only in normal times can you trust in the nice smooth clichés of politics like "beat them at their own game". The moderates fail by this policy of "no enemies to the Left" to reconcile these enemies to the Left; and they make it quite impossible to rally to their support any of the not yet quite negligible conservatives. Then, after the moderates get thoroughly frightened about the threatening attitude of the extremists, they turn for help to the conservatives, and find that there just aren't any. They have emigrated, or retired to the country, hopeless and martyred in spirit. Needless to say, a martyred conservative is no longer a conservative, but only another maladjusted soul. This last turn of theirs toward the conservatives, however, finishes the moderates. Alone, unsupported in control of a government as yet by no means in assured and habitual control of a personnel, civil or military, they succumb easily to insurrection. It is significant that Pride's Purge, the French crisis of June 2, 1793, and the Petrograd October Revolution were all hardly more than *coups d'état*. [Pp. 147–148]

At the stage where the extremists have just displaced the moderates, Brinton finds a second uniformity:

The dictatorship of the extremists is embodied in governmental forms as a rough-and-ready centralization. In detail these forms vary in our different societies, but the Commonwealth in England, the *gouvernement révolutionnaire* in France and the Bolshevik dictatorship during the period of "war communism" in Russia all display uniformities of the kind the systematist in biology or zoology would not hesitate to catalogue as uniformities. Notably the making of final decisions in a wide range of matters is taken away from local and secondary authorities, especially if those authorities have been "democratically" elected, and is concentrated on a few persons in the national capital. Though names like Cromwell, Robespierre and Lenin stand out as those of rulers, and although these men did exercise power in many ways, the characteristic form of this supreme authority is that of a committee. The government of the Terror is a dictatorship in commission.

This centralized executive commission—Committee of Public Safety, the All-Russian Central Executive Committee (Vtsik)—rests on a supine if talkative legislative body—Rump, Convention, All-Russian Congress of Soviets—and gets its orders carried out by an extemporized bureaucracy, largely recruited from party workers, and from that club-sect-pressure-group we have seen as the body of the extremist group. The old law courts cannot work, at least in their traditional manner. They are therefore supplemented by extraordinary courts, revolutionary tribunals, or are wholly transformed by new appointments and by special jurisdictions. Finally, a special sort of revolutionary police appears. [Pp. 179–180]

Another uniformity that Brinton notes involves religion:

The history of the accepted religious faiths of the old regimes is then one of the very clearest uniformities our study of revolutions affords. One might almost make a graph, in which the prestige of the old organized faith might be seen to follow a fairly regular curve, lowest at the worst of the Terror, gradually climbing back during the Thermidorean reaction to a position almost as high as that from which it had started in the old regime. [P. 229]

Brinton's most interesting and most characteristic explanation is probably the one resulting from his analysis of the reigns of terror occurring in at least three of his revolutions. He prefaces it with this statement of intent:

In the crisis periods of all four of our revolutions we may distinguish the same set of variables, differently combined and mixed with all sorts of contingent factors to produce the specific situations the narrative historian of these revolutions tends to regard as unique. There are no doubt a very great number of these variables, but for the purposes of a first approximation we may here distinguish seven. These seem not to be related one to another in any important one-way causal relationship. They seem, indeed, more or less like the independent variables of the mathematician, though it is inconceivable that they should be strictly independent. The temptation to single out one of them as the "cause" of the Terror is, like the temptation to find a hero or a villain in any situation, hard to resist. And each one of them has a history, goes back at least to the last generation or two of the old regime.

They are all woven together in a complicated pattern of reality; but without all of them—and this is the important point—you would not have a Reign of Terror, would not have a full crisis in the revolution. The problem of their possible independence need not worry us. Temperature and pressure are independent variables in the mathematical formulation of the laws of thermodynamics; but ice can form at 0° centigrade only if the pressure is negligibly small. We have already stressed this point, perhaps beyond the bounds of good writing. But the old notion of simple, linear, one-way causation is so rooted in our habits of thought, is indeed so useful to us in daily life, that we almost instinctively demand an explanation of a complex situation like the Terror

144

which will enable us to isolate a villain-cause—or a hero-cause. [P. 208]

What is important to notice here is that Brinton sets out to give a causal explanation. In conformance with good scientific practice, he refuses to single out one factor and call it *the* cause, and he refuses to think of causation in history as a simple connection between two kinds of phenomena. Still, as we have seen and as Brinton points out, the situation is much as it is in science and, when he is done, he will have given a causal explanation in the same sense that the scientist gives one.

In order to see how far his account is from a fully scientific one we must look at each of his variables in turn and see how hard it would be in each case to attach a numerical index. The first variable is what he calls the habit of violence: "the paradoxical situation of a people conditioned to expect the unexpected." This variable is a measure of the attitudes of large numbers of persons, and a social scientist would most naturally use questionnaires to assess these attitudes. However, since this is impossible in doing history, it might be possible to set up an objective measure of the amount of violence that did occur, measured, say, by the proportion of arrests by the secret police or by summary executions for given units of population and of time. One would then infer that people would expect violence to occur roughly in proportion to the amount of violence that actually had occurred in the recent past. The habit of violence could then be measured in an indirect and historically possible way. A high index for this variable would then satisfy one of the necessary conditions for the terror.

A second variable, the pressure of a foreign or civil war, could be measured numerically in a number of ways. One might, for instance, take the ratio of casualties in the war, on both sides if it is a civil war and on one side if it is a foreign war, as compared to the total population. Or, if it seems more suitable, one could compute the cost of the war per year and compare it to the gross national product. Again, the more pressure of a war, the more likely it is, all other things being equal, that a reign of terror will arise.

The third variable, the newness of the machinery of the new centralized government, is harder to measure. In one sense one could study each government department and bureau at the relevant date to see how old it is or how long it had gone without a major reorganization by the revolutionary government. One might then weight some bureaus as more important than others and compute an index or weighted average for the governmental institutions which could be compared to corresponding figures for other contemporary societies. One could then assign the revolutionary society a percentile grade in terms of the corrected average age of governmental machinery. The only trouble is that it is not really the newness of the machinery that is important but the level of efficiency with which it functions, and this is harder to measure. Brinton's reasoning is that new machinery will not work very smoothly and he thinks that, when it bogs down, personal conflicts will arise within the government and violence will be used to settle them. If we took the efficiency of the government as our variable, we would have to break it down into various subcategories corresponding to the different areas of government operation in order to get a measure. One could then compare, say, the judicial system of revolutionary France with the judicial systems of other contemporary societies by comparing such factors as number of cases handled, average backlog of cases, number of judges per unit of population, number of convictions, etc. One could then in theory order the judicial systems of the various countries as regards efficiency and assign each a numerical percentile grade. One difficulty, of course, would be that we are not likely to have sufficiently detailed historical information to allow us to compute such things as the number of cases handled and the number of judges. Further, even the subvariable would have to be refined further in order to make it workable. In one sense a judicial system which quickly convicts and executes anyone who comes into court is the most efficient one, but we would probably want to take other factors into account in assessing the efficiency of a judicial system or any other branch of government. In this instance there is quite a gap between Brinton's account and a fully scientific account, and much more work would have to be done in order to bridge it.

The fourth variable concerns the presence or absence of an acute economic crisis with large groups of the population bordering on starvation. Here the problem is a fairly simple one since there are any number of good economic indices of the severity of a depression. The deeper the depression the more likely there is to be a reign of terror.

The fifth variable, a more difficult one to measure, involves class struggle. Brinton remarks: "At any rate, by the time of the Terror the different antagonistic groups within the society have polarized into the orthodox revolutionists in power and the somewhat mixed bloc of their enemies" (p. 211). Here it is again a question of the attitudes which one group of persons has towards another group and the most natural sociological approach would again be by means of a questionnaire. A good substitute approach, which Brinton has used in other writings, is to try to get an idea of the social background of the revolutionists and their opponents. If, by taking as complete a sample as possible, one discovers that the revolutionists have a very homogenous social background and that the opponents can be divided into several interacting groups, each one of which is highly homogenous, one will then have demonstrated the existence of an acute class struggle. Here one could set up a number of criteria, each admitting of a yes or no answer, for membership in a particular social class; having answered these questions for each member of the sample, one could then tabulate the answers and get a statistical measure of the homogeneity of the group. As before, a numerical index would be possible, assuming there to be a sufficient body of available background information which would allow us to place a good sample of the revolutionists and their opponents in their respective social classes.

The sixth variable is, as Brinton notes, of a quite different sort and involves the personalities of the radical leaders:

> Like all politicians, they have learned the skills necessary for success in their trade; they have come to feel their trade is something like a game, as indeed it is; but they are reckless players, apt to play to the gallery, and always trying for a home run. No good revolutionary leader would ever bunt. Moreover, they are at least as jealous of one another as, to use another comparison, actors, and each one must always try for the center of the stage. What in more ordinary times has been lately no more than a conventional struggle for power among politicians is thus in the crisis period of revolutions stepped up to a murderous intensity. [P. 212]

This time we are confronted with a psychological rather than a sociological question. The psychological theory of personality abounds with categories for personalities, and these personality types might often be operationally defined in terms of certain kinds of numerical measures ranging anywhere from measurements of body types to scores on thematic apperception tests and intelligence tests. The only trouble is that the psychologist has no special interest in the particular type of person who becomes a revolutionary leader and emerges into particular prominence during the crisis stage. It may be possible to study that particular kind of personality and, perhaps, to set up tests to measure the degree to which an individual has that kind of personality; these tests might even be such that we could apply them roughly, after the fact, to historical personalities. It is just that the revolutionary personality has not been a subject for psychological research and is not likely to be as long as there is the present gap between history and psychology. The situation is that the psychologist has no reason to study this particular personality type, and, while the historian is interested in it, he has traditionally made no attempt to describe it in terms of the categories which psychologists use and can test for. Hence, the project of making this variable numerical looks hopeless at first, and would certainly be very difficult. Still, there is no reason to believe that the measurement of revolutionary fanaticism is any more difficult than the measurement of intelligence, and it is reasonable to assume that as much progress could be made with one problem as with the other, given a similar amount of effort directed at it.

Brinton's seventh variable is the element of religious faith, which he defines in such a way that it includes fanatical atheistic Marxism as well as the Independents of the English revolution, and the Jacobins. This variable could be treated in either of two ways. One might look at it as a personality variable, in which case it would present the same sorts of difficulties as the sixth variable, or one might measure it in an entirely different way. For instance, one could treat it as a social phenomenon and try to measure the difference between the behavior which the revolutionary leaders recommend to the masses and the actual behavior of the former. Or one might see whether and to what extent the revolutionary slogans are merely ritualistic. Since these factors would be just as hard to measure numerically and would have to be broken down further before such an attempt could be successful, our conclusion is that some of the variables can be made numerical rather easily while others show considerable resistance to such an approach. Still, we have found no reason to think that such an approach is theoretically impossible although it may often be practically impossible because it would often demand the kind of detailed information about a particular historical period which we do not happen to have.

In his last chapter Brinton qualifies many of the conclusions which he has reached earlier. For one thing, he thinks that his four revolutions may constitute only one kind of revolution and that the generalizations which hold for these four may not hold for all revolutions. He abstains from any sort of large-scale generalizations and predictions about history:

> It is even more tempting to try to fit these revolutions into something like a philosophy of history. But the philosophy of history is almost bound to lead into the kind of prophetic activity we have already firmly forsworn. It may be that mankind is now in the midst of a universal "time of troubles" from which it will emerge into some kind of universal authoritarian order. It may be that the democratic revolutionary tradition is no longer a living and effective one. It may be that the revolutions we have studied could only have taken place in societies in which "progress" was made a concrete thing by opportunities for economic expansion which cannot recur in our contemporary world, with no more frontiers and no more big families. It may even be that the Marxists are right, and that imperialistic capitalism is now digging its own grave, preparing the inevitable if long-delayed world revolution of the proletariat. There are many possibilities, as to which it is almost true that one man's guess is as good as another's. Certainly a conscientious effort to study four great revolutions in the modern world as a scientist might cannot end in anything as ambitious and as unscientific as social prognosis. [P. 276]

Some of his remarks here and elsewhere in his last chapter seem inconsistent with our interpretation of his earlier conclusions, but much of this apparent inconsistency is due to ambiguous terminology. We earlier held that for these uniformities to be significant and interesting, it must be possible to generalize beyond the four revolutions which Brinton discusses. Such an extension does not imply that the uniformities can be generalized over all revolutions, however, and he is quite right in rejecting that temptation. Suppose, then, that the four revolutions he discusses form one distinct kind of revolution and that there are other revolutions which do not belong to this class. It is still the case that if any other revolution is of the same kind and we can set up criteria for saying what that kind of revolution consists in, then the uniformities which Brinton has discovered can be projected over that revolution. While Brinton does not try very hard to characterize in the abstract the sort of revolution that he is interested in, he seems to feel that this is something that could be done. That having been done, we would then have a legitimate field for generalization. Again, the historical situation is like any other scientific situation. No scientific findings can be generalized indefinitely, but there always has to be a certain class of phenomena which can be independently specified and over which we are implicitly generalizing. When Brinton seems to suggest that his conclusions cannot be generalized at all he sells himself short, which perhaps explains why he does not put sufficient effort into specifying the class of revolutions over which his results could be generalized.

Similarly, when Brinton decides that prophecy and social prognosis are illegitimate he seems to have in mind very sweeping sorts of predictions. Certainly he has said nothing from which we can legitimately deduce predictions concerning what will happen in, say, the twenty-first century. On the other hand, we can deduce from Brinton's account the prediction that *if* a revolution of the relevant kind occurs in the twenty-first century and the seven variables he mentions are satisfied in very high degree, *then* there will be a reign of terror. That is, one cannot deduce categorical predictions from this kind of starting point, and Brinton seems to assume that these are the only kinds of predictions that there are. However,

151

conditional or hypothetical predictions like the one illustrated above are also perfectly genuine predictions and
are deducible from any sort of scientifically established
uniformity. Further, someone in the twenty-first century
who knows that a revolution of the required sort is occurring and that the seven variables are satisfied in high
degree would then be able to predict categorically that a
reign of terror will occur in very short order. Consequently, it seems that if Brinton means what he says in
the first nine-tenths of the book and is trying to establish
a sort of non-numerical scientific account of revolution,
then he qualifies too much in the last chapter when he
seems to say that generalization and prediction of all
sorts are really impossible after all. We interpret him to
mean only that the most extreme forms of generalization
and prediction are illegitimate. In general Brinton is working toward a sort of ideal historical methodology which
would also be a scientific methodology; but he encounters
certain obstacles and, by his own admission, can only
get part way towards this goal.

13 Conclusion

In surveying types of historical thinking, I have
taken some pains to note all the diverse forms of argument which it is possible to find in historiography. Interesting as some of these differences may be, however, it
is more important to note the uniformities. I have already
remarked on the usefulness of the technique of sympathetic identification in suggesting interesting historical
hypotheses. Still, there is an important difference, in any
scientific field, between the way in which hypotheses are
first arrived at, the form and content of those hypotheses,
and the way in which they are finally verified. These

elements are, of course, closely related. A particular method of discovery will produce hypotheses of a certain sort, and the nature of the hypotheses will then determine the way in which they can be verified. I have previously placed the emphasis on the method of discovery, but I have also stated the conclusions arrived at in some detail, and it is now time to make some generalizations over those conclusions. Most of the rest of the book will be concerned with methods that can be used in verifying the hypotheses of history.

It was pointed out in the introduction that most historical conclusions assert causal connections between events and that these give rise to counterfactual statements. While I have often noted these implications, my present claim is that *every* piece of historical writing contains them, and it would have been tedious to reiterate this point with each sample. In order to substantiate my claim I list below a set of counterfactuals, one of which is implied by each sample that we have considered. For convenience, brackets have been used to enclose the antecedent of each conditional, and in each case that antecedent is believed to be false even though the conditional statement as a whole is implicitly (and in some cases explicitly) asserted.

1. (Granet, pp. 18–20). If [an ancient source had contradicted the theory that great sages appear every five hundred years], the Chinese annalists would have altered the text.

    Granet first argued for this premise, and then took it as a premise in later arguments. He took this principle as a *general* one, and hence implied that, even in the case of a text that did not contradict the five hundred year theory, if it had contradicted the theory it would have been altered. A physical causal law such as "If water (in a pure form) is below 32 degrees F., it freezes" has counterfactual force of the same sort; it also entails of a body of water above 32 degrees that, if it had been below 32 degrees, it would have frozen.

2. (Granet, pp. 24–26.) If [the ancient Chinese had not been acquainted with hibernating animals], they would not have had such rigid rules of winter conduct for themselves.

The principle here is that the ancient Chinese were trying to copy nature in general and the animals in particular. Consequently, if the animals had behaved in a different way, the people would have behaved in a different way.

3. (Bullock, pp. 31–36.) If [the Papen-Hitler meeting at Schröder's house had not involved an attempted conspiracy against Schleicher], then Schröder would not, at Nuremberg, have said that it did.

4. (Parkes, pp. 44–47.) If [the torpedo had not been invented], the design committee for the *Dreadnought* would have been much less interested in speed.

5. (Mowat, pp. 57–62, 64–65.) If [parliament had realized that the passage of the Addison Act would lead indirectly to large scale public housing], it would have been more strongly opposed.

6. (Duyvendak, pp. 72–74.) If [the phrase "k'o tao," which appears in the first line of the *Tao-te-ching* had had the meaning "is said" as opposed to "is truly regarded as" for the Taoists], then it would have occurred in other Taoist texts with that meaning as an alternative to "yen."

7. (Tilly, pp. 87–88.) If [the Vendean counterrevolution had been caused simply by the peasants, nobles,

and priests, as opposed to bourgeois elements],
then the total number of peasants, priests, and
nobles would have been proportionately greater in
counterrevolutionary districts than in revolutionary
districts.

8. (Campbell, pp. 96–97.) If [the panic and depression
of 1893 had not occurred], then (all other things being equal) the Norfolk and Western Railway would
not have gone bankrupt.

   One should not attach too much importance
to the qualification in parenthesis because as we
shall see, some such qualification is presupposed by
every counterfactual on closer analysis.

9. (Huizinga, pp. 101–103.) If [the spirit of chivalry
had not been a dominant influence at the time],
then the later crusades would either not have taken
place or they would have been aimed at the Balkans
rather than the Holy Land.

10. Piecemeal history gives rise to less striking counterfactuals than the more general sorts of history, but,
even here we can find entailed counterfactuals.
Wank implies (pp. 117–118) that if [Berchtold
had been Aerenthal's first choice as his successor],
then von Merey and von Schiessl would not have
written as they did. Thomas implies that if [Mr.
Roberts had made all the speeches attributed to
him by Cavendish (pp. 119–120)], there would have
been strong similarities as to style, subject-matter
and content. Finally, Nixon implies that if [the
seamen on the slavers had not been treated so
cruelly on the "middle voyage"], a much higher
percentage would have returned to England (pp.
120–121).

11. (Namier, p. 130.) We noted before Namier's view
that if [an Anglo-Russian alliance had been suc-

cessfully negotiated in the spring of 1939], the Second World War would either not have broken out, or the Germans would have been defeated more quickly.

12. (Brinton, pp. 145–147.) Again, we must recall Brinton's assertion that if [there had been no habit of violence, or no economic crisis], then there would have been no reign of terror in the French revolution, or any other similar revolution.

We could go on noting such counterfactuals almost endlessly, and we take it as undeniable that counterfactuals are part and parcel of historical writing as it is actually practised. We have also spoken of ethical judgments of a special kind as being a very pervasive, though not universal, feature of historical writing. They were particularly evident in Namier's *Diplomatic Prelude,* but present, though not so obvious, in other samples. Brinton does not make ethical judgments about anyone in quite the way that Namier condemns Chamberlain, but there are still some ethical judgments to be found in his work. For example, Brinton points out that the moderates who first take control of a revolution (p. 142) invariably play a rather pointless and stupid game in which they end up alienating everyone and being ousted. He does not, of course, say that someone like Kerensky or Lafayette is immoral, but he does say that such moderates are guilty of bad strategy. The evaluation implicit here might be paraphrased as "If someone accepts a public office in the first place, he invariably enters a power struggle of one sort or another (ranging from competition with other persons to competition with other nations), and it is irrational for him not to adopt a good strategy and make a realistic attempt to win that struggle." In ordinary life our ethical judgments are not limited to calling people crooks and whores. We also make them when we say that someone is stupid or irrational. These latter judgments may not imply the immorality of the person concerned, but they are still evaluative in a different way. In fact, most philosophical specialists in ethics treat moral judgments as a special kind of ethical judgment, and emphasize what moral judgments have in common with other sorts of ethical judgments.[31]

Huizinga is also given to making ethical judgments, as in his remark that a barbarous age, like the Middle Ages, should set itself particularly high ideals in order to offset the barbarism. Although this idea is not really integral to his study, it should be remembered that he attributes chivalrous motives for an action only when it cannot be justified rationally. One can thus see that evaluations of rationality are integral to Huizinga's historical method.[32]

Even in the passage from Campbell's railroad history, we again have the feeling that railroad managers are being judged according to how well or badly they play a certain sort of game. Some managers are blamed for making gross mistakes while the executives of the Norfolk and Western are actually exonerated for making basically wise moves which would have worked out well except for the occurrence of a depression which we cannot reasonably have expected them to foresee.

More surprising still, we find some particularly striking ethical judgments involved in our samples of piecemeal history. Much of Wank's motivation in writing his essay seems to be to exonerate Aerenthal from sharing the blame for Berchtold's policies, which helped bring on the First World War. This is done by showing that Aerenthal did not really want Berchtold and his policies in the first place. Similarly, it is hard to write about the slave trade without getting involved in ethical judgments (this time moral ones), and part of the point of Nixon's note is to show that the slave trade was cruel, not only in its treatment of slaves, but in its treatment of seamen as well.

Again, in Parkes there is an implicit commendation of naval staffs and designers who turn out superior ships, and Fisher is particularly praised since he played such a clever and subtle role in getting the *Dreadnought* built. Here, in fact, one gets a particularly clear delineation of the kinds of ethical judgments that the historian typically makes from the ones that he typically refrains from making. Fisher is not commended because he just happened to be successful in getting the *Dreadnought* design adopted. It is rather because he used a strategy which would work in most similar cases, and which would be capable of surmounting considerable obstacles. That is, he won, not by accident, but because he played well. Parkes does not, however, in any way attempt to say whether it was proper for Fisher to mislead people in the way that he did. The historian's notion of "objectivity" allows him to rate historical figures for their effectiveness, but it ordinarily prevents him from himself making *moral* judgments about the strategies used or the persons using the strategies. Of course, a good history may present the relevant facts so that the reader can make moral judgments of his own, but that is a very different matter.[33]

Similar ethical judgments could be found in the samples taken from Bullock and Mowat, and, indeed, from most historical works. Still, we have had some samples of historiography which have not involved any ethical evaluations, even of the limited kinds mentioned above. Thus, Tilly, in contrast with the politically inspired historians, tries simply to isolate the conditions under which the counterrevolution occurred. He not only abstains from moral judgments about the counterrevolution itself, but he does not even try to say how effectively the counterrevolutionists went about their business. Similarly, one should not try to read ethical judgments into Granet's attempt to fix ancient Chinese chronology. Although the ancient annalists may have done peculiar things, Granet does not really say that they should not have doctored the texts. He merely points out that it was natural for them to do this and that their attitude and motivation was very different from that of, say, a present-day forger of old paintings and books. Granet's discussion of social customs in ancient China, Thomas's checklist of M. P.s, and the controversy between Waley and Duyvendak over the *Tao-te-ching* also seem to contain no evaluations. However, these samples are all relatively detailed and specialized, and were probably written for other scholars as much as for the general public. To say that these are attempts to "get the facts straight without interpreting them" would be a distortion because we have already seen that work of this sort is often very subtle, and may involve a great deal of interpretation and hypothesizing. What is true about this slogan is that, even after the facts have been established, there is still a great deal of room left for *further* interpretation of them, and for a *different kind* of interpretation of them. Simply getting the facts straight makes other work possible, and, as we ascend the pyramid, we typically get more general historical work, which is aimed at a larger audience, and in which evaluative judgments play an increasingly important role. While counterfactuals appear at all levels of historical writing, it is typical for ethical judgments to appear only at the higher levels. We are, nevertheless, justified in saying that the making of ethical judgments, like the asserting of counterfactuals, is essential to the historical enterprise when it is taken as a whole.

part 2 A METHODOLOGY FOR HISTORY

One of the conclusions of Part I was that counterfactuals and ethical judgments are essential to historiography as it is now practised. In this part we will try to provide a methodological framework not only for traditional historical assertions and hypotheses but also for counterfactuals and evaluative judgments. Part I indicated also that historical reasoning has two other main characteristics. First, historical reasoning consists largely of the same inductive and deductive reasoning used in science, again with particular emphasis on the forming and testing of hypotheses. It differs mainly in that it is often impossible to find suitable numerical indices with which to measure the relevant historical factors. Secondly, the historian almost always depends upon implicit psychological general laws for which our everyday common sense provides support, but which are not dealt with in the science of psychology proper, or in any other science. To make good this lack the historian usually has recourse to something like Collingwood's imaginative reenactment —that is, he imagines himself to be as much like the historical figure as possible, imagines himself to be in the position that the figure was in, and then imagines what he would try to do. He then concludes that the historical figure would, in all probability, have been motivated in similar ways. Further, this method is not used just as a means to an end, but also as an end in itself. Much of the satisfaction and understanding which historians and readers of history derive accrues because their research and reading has made possible this sympathetic identification. We take this as the second main feature of the methods used by most historians and we take it as a necessary condition for an adequate historical methodology that it both make history as much like an empirical science as possible and that it preserve this element of sympathetic identification.

1 Models in Mathematics and the Social Sciences

It is my thesis that models have a place in historical understanding, and that one who has historical understanding in high degree already has the knowledge that would enable him to construct a model of the historical situation which he understands. There is, however, a great deal of vagueness and confusion surrounding the word "model" and its use. Consequently, I will first explain what sort of a model I have in mind and relate this concept to the concept of a simulation and to the concept of a game. I can then specify the exact role of models in historical understanding.

We noted much earlier that the methodological framework to be suggested for history hinges on applying operations research to the real past as opposed to the conjectural future. The most important concept of operations research is probably that of a model, and, since there is an immense amount of confusion centering on this concept, we cannot pass over it lightly. The concept of a game is important for a different reason. We could develop our framework without talking about games at all, but it must be remembered that we are trying to reconcile the view of history as science with the view of history as a kind of *Verstehen* or complete intellectual fulfillment in itself. In this last respect it is helpful to draw on our intuitive notion of what it is to play a role in a game. By then making a connection between a certain kind of model and a game we can see historical figures as playing roles in games that we can reconstruct. We can then understand historical figures as people even while we are constructing a model of the past.

The clearest definition of "model" is that given by mathematicians. Here we conceive a mathematical system in a purely abstract way and we let the key terms of the language of the system remain undefined. There may be definitions in the system, but the definitions lead back eventually to these primitive terms. These latter are regarded as not having any meaning at all in themselves. They may be given a particular meaning for some specific purpose or application, but this does not in any way affect the status of the system itself or give the primitive terms any "permanent" meaning. Hence, the language of the system, based as it is on the primitive terms, is open to any interpretation that we might want to give it. The axioms of the system are, of course, stated in this language, and they must then, considered in themselves, be meaningless statements. Again, when the system is interpreted, they take on a particular meaning, and they may become true or false under those circumstances. But since they have no meaning in themselves they can have no truth value, apart from a particular application. We then speak of a model of the system as a state of affairs which, on a given interpretation of the primitives, is truly described by the axioms. That is, we find a model when we find some way of interpreting the primitives such that the axioms all become true statements about a particular state of affairs. It is occasionally possible to find a model of a mathematical system in the physical world in such a way that one can see that the axioms of the system really do accurately describe an aspect of the world on the appropriate interpretation. In most cases, however, one finds a model of one mathematical system in another system. Here it is not a case of seeing that the axioms truly describe some state of affairs, but of proving that a certain relationship holds between the two systems. One system, S, has a model in another system, S', if the following two conditions are met. First, the primitive terms of system S must be introduced into the language of S' as defined terms. Secondly, the axioms of S must be proven as theorems in S'. This amounts to collapsing S into S' and viewing the former as a part of a more extensive system. Of course, as noted before, we do not *have* to interpret the primitives of S in this way, and it still remains as an autonomous system quite apart from this special relationship to S'.

A simple example of such a relationship is afforded by group theory. Here the primitive terms will be G (usually interpreted to be the set of elements which constitutes the group), "o" (this symbol is placed between variables and $x \, o \, y$ can be read as "x operation y"), and the prime symbol (the prime may be affixed to a variable and x' is read "x inverse"). The last primitive is the symbol e (which is called "the identity element"). The axioms are then as follows:

A1. If x and y belong to G, then $x \, o \, y$ belongs to G.
A2. $x \, o \, (y \, o \, z) = (x \, o \, y) \, o \, z$.
A3. For any $x, x \, o \, e = x$.
A4. For any $x, x \, o \, x' = e$.

One interpretation of the primitives is as follows. Let G be the set of integers, "o" the operation of addition, let e

be *0* (zero) and let the prime symbol be interpreted as the minus sign. It can now be seen that all the axioms are satisfied on this interpretation. The sum of any two integers is an integer, and association over addition also holds for the integers. Axiom 3 is true because any integer plus zero is equal to itself, and axiom 4 now says, truly, that the sum of any integer and its negative is equal to zero. Inasmuch as these axioms, as interpreted, can be proven in the system or arithmetic, a model has been found for group theory in arithmetic.

We can find a different model in arithmetic by giving a different interpretation to the primitives. This time we will take *G* to be the set of rational numbers (fractions with integral numerators and denominators) greater than zero, "o" the operation of multiplication; we will let *e* be 1 and *x′* will denote the reciprocal of *x*. Axiom 1 will now say that the product of any two rational numbers greater than zero is a rational number greater than zero, and this is also true. Similarly, association holds for multiplication as well as addition. Axiom 3 is now true because any rational number multiplied by one is equal to itself, and axiom 4 is true because the product of a fraction and its reciprocal is always 1. Thus we again have a model for group theory in arithmetic.

These examples illustrate the precision of the mathematical concept of a model, but, unfortunately, models of this sort do not play any part in historical understanding. It is rather the social scientist's conception of a model which promises to be useful, and this concept is at once very different from and much less clear than the mathematician's concept of a model.

By a model a social scientist means, roughly, that if we have two systems or situations, *A* and *B*, such that *A* is a model of *B*, there is then an analogy between the operations in *A* and *B*, and that *A* is artificially created: further, *A* must be created in such a way that it is easier and simpler to understand than *B*. Thus, for the social scientist and others who use the same sorts of models, the situation to be modelled comes first, and one afterwards sets up an artificial model which resembles the actual situation in certain crucial respects, but which leaves out many complexities which are involved in the real situation. It can easily be seen that the social scientist's conception of a model is almost directly opposed to that of the mathematician. Suppose, for instance, that we find a model for a system of geometry in the world by interpreting the lines of the system as paths of rays of light. In the mathematical sense the physical system will be a model of the mathematical system, but it is the geometrical system which has been artificially created as opposed to the model for it. Further, while the interpreted geometrical system describes a part of the world, it is totally incapable of talking about most aspects of the world and is consequently simpler and easier to understand than the physical world or any part of it. Hence, on the social scientist's conception, it would be the geometrical system which is a model of the physical world rather than vice versa. It is now clear why there is so much confusion over this issue and why the mathematician often thinks of the social scientist as a bungler who is always getting things backward. There is, of course, no real difficulty as long as we are clear what we mean by a model, and, from this point on, we will adopt the social scientist's concept of a model as a starting point and attempt to make it more precise.

Models of the social scientist's sort cover a great deal of ground ranging from physical objects which are imitations of other physical objects to the most complex of computer simulations and artificially constructed games. Even though some of the models are physical entities while others are conceptual entities, they are all imitations of some state of affairs or situation or system, and they can all be thought of as simulations.

From a theoretical point of view, one of the simplest simulations is that of an actual model ship in a model basin. Here the size of everything has been scaled down to a point where it can be artificially controlled, and the naval architect can test one ship design against another while excluding such complexities of the real world as wind, tide, bad fuel, and drunken chief engineers. The situation of the model in the model basin is then easier to understand than the passage of the real ship through the water, but the crucial factor, the action of water on various hull designs, is the same in the basin as in the ocean. In a similar way, the airplane model in the wind tunnel is a simulation of the airplane's flight through the sky, but we cannot go so far as to regard a mouse's eating of a piece of cheese as a model of human eating habits. Since models (simulations) are artificially created, a mouse in itself is not a model of anything. Nevertheless, it is still possible to include mice, or other animals, in a complex artificially created situation which might constitute a model of some other situation. Thus, putting mice in an artificially created maze and giving them various stimuli may give us a model for a part of human behavior, or some other sort of behavior. Actually, our restriction that a model be artificially constructed may be unnecessarily tight. It is logically possible that a psychologist who is about to construct a maze with mice to simulate a part of human behavior might find that a maze of the appropriate sort already exists, by a freak of nature or by children in his back yard. It might even be complete with mice. Such a natural object might, by extremely long odds, turn out to be exactly what was wanted and serve as a model. However, we are not likely to have to deal with models of this sort, and it will be convenient to treat "model" and "simulation" as synonymous and limit both to artificially created systems.

One of the essential features of the model is that it must be easier to understand than the actual situation for which it is a model. Of course, a model of any degree of complexity simulates some features of the actual situation closely while leaving others out altogether. That in itself makes the model easier to understand, but it usually allows us to concentrate our attention on the most important features in other ways as well. Suppose, for instance, that we are looking at the game films of a football game and that we want to understand what happened on a particular play in more detail. We might then take a large board in the shape of a football field and twenty-two markers or figures to represent the players. By consulting the film we could then move the players an inch at a time (varying slightly with the speed of the players) so that we would have a representation of their relative position at each moment during the play. The play itself, or even the movies of it, would present a confusing blur of activity, but in the simulation we would be able to see exactly who was where when. The artificial construction of a simulation often makes possible a degree of control which we would not have over the real situation. In this case we can stop the play wherever we wish and look at it for as long as we wish. Or we can run it backwards, or run it over again, or set up several boards simultaneously representing the play at different stages. All this allows us to isolate a small temporal unit of the play for close study. When we are looking at the play itself or the film we are limited to a particular angle and we do not see any single stage of the play long enough to take it in properly. Further, the simulation also allows us to concentrate our attention on a small spatial part of the field in a way that is difficult when observing the actual play. A trained scout can watch a number of players at once and remember what each does during the play, but the average observer, not knowing where to look, sees little or nothing by trying to look everywhere. As mentioned above, a model has to allow us to isolate certain features for study, and it often allows us to study slowly what happens fast in actuality.

The kind of simulation which is represented by our recreation of a football play is relatively limited in its usefulness. In particular, it is hard to see how we could really learn anything very new from it. There has to be someone who understands football and who knows how to interpret films in order to set up the simulation. Its main use would appear to be in explaining the action of the game to someone who lacked understanding of it. The simulation also has a sort of visual clarity in that one can look at the board from many angles and easily assess the distance between any two players in a way that would be difficult from the film alone, where some of the angles would distort the actual space relationship. In this way it might be useful even to the person who set up the simulation, but since the simulation is based directly on the game film, it cannot tell us much that we could not have gathered just by looking at the film. In general, one can say that a simulation based on a single piece of evidence can only convey the information contained in that evidence in a more perspicuous form. As opposed to this, a simulation which is based on many different sources and which "puts them all together" may show surprising results, even to those persons who are thoroughly familiar with the sources.

What sort of understanding will the kind of simulation represented by the recreated play provide? We have already seen that it has a kind of visual clarity which the game films do not have, and this might lead us to notice things that we had not noticed before. We might, for instance, notice that a particular player did not get into proper position to make a particular block. Thus the simulation may be a *psychological* aid in making certain discoveries, but the simulation cannot provide us with any evidence in itself since all the evidence for what might have happened has to be traced directly back to the film. In fact, it is questionable that a simulation such as this can give us any historical understanding at all. It is a historical event—part of a football game—that we are studying, but the method that we are using is not a historical method. If one wanted to study an earthquake one could also line up a series of models of the area affected at different times during the disturbance, and these might be based on films taken from an airplane. Again, this might yield a certain amount of insight into what happened, but this time it is a natural event rather than a historical event that is being studied. Of course, earthquakes may enter into history, but when they do it is because of the effects they have had on human societies, and an earthquake that affects no one has no more to do with history than an eclipse of the sun which took place before there were any human beings. Events such as this are of interest to geology or astronomy, or whatever special science is involved, but not to history. The football play, on the other hand, involves persons and might have varying effects on the players, spectators, and others. But when we recreate it in the way just brought forward, we are not throwing any light on the effects it may have on human society or on individuals. Further, we do nothing to explain why any of the events took place with respect to human goals and motivations, or, indeed, with reference to anything else. We are studying the event in such a way that we take account only of the action of one physical body as it moves along the ground or hits another. We are studying it in the way that we might study a natural event, and it would not make any difference to our simulation if the players all turned out to be automata who ran the same play over and over again hundreds of times a day in connection with a beer advertisement. In view of this, let us say that an event can form part of the subject matter of history only to the extent that it is related to human society in some way or other. A historical method is then a method that can be used to establish such relationships. Thus, to do history, one has to study historical events and one has to use a historical method in studying them. In our simulation of the football play we have been studying a historical event, but we have been using a non-historical method in studying it.

It is sometimes said that the historian is only trying to find out what happened, but we can see that if he is interested in what happened in such a narrow way that he only takes account of physical events to the exclusion of such "mental" events as motivations and beliefs, he ends up by not doing history at all. In fact, when historians talk about merely trying to establish what happened, they mean that they are trying to establish what happened *from the point of view of the persons involved.*

We can now distinguish between what I will call 'dumb' and 'dynamic' simulations. A dumb simulation is one, like our simulation of the football play, in which we merely attempt to recreate an event which has always taken place by constructing some sort of mock-up based directly on available evidence. A dynamic simulation involves a much broader view of the situation which we are trying to simulate. It is here supposed that what happened happened in accordance with a larger number of rules and principles which can be discovered. It is also assumed that what happened was only one outcome among other possible ones, any of which could have followed according to these rules and principles. In a dynamic simulation we recreate not only what happened but attempt to represent in some way or other the unrealized potentialities, and we give some representation of the rules and principles which we take to govern the whole situation. This comes much closer to historical understanding because in history our study is always of persons and the plans they make for achieving one goal as opposed to others. We find that they are always considering various possibilities which, to them, lie in the future. But to understand what they were doing we have to have some idea of these other possibilities which were to them future, but which are to us might-have-beens. It is only a dynamic as opposed to a dumb simulation which promises us any knowledge of these possibilities. It is then only a dynamic simulation which holds out any hope for explaining human actions. Another characteristic of a dumb simulation is that no counterfactual statements are presupposed by it or are implied by it. One might suppose that one could look at such a model as the dumb simulation of the football play and see that so-and-so has the hardest block to make on a certain sort of play. One might, in fact, arrive at that conclusion by looking either at the model or the film or the actual play. However, the dumb simulation is not any kind of conceptual entity but a physical object (board and markers) which represents the actual play in basically the same way that a ship model represents a ship. It is just that the markers on the board always bear the same spatial relationships to one another as the players on the field. One may look at any physical object and make dispositional or counterfactual statements about it, but one reasons from all sorts of general principles which are explicitly or implicitly accepted, and this kind of model itself does not generate or imply these counterfactuals any more than does the situation itself. For that we have to have a conceptual model which incorporates, as a part of itself, general rules and principles from which counterfactuals could be derived.

Let us now contrast this dumb simulation of a play with a dynamic simulation of the same play. We might start with the same board and the same markers, but we would now have rules governing the distance each player can move during a simulated period, say, a second. We would then stop the game every second and move the players the appropriate distances. The difference is that instead of moving the players in the way that they actually did move during the play in question, we are free to move them in any legal way, and we eventually will have criteria for saying when the ball carrier was tackled, whether a pass was complete, and so on. Among other things, we are free to move the players in the way that they actually did move on a particular occasion and, if the simulation is an accurate one, we should get in the simulation the outcome that actually occurred in the game. This dynamic

172

simulation no longer consists solely of the board and markers but contains conceptual elements which are much more important to it. These consist in the principles according to which we move players and the criteria we have for deciding the outcome of the play. These principles and criteria allow us to make genuine discoveries of a kind which were impossible with the dumb simulation. They also allow us to infer counterfactuals. For instance, we can take the original play, alter a blocking assignment, and see if it makes the play more or less successful. We can also alter the ball carrier's path and make other changes, or we can substitute a different play altogether to see whether it would have been more successful. We might come to the conclusion that the play that was actually run promised the greatest chance of success in that situation, or we might come to some other conclusion. This possibility of vindicating the quarterback's judgment takes us far beyond a dumb simulation, but it also preserves many of the advantages of the dumb simulation. We can still stop whatever play we are running whenever we wish, and we can still localize our attention on certain parts of the field in a way that is difficult when watching the actual game. Further, all the pedagogical advantages of the dumb simulation are preserved here. In fact, it was pointed out that we can still move the markers in the same way that we did during the dumb simulation even though we would now be moving them according to the rules of the simulation as well as consulting the game film. It thus appears that the dumb simulation is, in a certain sense, a proper part of the dynamic simulation. That is, the dynamic simulation can be used to re-create the situation that actually occurred, but it can also be used to reproduce possible situations that might have occurred but did not. Consequently, the dynamic simulation is both logically different in kind from the dumb one, and is much more powerful.

Since historical understanding involves not only finding out what happened in the narrowest sense, but explaining why people acted as they did, we must consider the unrealized possibilities which the historical figures took into account in making their plans. Since only a dynamic simulation can deal with these it will always be dynamic simulations that are relevant to historical understanding.

In return for the increased power of dynamic simulations the price we have to pay is that it becomes much more difficult to check the accuracy of the simulation. The dumb simulation could be checked against the game film at every stage, and any inaccuracies could be easily discovered and corrected. However, no dynamic simulation can be based directly on a single piece of evidence in this manner. Since the dynamic simulation deals with other possibilities than those that actually occurred, it has to be based on the principles and natural laws which are taken to operate in the real situation. Of course, it is much more difficult to discover what principles govern a particular situation, or type of situation, than it is to discover what events took place in the narrowest sense, at least given an accurate record or transcription of some kind.[1] Further, the real difficulty lies not just in discovering which principles and laws are correct, but rather in trying to get a complete list of all such principles which are relevant. In constructing a dynamic simulation it is very easy simply to overlook a factor which operated in the real situation and thus to leave out any representation of that factor in the simulation. There can never be any certainty that one has a completely accurate dynamic simulation, and, as in most scientific areas, we just have to do our best and try not to omit anything important. We do have a way of verifying the accuracy of the simulation to some extent. If we start with the initial conditions that obtained historically, the rules of the simulation should take us to the outcome that occurred historically. However, this test is certainly not conclusive because we will never have *all* the relevant initial conditions in the simulation, and the fact that a dynamic simulation passes the test does not relieve us of responsibility in trying to perfect it further.

Moving from dumb to dynamic simulations we find that still another element enters the picture. In the dumb simulation of the football play we could recreate the play while ignoring altogether its relative success or failure. In a dynamic simulation of football we can also experiment to see what will happen without making any sort of ethical judgment about it, but at some point we will have to take account that there are certain goals in the game and that the strategies and tactics employed are intended to achieve them. In the dumb simulation there is no attempt to explain why anyone does what he does, but in the dynamic simulation we can ask why a certain strategy was used. A strategy is a plan for achieving a certain outcome and, once we have strategies, we must also have desired outcomes, and within the dynamic simulation these must also be represented.

In the dynamic simulation of a game like football certain rules must be set up which govern what can be done in the simulation and which moves can be made. These rules of the simulation will reflect not just the rules of football, but also the physical potentialities of the players, and will tell us what choices are open to one side or the other, and to what extent these choices are limited. In the actual game the choices are limited in the sense that a team cannot do anything illegal without penalty, but, even more important, the possibilities open to the quarterback are limited by the potentialities of his players. Certain players simply do not have it within their power to run a hundred yards in ten seconds or less, and others cannot possibly make certain blocks or tackles. Consequently, what we call the rules of the simulation are much more extensive than the rules of football, or the rules of any similar game. The rules of the simulation will have to be so extensive that, given the choices which are made as well as certain chance factors, they will allow us to infer exactly what has happened at every stage of the simulation.

If we are now interested in evaluating the choices of the quarterback, as we probably would be, we must distinguish between what could reasonably be expected of the players and their actual capabilities at the moment. If one of the backs pulls a muscle at the beginning of a play and can only run at half his usual speed, and the play therefore fails, one can hardly blame the quarterback for having made a poor choice of plays. In the simulation of football under consideration, the actual capabilities of the players would be reflected, at least to the extent that these can be accurately determined. However, we can see even here that in evaluating decisions we must take into account what could be reasonably expected of the players, and these reasonable expectations are so far not built into the simulation. We will later see how these evaluations can be handled in the context of a simulation.

A dynamic simulation constructed in this way should allow us to try out unactualized possibilities to see what would have happened under varying circumstances. It does not necessarily follow that a given possibility would have been fulfilled in the actual situation for two main reasons. First, the simulation may not be complete enough to give us any assurance that what happens in the simulation would have happened in the actual situation. Secondly, there are always many circumstances which we do not believe to be relevant to the main events in which we are interested and which we exclude from our simulation. But, as we will see later, it is conceivable that almost anything might affect almost anything else, and in the real situation there is always the possibility that one of these seemingly irrelevant factors might have made a difference. Thus, there is a certain gap between what happens in the model and what would have happened in the actual situation, but this is to be expected since we are doing a kind of empirical science; there are always ways in which the conclusions of inductive science can turn out to be mistaken or ill-founded. The whole issue will be discussed later in much more detail.

Up to this point our examples have been somewhat parochial since they have been drawn from games like football, but we can easily simulate situations which are not games in this ordinary sense. However, from the point of view of a simulation, there is less difference between a game like football and an activity like warfare or politics than one might think. We saw that in football the range of choices that one can make is limited by two factors: rules in the strict sense, which tell us which actions would be illegal and the physical limitations of the players. In almost any human activity there are obviously going to be physical limitations. One cannot conquer Russia with an army of a few dozen, and one cannot be nominated as president of the United States without any political background, fame, or money. One might suppose that in such situations there would be nothing analogous to the rules of football. Nevertheless, it turns out that there is another factor which limits choices and which is rather like following the rules of a game. Historical figures are usually limited not only by the possible but also by their own unquestioned assumptions as to what is possible. Further, the historian looking back to almost any age can see possibilities for action that did not occur to any of the principal actors either because they were alien to the contemporary culture in a certain way or ignorant of certain facts of nature. For example, it might have been physically possible for a Roman general to construct balloons and land some of his men behind the enemy, or use them for scouting purposes. However, it is an unquestioned assumption of the general that his men cannot be made to fly, and such a possibility never occurs to him. In simulating battles of the time we would probably also leave such possibilities out of account because we want to simulate the strategy and tactics of the time and we want the same sorts of choices and decisions to arise in the simulation that would or did arise on the actual battlefield. Hence, as far as our simulation goes, we would probably decide to ignore certain physical possibilities, and one might classify them as being contrary to the rules.

Other sorts of unquestioned assumptions might be moral ones. For instance, it might occur to a British prime minister in his daydreams to invite all his political opponents to a dinner and then poison them Borgia-fashion. But it never seriously occurs to him that he might actually do it, and one consequently cannot really say that he decides not to do it. Certainly, in British politics, the decision not to poison one's opponents is not a strategic or tactical decision. It is not that it might not work if done cleverly and selectively, but it is just that British politicians have always come from a social class which is encouraged not to do such things. This habit of not doing certain sorts of nasty things, first inculcated on the playing fields of Eton, is reinforced to the point where certain possible actions are removed from the politician's repertoire. Again, following the mores of one's society is not quite like complying with the backfield-in-motion rule, but from the point of view of the simulation we can still distinguish between actions which would be physically impossible and those which are physically possible but not considered seriously by the persons concerned for one reason or another.

A glance at the list of counterfactuals given above indicates that the antecedents, while false, do not represent either physical impossibilities or possible actions which would not have been considered seriously by the actors. On the first score it seems that the ancient Chinese might not have been acquainted with hibernating animals, that parliament might have recognized the probable consequences of the Addison Act, and that chivalry might have been less influential. We will see later that such assumptions, when combined with the rest of our knowledge, may lead to difficulty, but none in itself represents a physical impossibility comparable to supposing that a pail of water which is held at 13 degrees Fahrenheit for an hour under normal conditions is not frozen.

Moreover, every counterfactual that is mentioned refers to a state of affairs that is not only possible from our point of view, but which would have been considered possible from the point of view of the historical figures. Even if the torpedo had not been invented, the design committee for the *Dreadnought* would not have been nonplussed, and could still have designed a ship. Similarly, if the panic of 1893 had not occurred, the directors of the Norfolk and Western could have continued business as usual in a way that they could not if they had discovered that the locomotive wheels might melt at any moment, or even if they had thought that their competitors had access to atomically powered locomotives. More generally, a counterfactual will be of historical interest only if it can be stated within the rules of the "game" concerned.

We saw before that in dynamic simulations we have to take account of the element of success and failure in a way in which we would not in the case of dumb simulations. However, when we come to simulate such things as politics and battles, which are not games in the narrow sense, we must recognize that there is usually no single goal which is recognized by all the participants. Rather, there is likely to be a whole array of goals which may be graded in some order for each participant, but which may not be entirely common to all the participants. Further, the participants in some cases may not have a clear idea of their own goals, or they may not be entirely decided as to the relative value of various goals which they seek. In short, they may act more or less instinctively without fully articulating what it is that they are trying to do. In order to construct a dynamic simulation of such a situation we very likely do have to be clear about the goals, and their relative value. This may involve being clearer about the goals of the participants than they are themselves. In such a case we would be in the position of constructing a theory as to what the real goals of the participants are. The test of the adequacy of such a theory would then be to see how well it explains the recorded behavior, disappointments, and claims of success made by the participants and the people surrounding them. While we might have to suppose that the actions of the participants are typical of those of a certain social class, or other sort of class, at a certain time, there may be some basis for such an assumption, and we may be able to thereby infer the probable motives and goals of the people concerned. This is one of the many places where a dynamic simulation may presuppose a specialized historical investigation. We will eventually want to say that dynamic simulations can play an important role in historical understanding, but it should be clear from this point on that it cannot replace the sort of specialized historical investigations that have traditionally been made. Rather, its function will have to do with the direction of these investigations, and the putting together of the results arrived at.

It is now clear that all models in the social scientist's sense are simulations of actual situations. Further, it is also clear that such persons as sociologists, social psychologists, and political scientists are all sufficiently interested in causal connections so that dumb simulations will be practically useless to them. For all practical purposes, then, we can think of a social scientist's model as a dynamic simulation of an actual situation. However, the historian studies the same sorts of situations and circumstances as the social psychologist, the political scientist, and the others. The only difference is that the situations the historian studies lie in the past as opposed to the present or the future. Nothing about a dynamic simulation ties it in any way to either the past, the present or the future, however.

I will now attempt to show how dynamic simulations can be useful to the historian.

2 Games

It should by now be obvious that there is a close connection between simulations, particularly dynamic ones, and games. I will now try to make this relationship clearer. To clarify this relationship, it is first necessary to make the concept of a game itself clearer, and, in view of Wittgenstein's disquisition on games, one might wonder whether it is possible to give any sort of definition for the concept. Wittgenstein argued that there is only a family relationship between games and that no single common feature is essential to games as such. That is, given any game, there will be many features which it shares with other games, and one can often decide that something is or is not a game by noting the presence or absence of these shared features; it does not follow, however, that one can lay down any set of characteristics that must be shared by *all* games. Definition of the concept, in the usual sense of 'definition', is hence impossible.

All this is very likely true of 'game' as it is used in everyday conversation. Nevertheless, I will use it here as a technical term and narrow the concept in such a way that fairly precise limits to it can be set. In so doing I will exclude some activities, such as ring-around-a-rosy, which are ordinarily called games, and count as games certain activities which have much in common with many ordinary games, but which are sufficiently complex and esoteric to be denied the title in ordinary language.

181

My artificial definition of a game will allow it to have any number of players from one upwards. Each player will have an object or array of goals which he is trying to reach. These will ordinarily be shared by the players, but shared goals are not essential to this concept of a game. This restriction in itself excludes ring-around-a-rosy if one construes it as an activity that children engage in just to amuse themselves without there being any competitive element and without anyone's striving for any goal. There must also be some sort of a distinction between the rules and whatever strategic and tactical principles a good player might follow. Activities which are purely mechanical and in which the rules always specify what move must be made next will not be considered as games. A dumb simulation, being such an activity, would not count as a game. This restriction means that there are always free choices to be made by the players, and further that these free choices must be capable of making a difference to the outcome of the game. Where there are such choices to be made there is always the possibility of making them badly or well, and there will usually be a set of heuristic principles which will help the players to improve their choices. Hence, there will always be a distinction between principles which have to be obeyed (rules proper) and principles which one can elect to follow or not. I will not include as a game the sort of activity where there are desired outcomes and where one can make free choices, but where there are no rules. One can, for instance, imagine a dance-hall activity (some of the new dances may approach this) where the object is simply to make oneself conspicuous, and where one can do whatever one wants to that end. There might well be considerations of strategy and tactics involved in such an activity, but I prefer arbitrarily to limit the concept of a game in such a way that it will only include activities which are structured by rules.

I mentioned earlier that there is a considerable

resemblance between the rules of a game in the strict sense and the unquestioned assumptions which are made in many areas of life. In fact, the resemblance is so strong that one may allow assumptions of this sort to count as rules, thereby extending the range of the concept. In particular, I will allow as games those activities which would come under the ordinary concept except that the stakes are so high and the involvement of the players so often involuntary that the man in the street would hesitate to refer to them as games. The rationale here is to treat a principle which operates as a rule as a rule whether or not it is so labeled and whether or not the participants are fully aware of its status. Nevertheless, it will still be difficult to make an absolute distinction between unquestioned assumptions and very basic strategic and tactical assumptions which are *seldom* questioned. Consequently, there will still be some vagueness surrounding the range of application of the concept of a game. But the vagueness is now sufficiently limited so that it need cause us no concern.

We saw it to be essential to any dynamic simulation that attention be concentrated on certain specified kinds of outcomes, and that we be able to proceed with the simulation until these outcomes are determined. Speaking now of games, we can go even further and introduce the factor of success or failure. We still concentrate our attention on certain outcomes, but we do so now because these outcomes determine which of the players are successful and which unsuccessful, and the degree of success achieved in each case. Thus, one of the respects in which a game differs from even a dynamic simulation is that there *must* be an element of competition in a game where there need not be in a dynamic simulation. It is essential to the concept of a game that the players play it in order to win, even if they do not want to win exactly the same things. The dynamic simulation, on the other hand, can be played from a great variety of motives, and we can deduce from it nothing about the motivation of the participants.

There are still other activities which I will exclude from the class of games. Suppose, for instance, that I go down the street to buy a chocolate bar. This activity has a player, myself, it has an object, the getting of the chocolate bar, and there is a possibility of success or failure, which is also essential to our concept of a game. I may be hit by a car before I get there, or the store may be out of chocolate bars, and so on. Further, there are unquestioned assumptions about permissible tactics operating here. I could lie on the street as if injured so as to get a ride from a passing motorist, and I could then "recover" when passing the candy store, get out, and buy my chocolate bar. These tactics might work, and work better than any alternative, but they are beyond the range which I am willing to consider. Still, this activity is not to be counted as a game, although it could be simulated in such a way that the simulation *would* count as a game. That is, one might have a board and move one's marker a certain number of spaces each turn, roll dice to see if one must wait for a traffic light, to see if one is hit by a car, and finally to see if the store is out of chocolate bars. But the reason that the simulation is a game whereas I do not count the event simulated as one is that in the latter case I do not raise the question to myself, or to anyone else, of what is the best way to get the candy bar. The only question that I consider is whether I want one; having decided that I do, the next steps are obvious even though there are actually many choices as to route, speed of walking, etc. To play a game it has to occur to one that there are better and worse ways of achieving the goal either in the sense of achieving it to higher or lower degree or in the sense of maximizing or minimizing the probability of realizing a fixed goal; one must then consider the question of what method to use in trying to realize it. Even such games as sprinting would not be games in this sense if there were not various ways of running and other decisions of tactics to be made. There is no reason to think, for example, that a race between two dogs for a bag of meat is a game as far as the dogs are concerned. It may be a game for the handlers or owners of the dogs, but then only if there is a question of training the dogs in one way rather than another, starting them from different positions, etc.

We saw before that one can go through or play a dynamic simulation as if it were a game except that one need not play with any particular goal in mind. In a similar way one might play it absent-mindedly without realizing the opportunity within it for varying tactics and strategies. It is nevertheless characteristic of a dynamic as opposed to a dumb simulation that there is always the *opportunity* for the employment of different strategies whether one realizes it or not.

Another distinction between kinds of games probably has more apparent than real importance. In some games such as chess the emphasis is on certain decisions or choices, such as where to move one's rook pawn, and the move itself is then performed very easily and trivially. In other games, such as baseball and football, it may be easier to decide what move to make, but the move itself involves running, throwing, and other arduous activities. Consequently, we can distinguish between decision games and action games. In a decision game the important thing is to decide what to do and the move itself involves only doing something that anyone can do without appreciable effort. In an action game, even after one has decided what to do, there is a real question as to whether one can really carry out the move. Further, there are different kinds of action games, and the moves may be hard to make for varying sorts of reasons. In the instances cited there may be physical difficulties in throwing a pass the required distance or hitting a ball in the right direction, but in other games, such as the game of politics, the moves, such as making a particular kind of speech, may be difficult because they expose one to the slings and arrows of the masses or to the condemnation of one's social class. Thus, a move may be hard to make from a moral point of view, or it may be risky and fraught with dire consequences to oneself and one's regime. Or again, the player may be sure that he wants to make the move, but the move may involve persuading others to take certain courses of action, and this may be difficult. Hence, the moves of action games may be difficult to perform in various different ways. There will also be some cases where a difficult move in an action game can actually be broken down into a series of moves in a corresponding decision game. Thus, again, there may be no black-and-white distinction between action games and decision games.

The next step is to lay out the relationship between games and simulations more explicitly, and consider, among other things, whether all games are simulations and whether all simulations are games. It is obvious from the start that not all simulations are games because simulations include dumb ones as well as dynamic ones. But a dumb simulation proceeds always according to fixed rules, and the process of playing it out is mechancial. In a game there are always issues of strategy; hence no dumb simulation is a game. Narrowing the question, one can then ask whether all dynamic simulations are games, since there is always a nonmechanical element in a dynamic simulation which gives rise to questions of strategy. But we have also seen that in the playing of any game there are goals. In a dynamic simulation there are outcomes which would ordinarily represent the goals of the situation being simulated, and the simulation can also be played by one or more players and treated as a game. In fact, if the players actually try to achieve these goals it *is* a game but, as we have just seen, one can play a dynamic simulation in an offhand way without striving for any outcomes as goals, all the while making arbitrary or random decisions of tactics and strategy. It then follows that people who play a dynamic simulation in such a way are not playing a game, but in that case all that keeps the dynamic simulation from being a game is the attitude of the players towards it. One can say that a dynamic simulation can always be treated as a game if we choose to play it to win, and try to win in an intelligent and nonmechanical way.

As to whether all games are simulations, one's natural reaction is to say that there are some games which are not simulations. For example, the game of baseball qualifies as a game under the restricted definition of the concept, but it does not appear to be a simulation of anything. Played for its own sake, it does not seem to bear any special relationship to any other activity which it might be taken to simulate. In contrast to baseball, there does appear to be a class of games which are presented as quasi-simulations, for example, children's board games where markers are moved along the board according to the throws of dice. The markers usually represent animals or persons, and the children who play the game are supposed to make the connection between the moving of markers around the board and a race between the animals and/or persons represented. However crude the game may be, there is the idea that it simulates something else. Similarly, the game of Monopoly is in some sense a simulation of the hotel and real estate business, but again, it is too crude to be taken seriously as such.

One might suppose that it is action games that are played on their own account and that decision games are simulations of something else. This would be a false dichotomy, however. In the first place, there is relatively little difference between action and decision games. A decision game, which involves, say, the moving of markers, can always be transformed into an action game by making the moves themselves athletic events. The Russians have done this with chess, staging public chess matches in Dynamo Stadium in which ballet dancers are substituted for the pieces and moves have to be made in the proper ballet style. Further, an action game still involves strategic decisions, and one can transform it into a decision game by regarding the players as the persons who give orders to the persons actually making the moves. Thus football is a decision game from the point of view of the coaches of the rival teams. In the second place, there are some decision games, such as chess, which are not obviously simulations of much of anything. Consequently, one must look further for the relationship between a game and a simulation.

Reviewing the difference between a simulation and the situation simulated, we note that the simulation is simpler and easier to understand in that we can focus our attention on spatial and temporal segments of the simulation more easily than in the case of the situation simulated. This much is true whether or not the simulation happens to be a game. If we then have a game we can treat it as a simulation of another situation if there is similarity between the sorts of strategic decisions that can be made in either case, provided, of course, that the situation simulated is more complex than the game. Hence, given any game, we can always imagine a more complex game, constructed along similar lines, such that the first game is a simulation of the second. Even in the case of a game like baseball, one might imagine a very stylized sort of warfare of which it would be a simulation. In warfare of this kind movement might be restricted to pathways along the side of a square, the bases might represent natural havens, and so on. Granted that there has never been warfare of this sort, and that it is extremely unlikely that there would ever be, it is still imaginable as a situation which baseball could be taken to simulate. Actually, one need not even go as far as this to find a situation which baseball would simulate; one need only imagine a game which has all the features of baseball plus some other complexities not characteristic of it. In this way any game at all can be taken as a simulation of some possible situation, even though that situation may not exist in the world.

I have stated the condition that a game must have a goal which the players must try to reach. However, I still allow the concept of a game to include both the case where people play for fun and the case where they play in deadly earnest for the highest stakes. One can ultimately draw no sharp distinction between playing for fun as opposed to gambling, playing the stock market, engaging in business, and so on. In all these cases there are goals and, as far as the game goes, one can disregard the reasons that people may have for trying to reach the goals. With whatever seriousness a game may be played, the earlier conclusion that any of them can be treated as simulations still holds. Further, the situation simulated may itself be played for fun, or in earnest, or it may simulate some further situation, in which case it may, or may not, be a game itself.

In any dynamic simulation there have to be events which take place, and these can be divided into two classes: those corresponding roughly with the aspects of the real situation to be simulated and those which may be essential to the simulation, but which we are willing to let happen in a random way as opposed to their happening in the ways, and for the reasons, that they would happen in the real situation. That is to say, in any dynamic simulation there will be places where we throw dice, or do something similar, to see what happens next. If, in a simple board game, we throw dice to see if Peter Rabbit can get by the hairless one-eyed monster, we are not suggesting that there is no predicting whether a real Peter Rabbit would get by the monster, and we are not implying that there are no causal factors involved. We recognize that whether one gets by the other is going to be determined by such things as the relative speed and manoeverability of the two actual participants, whether one slips in the mud, the general emotional state of the participants, and an indefinite number of other factors. In some games we might try to simulate this aspect of the situation in as much detail as possible, but in the average children's board game we are content to simulate very little and to consign a great deal to the area of "pure chance." Further, more sophisticated games and simulations differ from this only in degree; we may try to simulate more events in more detail, but there will always be some aspects of some events which are not simulated. Some kind of indeterminacy is essential to the notion of a simulation; if it were not, the simulation would not be a simplification of the actual situation. It would be no easier to understand than the actual situation itself.

Contrasted to these events which are left to chance, there are other events in a simulation whose outcomes are determined by the rules in conjunction with decisions taken by the players and prior events. That is, there are some events which are such that we can deduce their outcome if we know what has happened in the simulation up to a certain point and what decisions have been made. Of course, some of these events upon which these outcomes depend will probably be themselves determined by chance, but the events which we are trying to simulate closely are also dependent on other factors. Ordinarily, if the game has a single goal, the question of whether it is achieved will probably belong to this latter class. This is because it would be pointless to play a game and then simply throw dice to see whether the goal is achieved, at least unless the prior progress of the game tells us which outcomes of the dice will determine a victory. If the course of the game or simulation has nothing to do with the achieving of the goal or the determining of the crucial outcome, then there would be no point in having the game or simulation at all. Similarly, however many crucial outcomes there may be in the simulation, it is these outcomes that tend to be the farthest removed from pure chance.

It has now become clear that one who constructs a dynamic simulation has a choice of what sorts of events to leave to chance and what sorts of events will be 'rule-determined,' as I will call them. It is a question of what aspects of the real situation one wants to simulate in the most detail. Usually they are the aspects of the real situation which are most bound up with human decisions. This fact reflects the motives we ordinarily have for constructing simulations, and it particularly reflects the purposes I have for dynamic simulations in this book. Whether a game or system happens to constitute a simulation of some other situation has, of course, nothing to do with the motives behind the construction of a simulation. Nevertheless, various simulations of the same situation may recreate different parts of it in varying degrees of detail, and in this respect the structure of the simulation usually reflects the motivation behind its construction. In history, and in the fields where simulations are ordinarily used, we are most interested in those aspects of the real situation which involve human decisions. Hence, it is natural to recreate *them* in the most detail in a simulation, and we will usually find in a simulation so intended that at least one class of decisions is removed from the area of chance.

At this point one might recognize that it is essential that dynamic simulations contain "chance" events but still wonder whether such a simulation can be historically useful *because* it must contain such events. The objection would be that since the real analogs of these "chance" events are determined causally, the simulation departs too much from reality to be useful. Nevertheless, it must be remembered that a dynamic simulation is supposed to simulate the world as it would have been if different decisions had been taken, or if some of the circumstances had been altered. Even then of course, there is no reason to think that there would actually have been *chance* events, and it does have to be admitted that the hypothetical world simulated is not exactly the world a historical figure would have had to deal with *in all respects*. But it *is* the world that he would have reasonably supposed that he had to deal with—the world as best he would have been able to foresee it. Suppose, for instance, that we are simulating the battle of Trafalgar and that in our simulation a certain rain-squall that was important in the actual battle does not take place. It would probably be a chance event in the simulation and, as such, it might not occur. While the rain may not be a chance event relative to the forces of nature, it is a chance event relative to the plans of the participants in the battle in that they had no way of predicting it. Thus, in evaluating their plans, which in no way involve rain-squalls, we are interested in Trafalgar-like battles which involve no rain as well as ones that do. Further, once we change some events in constructing a hypothetical world, we have no way of knowing whether the rain squall should be included or not, and we have virtually no choice but to leave it to chance. If it is important enough, however, we can construct a range of simulations involving rain, and another range involving no rain. We might then arrive at some such conclusion as the following: "Plan *A* promised the best chance of success provided that the weather remained good, but Plan *B* would very likely have worked whether or not it rained." In this way we can remove an unpredictable event from the area of chance if it is sufficiently crucial to justify the construction of two whole ranges of simulations.

Similarly, if we decided to simulate the situation in which, according to Campbell, the Norfolk and Western Railway found itself, the occurrence of a debt that could not be paid because of claims against the creditor would presumably be a chance event. As such, it might not occur in any given run-through of the simulation. As before, we would not be claiming that there was no explanation for the incurrence of a debt of that sort by the railroad, but it might not be a part of the simulation because the officers of the company could not have predicted it, and would not have allowed for it in their plans. But again, if we are really interested in whether or not the railroad would have gone bankrupt without the occurrence of such a debt, we can run simulations both with it and without it, and compare the outcome. It is, of course, harder to specify the connection between the non-payment of a debt and the resulting loss of public confidence in the company than it is to specify the connection between a rain-squall and its effect on gunnery. However, there is no reason to think that the connection is less real in the former case even though it may be more difficult to set up the simulation which represents that connection.

3 The Uses of Models

We have already touched on one use of simulations in our instance of the dumb simulation of the football play. But, this use can teach only what happened in the narrowest sense, without imparting understanding of the situation simulated. It is much more interesting to start with a system or game of some sort and hope to discover an analogy between it and some more complex and less understood situation or system so that we will be justified in saying that one is a simulation of the other. Since the first system is artificially constructed, we can understand its functioning in detail, and we hope that it will be useful in understanding some other system which is not artificially constructed and whose mechanism we do not understand.

There is, for example, a possibility that a digital computer furnishes us with a model for the brain processes involved in certain kinds of human problem-solving behavior. Here we begin with the computer which is artificially constructed and basically well understood. That is, we know from what sorts of components it is built up, how these components are arranged, and the ways in which it can be programmed. It is true that Newell, Shaw, and Simon, as well as others, have succeeded in making computers do things which we would not initially have supposed within their competence, but still we can see perfectly clearly how the computer arrived at the results once they were achieved. We also know that the human mind can arrive at similar results, in this case the proofs of theorems in logic, and we probably begin by supposing that there are brain processes corresponding to the various stages in the solution of the problem. However, we are ignorant of most of the brain mechanisms that are analogous to the computer mechanisms so well understood. We know that there is some analogy between the process of human problem-solving (again, in this case, doing proofs in logic) and what also appears to be the game of computer problem-solving. But we do not know how close the analogy is, and we therefore do not know whether the one is a model of the other. Or, to put it more accurately, we do not know in what respects the one game is a simulation of the other.

At this point, however, the suggestion that we may have a model here generates hypotheses which we can test. We know, for instance, that the computer is ultimately composed of two-state electrical devices (electrical devices which, like light bulbs, have to be either "off" or "on"). The question then arises whether the human brain, in this area of its functioning, can also be said to be composed ultimately of two-state devices electrical or otherwise. This is a question which we can bring under empirical investigation, and we can also ask such questions as whether there are any neural routings comparable to the circuitry of a computer. If the answers to these questions turned out to be affirmative, we would then be justified in saying that the brain stores its information in binary form, and that it performs arithmetical operations in the way that a digital computer does. If, however, the answers turned out to be negative, we might wonder whether an analog computer (where information is stored in continuous rather than in discrete binary form) would furnish us with a better model, or whether something other than a computer might furnish us with a better model. In dealing with questions of this sort, we should not ask whether, say, a digital computer furnishes us with a model of the brain; neither the computer nor the brain is a game in itself, and a computer, in itself, is not a dynamic simulation of anything. However, we can view either the computer or the brain as it is engaged in solving a problem, and it then becomes possible to ask whether the one is a dynamic simulation of the other; we will then want to know in exactly what *respects* one is a simulation of the other. This is not a case of setting up a model and then inferring the probable behavior of the situation simulated from the behavior of the model. Rather, we compare the two systems to see how close a simulation there is. At the beginning, of course, we cannot answer this question, but the mere suggestion generates hypotheses which can be tested. Thus, in this use of a dynamic simulation, we cannot derive results directly, and the value of the simulation lies entirely in its suggestiveness.

The other main use of simulations is in the construction of a system or game which we know to be a simulation of a real situation in which we are interested. In this case the real situation must be sufficiently understood so that we will know how to construct a model of it, and know that we have a model when we are finished. However, it may still be complex enough so that even though the basic mechanisms of the real situation are well understood, we may not know how it will act in all circumstances. In such a case the model will yield predictions about the real situation in that we can try out various possibilities in the model, see what happens, and then extrapolate our conclusions and apply them to the real situation. This is one of the basic techniques of operations research. Consider, for instance, a possible nuclear war between Russia and the United States. We know the basic capabilities of the weapons and the men involved, and we also have a good deal of information about the various kinds of weapons and men. However, in a war of this complexity and scope there is simply too much going on to be able to easily assess the probable outcome, or even to predict the probable outcome given certain strategic and tactical decisions on both sides. In this sort of case it is very helpful to construct what is known to be a simulation of the more important aspects of the war in detail, leaving the less important aspects to chance. We can then play the game out to see what the outcome is, or, better, use a computer to play the game out thousands of times to see what the average outcomes will be. In this sort of use of a simulation the motivation is much more practical than it would be when one is considering whether a computer can give us a model for a set of brain processes. In our war game the Defense Department is using the simulation to discover what kinds of decisions to make now, what kinds of problems are likely to arise in the future, and how to solve them. Thus, there is a great emphasis on simulating as closely as possible those aspects of the real situation in which human decisions about tactics and strategy are most involved. If, for example, one knows that the probability of a missile's landing within a mile of its target is .66, and one is firing a hundred missiles at the same target, one leaves it to chance whether any given missile will hit its target. One does not attempt to simulate the flight of the missile and the effect of the various relevant factors on it. There is no point in doing that in this kind of game, since, once the missile has been shot off, no further human decisions are made concerning it and there is nothing one can do to guide its flight. On the other hand, we want to know in as great detail as possible the consequences of shooting a missile or set of missiles at one time rather than another, or aiming them at one place rather than another, because this is something that is subject to human decisions. In operations research the point is to gather from the model the information which will make it possible to make rational decisions in matters such as this when the need arises.

4 Operations Research and History

My main suggestion in this section will be that operations research can be applied to the past even more effectively than to the present or the future. I will further argue that when it is applied to the past it can give us historical understanding. In particular, historical understanding can be achieved by constructing simulations of situations that have already occurred as opposed to ones which are expected to occur in the future. There are advantages in doing this because we usually know more about the past situation than we do about the future one, and we are in a position to construct a more reliable simulation in that we know better what to include, what to leave out, and so on. In warfare we have much more complete information about the relative effectiveness and reliability of the weapons of, say, the First World War than we have concerning the weapons of the Third World War. Information of this sort is very important to a simulation and, for this reason alone, we are in a position to simulate the First better than the Third. Similarly, we have a quite complete knowledge of the dynamics of politics for the better known periods of history; this is contrasted with the difficulty in predicting what the crucial political issues will be and what will sway the voters in some twenty or thirty years. The same situation holds for most of the fields which history covers.

Another advantage to simulating the past concerns the verification of the accuracy of our simulations. When the defense department constructs a model of the Third World War, there is not much that can be done to verify the accuracy of the model except to wait for the war to occur. If it never does occur, it will be very difficult to say how accurate the model is even though, in the course of time, we may acquire additional relevant information about the military hardware, the political forces, and the other influences involved. When we have a simulation of the past we can simply plug in the constants which represent the past situation, as nearly as we can determine them, and play the simulation out a large number of times to see if the average outcomes are the ones that actually occurred. As mentioned before, this process does not yield a conclusive verification of the accuracy of the simulation, but it certainly helps, and we here have a technique which is not available to ordinary operations research as applied to the future. Now, it happens that operations research, as applied to the future, is a fairly well-entrenched applied science. The fact that very large sums of money are invested in it is perhaps not relevant here, but it is generally assumed to have a fair degree of reliability and no one seems to look upon it as a form of magic. Further, it yields detailed information and predictions about the situations simulated. If, then, the method is more reliable when we turn it on the past, it would seem that it should command the consideration of historians. To turn it on the past is particularly tempting because it allows us to extrapolate from the available evidence enough to reach surprising conclusions which were not explicit in any way in the original evidence. According to Collingwood, the best historians have always succeeded in one way or another in deriving more information from their sources than they appeared to contain at first sight. The technique of dynamically simulating the past now gives us a systematic way of achieving this goal.

Of course, when we are simulating the future, the model gives us predictions, but when we are simulating the past the dynamic simulation gives us, not predictions about the future, but assertions about what would have happened under varying circumstances. We saw earlier that the dynamic simulation gives us a more thorough understanding of the situation than the dumb simulation because to the extent that it can be carried out it allows us to assess the consequences of all sorts of events which did not occur. In particular, it allows us to assess the consequences of choices which were not made, but which might have been made. Thus the method of operations research, turned on the past, promises to tell us not just what happened in the narrowest sense, but what else might have happened. This, in turn, sets the stage for explaining what did in fact happen.

Operations research is generally associated with the use of computers. In theory these do not make anything possible that was not possible before since a human being can do anything a computer can do, albeit much more slowly. In practice, however, the use of computers makes the method of operations research much more powerful. We already know that in any dynamic simulation there will be certain chance factors, and that there is a convenient way of getting a computer to make these "chance" decisions. One starts by generating a random number in the computer and certain digits of it can be consulted whenever any random choice is called for. Thus, if there is an even chance between event A's taking place and its not taking place, we can say that it will take place if the last three digits of the random number, when viewed as a single number, constitute a number greater than 500. If the number is less than or equal to 500, then the event does not take place. Similarly, if there is a two-thirds chance of *A*'s occurring, then we can say that it will occur if the number exceeds 333, and not otherwise. Thus, given the odds for the occurrence of a chance event, the computer will say whether it actually occurs. However, the fact that chance events occur in a dynamic simulation means that no single playing of the game or outcome is decisive or even very significant. It may be atypical in that some of the chance events took place against long odds. Therefore, it is desirable to play the game a large number of times using the same strategies over and over again, and one is then in a position to say what the average outcome will be, given certain initial circumstances and particular strategies on both sides. The use of the computer makes it practicable to play the game a large number of times and to produce reliable results. The role of computers is, of course, unaffected when we turn operations research on the past; they can be used in the same way that they are in dynamic simulations of the future.

To simulate in most detail where human decisions are involved is, we noted earlier, a feature of operations research as applied to the future. Applying it to the past, we note the obvious fact that the decisions have already been made and our practical motivation—the discovery of what choices to make in the future—has now disappeared. However, we are still interested in human decisions in the past both because we want to evaluate them ethically and because most of our counterfactual possibilities hinge upon them. For example, we are interested in whether there would have been war with Germany if the Chamberlain government had decided to give high priority to forming an alliance with Russia, since this was a crucial step in Namier's evaluation of the Chamberlain government. Of course, the possibility of war would have been affected even more if the density of aluminum and the other light metals had been half again as great. In that case airplanes could not have flown, and Germany could not have had much hope of overcoming the Russian masses with technological superiority. But since no human decision is here involved, it is not the sort of counterfactual possibility that interests us. In fact, to understand history we have to put ourselves, as Collingwood says, in the place of the historical participants when they were making their decisions and were about to undertake their actions. Consequently, the historian of the late thirties is now interested in exactly those features which would have been of interest to the operations researcher (if there had been any) at that time. Thus, when we take the techniques of operations research and turn them on the past, we do not have to refocus those techniques since they already center on the sorts of crucial decisions and actions which interest the historian of the past in much the way that they interest the economic, political, and military planners of the present.

Whether we are dealing with the future or the past, there are still a number of important choices to be made in the construction of the simulation, even after we have decided to simulate in most detail where human decisions are most important. If, again, we are trying to simulate nuclear warfare between Russia and America, we can regard the game as having any number of different players. We could have only two players although this would be unrealistic because on each side there are a number of men who make important and relevant decisions. Consequently, we might want to populate our game with a number of players whose decisions are subordinate in various ways to the decisions of other players. On the other hand, if it is the American government which is paying for the operations research, we want to simulate the problems that the American leaders may have to deal with in the future, and we may not be nearly so interested in the problems of the Russian leaders. We may then eliminate some or all of the Russian players and substitute a set strategy which they are believed to favor. The strategy would then spell out the kinds of responses which would be made in certain kinds of situations; this strategy might be made part of the computer program. The game might then be played many times with that strategy assigned to the Russians in order to simulate strategic problems which the Americans would face. Or, more likely, we would think of a number of different possible Russian strategies and play the game many times using each.

There are still two main ways in which we can use the dynamic simulation. We can use the game in order to familiarize American leaders, or potential leaders, with the situations which they are likely to face, and simply have them play the game against set Russian strategies. In this case they would be making their own decisions intuitively, or in any way that seems natural to them, and they would have the opportunity to see whether they did well or badly. On the other hand, we can use the game not as a training instrument, but as a means to establishing certain hypothetical conclusions. For example, we might discover that if the Americans use such-and-such a defense two-thirds of the American cities would be obliterated in the first strike whereas another defense would result in only half the cities being obliterated; there is almost no limit to the number of similar hypothetical conclusions which could be derived from the dynamic simulation. If we use the simulation in this way we might also think of possible American strategies and build them into the computer program as well (one at a time). We could then match Russian strategy *A* against American strategy *B*, Russian strategy *C* against American strategy *E*, and so on. Hopefully, we could then discover the optimum American strategy given certain Russian opening moves. Or, if the Americans are to make the opening moves, we might then try to discover, perhaps by intelligence methods, the most probable Russian strategy and adopt in advance the American counterstrategy shown to be most effective.

When we apply operations research to the past,

both these uses of a dynamic situation will be relevant. Insofar as we wish to put ourselves in the place of a historical figure, we can include ourselves in the game in order to get a feeling for his situation. Insofar as we wish simply to derive counterfactuals about the past situation, it will be more effective to leave ourselves out of the situation and leave all choices to be determined probabilistically. Before describing this method in more detail, however, I must first deal with some general problems created by the presence of counterfactuals in historiography.

5 The Problem of Counterfactuals²

In modelling a past situation, the hypothetical conclusions generated will actually be counterfactual statements about the past. There are, however, some very basic questions which concern all counterfactuals and which imply the absurdity of some.

I will first consider various uses of hypothetical statements of the form "If *A* then *B*," where *A* and *B* stand for events which are either past, present, or future. The important distinction in the analysis of statements of this form is not between past events and future events, but between our knowledge or lack of knowledge as to whether the events *A* and *B* have taken or will take place. There are some interesting relationships between the use of hypothetical statements and our empirical knowledge and ignorance. To illustrate these I will suppose that we are in a position to question an oracle who is all-wise in the sense that he can tell us exactly what will happen or what has happened at any place and time. The problem then will be whether there can ever be any reason to ask him hypothetical rather than categorical questions. We might say that there is no reason to ask the oracle whether the hypothetical "If A then B" is true when we can just as well ask him whether A will occur and then whether B will occur. Suppose that A is known by everyone to be presently occurring and the oracle tells me, in response to a question, that "If A then B" is true. I can then deduce that B will occur, but has the oracle told me any more than that? It might be concluded that the oracle was asserting a causal connection between A and B, and in this case I would make further inferences. I might, for instance, conclude that A', which closely resembles A, will be followed by B', which closely resembles B, and so on. Thus there might be some advantage in asking the oracle a hypothetical question rather than just asking him whether B will occur. Nevertheless, this advantage will be short-lived because I can accomplish the same thing by also asking whether A' and B' will occur, and other similar questions. Up to this point, this kind of hypothetical question does not seem to be necessary, given the assumption that I can always consult the oracle. However, there still remains the explicitly counterfactual question where, knowing that A occurred, I ask "If A had not occurred, would B have occurred?" In this case I can find no alternative way of answering the question by saying of any number of events that they have or have not occurred. In fact, so far as I know, the oracle himself might not be able to answer this question. Even if someone were to know completely the past and future history of the world, he would not necessarily know what would have happened if Papen had not had his meeting with Hitler, or if the ancient Chinese had not been acquainted with hibernating animals. Thus, even such an oracle might lack historical understanding.

The conclusion here is that insofar as hypothetical statements do not entail counterfactuals, the information they impart could, under these conditions, also be imparted by categorical statements. We often use hypothetical statements of the form "If *A* then *B*" because we are ignorant about the occurrence or non-occurrence of *A*; however, as we have seen, under certain ideal conditions of knowledge they would be unnecessary if we were not also interested in the explicitly counterfactual case. Thus counterfactuals occupy a special position, and it is not surprising that they involve special problems; in view of this fact, it becomes initially more plausible to think that extra inductive assumptions are needed beyond those presupposed by the predicting of simple events.

This being the case, I will concentrate attention on these explicitly counterfactual conditionals as opposed to conditionals where the antecedent is not known to be true or false. When I assert "If *A* then *B*," knowing that *A* did not occur or will not occur, certain conditions have to be satisfied for the sentence to be plausible enough to be interesting. Specifically, it must be supposed that the speaker is not just making a guess, and that he has some sort of evidence for his assertion. This goes with the assumption that the occurrence or non-occurrence of *A* and *B* is not a matter of chance, and that it is possible to make rational predictions concerning them. When we consider the counterfactual possibility of *A*'s occurring, we usually assume that there are causal laws which, together with the occurrence of numerous past events, in fact brought about *A*'s non-occurrence. Thus, in order to suppose that *A* occurred, we have also to make other counterfactual suppositions concerning either the causal laws or the prior chain of events. We have to suppose that a whole range of events reaching into the past to an undetermined extent did not occur when we know that it did, or we have to suppose that certain causal laws which we ordinarily take to be true are in fact false, or we have to combine both suppositions in some way. The hypothetical counterfactual then tells us that if the universe had been different enough to determine *A*'s occurrence rather than non-occurrence, *B* would then have occurred.

This feature of counterfactuals is often not noticed by historians, perhaps because they are often not aware of the importance of counterfactuals in their enterprise, and do not give the matter much thought. In line with what I have just said the historian ordinarily supposes that there is a causal explanation for the falsity of the antecedent of the counterfactual. As an example, consider the view implied by Huizinga that if chivalry had not been a dominant factor at the time, the later crusades would not have taken the form that they did. Huizinga does not suppose that the rise of chivalry was a chance event, and, as an intellectual historian, he believes that such phenomena have causes. However, according to the reasoning above, we cannot suppose that chivalry did not occur without setting aside a number of other prior conditions, either particular events or general laws. The assertion then would be, in effect, "Given a world which is sufficiently different from the actual one so that chivalry need not have occurred in medieval times, the later crusades would either not have occurred or would have had a different goal." I will attempt to show that even counterfactuals which assert less than this one can turn out to be more dangerous than usually seems to be appreciated.

It is now appropriate to raise the question of determinism and its relation to counterfactuals both as they appear in ordinary language and in historiography. I do not think that there are any decisive arguments to support either determinism or indeterminism, but we can at least try to see whether either position is presupposed by the beliefs of common sense. A basic point seems to be that even if we believe that some events cannot be explained, we are not in a position to say which particular events. If we are indeterminists it is not because we think that there are some inexplicable events, but because we have doubts about all events being simultaneously completely explicable. Indeed, it is never improper to ask for an explanation of any particular event that occurs, and,

as Kant pointed out, empirical investigation of any subject matter presupposes that there is an explanation to be
found. Since there is no facet of the world which we com-
monly suppose to be uninvestigable, we collectively suppose at one time or another that any event open to ordinary observation does have an explanation. This is not
quite a deterministic assumption because common sense
never seems called on to make such an assumption about
every subject matter at once; rather, we only suppose that
the event we are talking about has an explanation. When
we assert a counterfactual we are engaged in a kind of
explanation, and we would be defeating ourselves if we
supposed the events surrounding it to be undetermined
and inexplicable.

Contrary to my position, J. L. Austin held that we
do suppose certain kinds of events to be inexplicable. A
complete argument to this effect is to be found in a footnote to "Ifs and Cans":

> Consider the case where I miss a very short putt and kick
> myself because I could have holed it. It is not that I
> should have holed it if I had tried: I did try, and missed.
> It is not that I should have holed it if conditions had
> been different: that might of course be so, but I am talk-
> ing about conditions as they precisely were, and asserting
> that I could have holed it. There is the rub. Nor does 'I
> can hole it this time' mean that I shall hole it this time
> if I try or if anything else: for I may try and miss, and
> yet not be convinced that I could not have done it; in-
> deed, further experiments may confirm my belief that I
> could have done it that time although I did not.
>
> But if I tried my hardest, say, and missed, surely
> there *must* have been *something* that caused me to fail,
> that made me unable to succeed? So that I *could not*
> have holed it. Well, a modern belief in science, in there
> being an explanation of everything, may make us assent
> to this argument. But such a belief is not in line with the
> traditional beliefs enshrined in the word *can*: according
> to *them*, a human ability or power or capacity is inher-
> ently liable not to produce success, on occasion, and that

for no reason (or are bad luck and bad form sometimes reasons?).[3]

The basic assumption here is that the speaker is correct in saying that he could have made the putt. If there is in fact an explanation of his not making the putt, then there is a sense in which he could not have made it. We can admit this and save the first "could" only by giving it a dispositional analysis, which I propose doing. We have just seen why Austin rejects "I would have made it under other circumstances," as well as "I would have made it if I had tried." It seems to me, however, that Austin has not considered all the hypothetical assertions that might be implicit in the remark. Let us suppose that when the unfortunate putter says "I could have made it," his partner replies "If you could have, why didn't you? That missed putt lost the game for us." A number of answers would be appropriate here: "I hurried it too much," "I didn't realize that there was a slight bank near the ball," "I let the pressure bother me too much," or he could mention any number of other particular factors. These answers are all consistent with the putter's having tried the first time, and with the circumstances remaining the same in Austin's sense. The putter implies that he would have made the putt if he had taken longer, etc., not that his missing the putt has no explanation. In fact, he is suggesting explanations (or making alibis) as it is natural to do in such a situation. He would be anxious to make it clear that he is not really as bad a putter as one might suppose. In fact the putter might even be so self-effacing as to say "I really don't know why I missed that putt." Here again, he is not saying that there is no explanation, and the utterance is comparable to "I don't know why I am hooking my drives"; any golfer who says anything like that will inevitably receive explanations and advice whether he wants them or not. Even if the putter makes a reply such as "Sometimes they don't go in" or "You can't win them all," he is not really saying with

Austin that a human ability is inherently liable to fail sometimes for no reason; the putter who makes such a remark more likely implies that he would rather not talk about the matter further.

Thus I think that we can stick to our prior conclusion that common sense does not hold any particular event to be inexplicable, and that it is always willing to consider possible explanations when it is not already satisfied with one. In the following examples of counterfactuals I will assume that there is a causal explanation for the non-occurrence of the antecedents.

The problem which now arises is that in supposing A's occurrence we have set aside either some of the causal laws seeming to govern the world, or some of the past history of the world, or both. We then assert that on the basis of the altered past and/or the altered causal laws B will occur; this is what "If A then B" means when it is explicitly counterfactual. However, in practice we never know to what extent we must change the actual world in order to let A occur, and it may be that in changing it we have set aside the very causal laws and/or past history which might bring about B's occurrence, or for that matter, B's non-occurrence. As an example, suppose that someone asserted the following: "If that baseball had been hit three feet higher Jones would not have caught it." If asked, he might defend this statement by pointing out that Jones cannot jump very well. This seems to be a relatively simple empirical statement which would be false if, for instance, it turns out that Jones can jump much higher than had been supposed. Let us assume, nevertheless, that there is good evidence for the statement and that we would be justified in believing it according to the usual standards for counterfactuals. On examination, the situation becomes more complex, however. In particular, there must be ways in which the ball could go higher than it did without affecting greatly the evidence for thinking that Jones could not catch it.

Let us begin with a very adverse case. One way to

allow for the ball's having gone higher would be to suppose a difference in the laws of gravitation so that there
would be less attraction between the ball and the earth,
resulting in a higher trajectory for the ball. It is obvious
that this counterfactual assumption would alter the whole
pattern of our solar system and might well result in an
earth which was not only unsuitable to baseball, but to
all other forms of life as well. Although this is clearly a
bad assumption to make, we cannot just suppose that the
ball went higher and that nothing else was altered; we
would then be supposing that in a particular instance laws
were violated which we believe to hold generally. Since
neither of these courses is attractive we would have to
make some other kinds of changes in the hypothetical
world. We might want to say that in the counterfactual
situation the ball would go higher and farther because it
is more resilient than the actual ball. This time we are
making a relatively local change which does not turn
the world upside-down. Even here things could turn out
badly for the wishful thinker, however. We know that all
balls which are used are carefully tested for uniformity,
and if this ball is to be more resilient, then it must be that
all such balls are more resilient. In that case the hypothetical Jones would presumably be used to this fact and
might play deeper. Thus he could have caught the ball
even if it had been higher, and for an unsuspected reason.
Of course, this is only one way in which the altered
resiliency might affect the situation; we could also ask for
the circumstances under which the baseball authorities
might have decided on a livelier ball, and the answer to
this question might affect the situation still further. It is
easy to see how diverse the effects of any alteration in
the physical world *might* be, and these effects will ordinarily involve further alterations, and so on. Of course,
it might be that the original situation would be unaffected
by these changes, but we will never know this. There will
always be the logical possibility that the situation would

be affected in unforeseen ways, and any attempt to decide the question inductively will result in inconclusive arguments which become increasingly obscure the further they are pushed.

The situation is further confused by the alternative sets of counterfactual assumptions that we can make. Since we have supposed that there is a class of counterfactuals which we are justified in asserting on the basis of evidence at hand, our problem is to find a set of counterfactual assumptions which would not affect the relevance of this evidence. Having found such a set of assumptions we should have *reasons* for thinking that the changes they would involve in the world do not affect the evidence. Even if we grant the assumptions which justify ordinary prediction (and these are not supposed to be counterfactual assumptions), we are not thereby provided with these reasons. We need not be concerned with the possibility of there being more than one adequate set of counterfactual assumptions. These assumptions are not entailed by the counterfactual and we could switch from one set to another without altering the meaning of the counterfactual. It is just that our reasons for thinking the counterfactual to be true evaporate unless this evidence is shown to be unaffected by at least one set of counterfactual assumptions. Even then, if the hypothetical world corresponding to these assumptions is too different from the actual one, the sustained counterfactual may no longer be interesting or relevant. All this need not imply that counterfactual induction is mistaken or unreliable, but there is a gap in our inductive assumptions which has not been filled.[4]

It is particularly important to notice the role of generalization in this process. Whenever we change an event we usually violate at least one general principle which holds true of the actual world. In order to save it we have to change other events, but they are instances of other generalizations which are supposed to hold, so the process is repeated over and over again, apparently with expanding consequences. The more we try to explain the original alteration the deeper we entangle ourselves. These problems do not arise explicitly in common-sense reasoning, but they are presupposed by it in that our ordinary language is filled with counterfactuals of all kinds, asserted without any qualifications whatsoever. Insofar as we do consider this problem at all we probably try to minimize it in the following way. We tend to make alterations in the hypothetical world until we come to a case of human agency, and there we stop. In the above case we would probably suppose that the batter swung earlier or harder for reasons of his own, and there our inquiry ends. It is not really that we suppose his actions to be undetermined at this point. On the contrary, the process of a batter swinging at a ball is a fairly mechanical one which seems much easier to explain than, say, a complex ethical decision. Rather, our inquiry ends because the causal laws operating here are less well known than the laws of gravity and resiliency, and much harder to state precisely. Psychologically it is much easier to set aside an unfamiliar law which we suppose to exist than to abrogate a perfectly well known law. Many find it more attractive than the alternative process of changing an indefinite number of events reaching perhaps infinitely far back in time in order to keep the generalizations the same. A scientifically oriented person might be willing to keep the generalizations the same at any cost, but the generalizations have no logical priority over the particular facts, and there is no reason why he should do so. The more natural tendency seems to be to abrogate some largely unknown and seemingly innocuous generalizations. As we have seen, from the point of view of counterfactuals neither process is particularly innocuous. It is logically possible that the consequences of changing one event in the hypothetical world would upset the applecart.

Let us now return to Huizinga's counterfactual con-

cerning chivalry and the crusades. Since it was not supposed that the occurrence of chivalry was a chance event,
we have to ask under what conditions chivalry might not
have arisen. One's first intuition might be that it had a
good deal to do with feudalism. Suppose, then, that we
set feudalism aside in the hypothetical world so as to
make possible the non-occurrence of chivalry. We then
have to ask what to put in its place: something akin to
modern democracy, the totalitarian rule of societies such
as Nazi Germany or the ancient China of the Emperor
Ch'in Shih Huang-ti, or something entirely different?
Having chosen one alternative we then ask whether it
would have been likely to have resulted in an invasion of
Palestine. Along the way we have to ask such questions as,
for example, whether any European society would have
been well organized enough to have mounted invasions
and whether the different countries could have cooperated
enough to have participated in a joint undertaking of that
size. There seems to be no rational way of answering these
questions, and, as a result, it appears that this counterfactual assertion demands too great a revision of the
actual world. Still, we will later see that there are rational ways in which the historian might arrive at *some*
counterfactuals, even though they may be more modest
ones.

Before proceeding further, two objections must be
considered. The first is that when we assert a counterfactual
we do not expect it to hold in all circumstances, but that
there is a list of conditions which have to be satisfied before we are willing to say that the consequent will follow
on the antecedent. Thus the counterfactual as uttered is
not complete in itself, but has to be amended by adding
a list of conditions to the antecedent. In our example these
might specify that everything about Jones and his en-
vironment remains exactly the same except for the flight
of the ball. The process is complicated by the fact that this
list of conditions may be very long or even infinite, and

hard to specify in any case, but it could be claimed that the counterfactual implicitly refers to those conditions. On this interpretation of counterfactuals, the counterfactual about Jones and the ball may not be without foundation after all. Even if the evidence for thinking that Jones would not have caught the ball is undermined by the counterfactual assumptions, it might be argued that Jones would be able to catch it only because one or more of the conditions implicit in the antecedent was not satisfied; thus the counterfactual might still be true.

Although this interpretation seems to me to be mistaken, it is partly correct in saying that we do not expect a counterfactual to hold in all circumstances and that there are conditions which we must believe to be satisfied before we expect the counterfactual to be true. It seems to me that when I use a counterfactual in an actual context, part of what I am asserting is that any conditions which may be presupposed by the counterfactual are already satisfied. If my counterfactual assertion is judged to be false, I am equally wrong whether my mistake consisted in not realizing that certain conditions were presupposed by the counterfactual, or my mistake consisted in thinking that these conditions prevailed when they did not. The counterfactual thus implies categorically that all conditions which may be presupposed obtain in fact. The difficulty arises because we usually do not know about all the presupposed conditions which have to be realized, and we can meaningfully assert the counterfactual without being able to specify them. When we assert the counterfactual we do not usually think of the possibility that the setting aside of an actual event in favor of a counterfactual antecedent may require us to alter the world in such a way as to affect these conditions. We are not aware of the fact that a counterfactual requires us to deal with a hypothetical world which may be different from the actual one in some respects; we tend to think of the counterfactual as being a statement about the actual world just as it is, except for the antecedent, and it is this misconception underlying the everyday use of counter-factuals that gives rise to the problem.

The second objection is that there are counterfactual statements directly derived from scientific laws, and these might be thought to be immune from the problems mentioned above. Such a statement might be "If the pressure of this gas had been double its actual pressure, and the volume occupied had remained constant, the temperature on the absolute scale would have been approximately twice its actual level." The ideal gas law, from which this counterfactual is derived, does not exactly describe the behavior of any gas, but let us treat the term "approximately" in such a way that this counterfactual is true of the gas in question. We might then argue that as long as the pressure is doubled and the volume held constant, nothing else matters; it is then inevitable that the temperature will be approximately doubled. This counterfactual differs from the others in that there seem to be only two presupposed conditions, and the list of conditions can thus be stated completely. Further, it seems intuitively unlikely that the substitution of the antecedent for the actual event in this case would require us to delete the ideal gas law from the hypothetical world about which the counterfactual is talking. This is always a logical possibility, but there is much more evidence than usual for dismissing it. While this is a very "safe" counterfactual, it is also a rather abstract one in that, unlike the one about Jones, it involves several terms which have to be operationally defined. When we define pressure and temperature at a given time in terms of readings which would have been obtained from certain instruments, our counterfactual assertion becomes more complex in that both the antecedent and consequent involve counterfactuals themselves. More important, these other counterfactuals are not directly derived from laws which can be completely stated in the sense that all their qualifications can be built into their antecedents. There are an indefinite number of factors which can adversely affect the best of pressure gauges and thermometers as well as the people reading them. Let us grant that the counterfactual derived from the ideal gas law is confirmed to a very high degree on the usual inductive assumptions as long as it is stated abstractly. But it is still just a restatement of the law and does not tell us what to expect in particular counterfactual circumstances, or in a particular hypothetical world. When we do fill in the operational definitions to obtain particular "predictions" about hypothetical worlds, we will encounter the same problems discussed above. In particular, the setting aside of the actual event (the actual pressure of the gas) might conceivably conflict with the conditions under which, say, the thermometer would work and be read properly.

In our discussion of Mowat we noted that he was presupposing some very general causal principles such as the one that says that a Bill in Parliament is more likely to be passed if there is a precedent for it. We also saw that such principles, which are part of Mowat's explanation sketch, differed from scientific laws in that we could not, in the historical case, distinguish the main hypothesis from the auxiliary hypotheses which are needed to describe the conditions under which it would be verified. We have here seen, however, that even in a scientific case, we cannot assert a genuine counterfactual associated with a law without becoming involved in assertions about those same conditions of verification, and we thus depart from the level of abstraction at which the law is stated. Thus, while there is an important difference between a scientific law and a "historical law," much of this difference disappears when we consider the counterfactuals associated with those laws. This again indicates that the *applied* science of operations research which attempts to discover the consequences of future *particular* events (which may not occur) can be applied equally successfully to the discovery of the consequences of events which did not occur in the past. In neither application does it have the generality and level of abstraction of physics, and the output of operations research is a set of hypothetical statements about events which are described, not in terms of a set of technical concepts, but in terms of our everyday concepts.

We can now summarize the problem apart from any particular examples. When we allow for the possibility of the antecedent's being true in the case of a counterfactual, we hypothetically substitute a different world for the actual one. It has to be supposed that this hypothetical world is as much like the actual one as possible so that we will have grounds for saying that the consequent would be realized in such a world. There are two extreme forms that this assumption might take. We might suppose that exactly the same causal laws hold for the hypothetical world. Since we are altering the event represented by the antecedent of the conditional, we will then have to alter an indefinite number of other events according to these causal laws. This chain will presumably reach back indefinitely far in time and affect events widely separated in space with the consequences noted above. The opposite assumption would be that we need alter only the event represented by the antecedent; we would then try to find distinct but similar causal laws which would allow the antecedent to be true. As we have also seen, the likelihood of being able to do this is small.

The most plausible assumption to be made in any particular case seems to be a mixture of the two kinds mentioned above. We alter a series of events until we get to a "natural" breaking-off place where we alter the minimum number of causal laws so as to limit the number of changes we have to make in the history of the world. Such a breaking-off place is one that provides as much continuity as possible. In the aforementioned example we would not keep the trajectory of the baseball exactly the same and then make it "jump" three feet because this would break up the continuity of a single event. It is more plausible to alter the causal relation between different kinds of events than it is to violate the simple laws of motion or make objects appear and disappear mysteriously. Thus the view of reflective common sense is not too far off the mark since it does seem to be a combination of the two kinds of assumption that gives us the best hope for an orderly hypothetical universe which will be as similar as possible to the actual one. It is just that there is no reason to pick out a case of human agency as the breaking-off point. The hypothetical world will thus have most of the same laws and much the same history as the actual world, but the differences which do exist between the two worlds might still involve very different futures.

These assumptions are affected by the fact that one can take various views of the actual causal structure of the world. On one view, we might suppose that there are a few causal laws which are very basic. This view would, of course, imply that there are only a very few *kinds* of uniformity in nature and that everything, or almost everything, that happens is an instance of one of these uniformities. The alteration of one event would either destroy these uniformities, or it would force us to change a great part of the history of the world. We would then have to assume in asserting a counterfactual that there are other uniformities, we know not what, which would still produce the expected result, or that the world had a different history, we know not what, which would produce the result. In either case a counterfactual for which we had good reasons in the ordinary sense becomes groundless. On another view of the world, however, causal laws would be less basic and more numerous; the uniformities would be of the form, "All events of the type A which occur under conditions B are characterized by C," where the relevant properties might not be subatomic. In this case the alteration of a single event or small number of events need not upset the whole causal structure of the world, but only one pattern of uniformity. The latter seems to be the view closer to common sense, and if true, would make it easier to justify the counterfactuals we assert by appealing to other uniformities which we suppose to be unaffected. This whole issue seems to be logically independent of the issue of freedom and determinism. Even if we suppose that there are a multiplicity of limited causal laws each describing different domains, it might still be that the causal laws all operate without exception within that domain. Determinism does not demand that the alteration of one event affect everything else in the universe; rather it demands only that the substitution of one event for another affect all the events within a certain class.[5]

Having stated what I take to be the basic problem of counterfactuals, I will compare it briefly with the problem Nelson Goodman finds, and then try to state the additional assumptions that will be needed to justify the assertion of counterfactuals. Goodman's basic goal is to state precisely the conditions under which a counterfactual will be true without using counterfactuals to specify them. For him the difficulty arises with the requirement of cotenability: the antecedent together with the relevant conditions must all be capable of holding at the same time according to the *actual* causal laws governing the world. As this requirement can only be stated in terms of counterfactuals, Goodman concludes that it is impossible to replace the language of counterfactuals with some other kind of language.[6] It is often pointed out here that the impossibility of such a translation shows not that there is a problem about counterfactuals, but just that they differ from other kinds of statements. In fact this problem arises only because Goodman never considers the possibility of changing the causal laws in the hypothetical world. On my account we are assured of cotenability in Goodman's sense because we keep altering facts and laws in the hypothetical world until they *are* all cotenable.[7]

In general my approach differs in that I have not tried to provide a way of reducing counterfactuals to something else. The problem I raise is simply that counterfactual induction depends on general conditions beyond those presupposed by ordinary induction.

To see why the usual inductive assumptions do not entirely support counterfactual induction, let us take for granted a strong inductive principle that would completely support induction by simple enumeration: all constant conjunctions of events which have held in the past will also hold for the future. This is such a strong principle that it is patently false and would never allow a prediction on the grounds of simple enumeration to be false, no matter how bad the sample; however, it will do all the better as an example. The counterfactual is not supported by the principle for several reasons. First, it is not a prediction and cannot be directly verified in the future in the way that statements about white swans can be. Of course, there are many non-counterfactual predictions which are not based on simple enumeration either, at least in any obvious way. In particular we make many hypothetical predictions which are not meant to be counterfactual, and the basis for these is usually the supposed operation of certain causal laws. If the evidence for the laws is indirect then the inductive principle supporting enumerative induction may not support the hypothetical predictions. However, we do suppose that the law, whatever it may be, has operated in the past, and we can now support the hypothetical prediction by adding the second assumption that the same laws which have held true of the past will hold for the future.[8] This second assumption does not provide a basis for the counterfactual because we cannot be sure that the changes in the hypothetical world involved in the counterfactual antecedent will not conflict with and undermine the evidence for thinking the counterfactual to be true. The relevant law brings about its effect only if the antecedent is realized and another list of conditions, only part of which can be specified, is fulfilled. In the first place, there might be a conflict between the antecedent and one of the unspecified conditions according to the laws which hold for both the actual and hypothetical worlds; thus we could be assured of the universal truth of the law, but still not know that it applies to the counterfactual situation. Secondly, it might turn out that it is convenient to set this law aside in the hypothetical world; in this case the law might always be true of the actual world, but not of the hypothetical world. The counterfactual asserts more than that the law holds for the actual world. It asserts that the same or similar law holds for the hypothetical world, *and* that it would operate to produce a certain effect in that world. In this way it goes beyond the ordinary hypothetical prediction.

Our conclusion then is that counterfactual reasoning, although a kind of induction, is so different from other kinds of induction that the usual inductive assumptions are not even relevant to it. Yet, it is not easy to state precisely the assumptions that are required. It seems possible only to lay down certain necessary conditions for the plausibility of a counterfactual. These, as stated above, will be (1) that the respects in which the hypothetical world differs from the actual one, apart from the counterfactual antecedent, are not related causally to the consequent to any great extent, and (2) to the extent that there is such a relationship, these laws are independent of other laws, and can be set aside without severe consequences.

Applying this general conclusion to the counterfactuals that will be generated in a model of a historical situation, we should notice first that there are two kinds of hypothetical statements that we can make when simulating the past. We can make a hypothetical counterfactual statement about the actual historical situation and say that if decision *A* had been taken, event *B* would have occurred. We can also make a hypothetical statement about the model to the effect that if decision *A* is taken event *B* will take place in the large majority of cases. This latter statement need not be counterfactual. We could, of course, say of a certain game that was played using the model that if decision *A* had been taken event *B* would have occurred. However, we really have very little temptation to make such counterfactual statements about the *model* since no single game that was played on the basis of the model has any great significance in itself, owing to the chance factors mentioned earlier. What is important is what will happen in the majority of games played according to the model and where decision *A* is taken. Hence, the statement we really want to make is, "If decision *A* is taken, an event of the type *B* will occur in such-and-such a percentage of the games played." Or we can phrase this differently and say that if decision *A* is taken in a game played according to the model the probability is such-and-such that the event will take place. Thus, we derive a hypothetical statement which involves a probability statement as one of its parts, but which is not counterfactual. These statements about the model are also very safe in that they can be verified in a painstaking way. One simply uses a computer to play out the dynamic simulation a large number of times, and one then compares the relative frequency of occurrence of event *B* with the predicted probability. The verification is, of course, never quite conclusive, but it can be as reliable as any that are ordinarily obtainable in science. These 'safe' hypothetical statements about the model are then to be contrasted with the 'dangerous' counterfactual statements about the actual situation.

It is tempting at this point to substitute the safe statements about the model for the dangerous ones about the historical situation, and to discard the latter entirely. However, this will not do. We can make safe statements about the model, or at least ones that we know how to verify, but these would not be historically interesting if

222

the model were simply an independent game, or set of games, and did not give us a dynamic simulation of some past situation. We have seen that counterfactuals are essential to historiography, and we cannot avoid them so easily. Nevertheless, it will be of considerable help that for every dangerous counterfactual statement about the past there corresponds a safe hypothetical probability statement about the model. Assumptions about hypothetical worlds will still have to be made, but they can be organized more scientifically than was possible before.

It was noted earlier that every counterfactual statement involves the assumption of a hypothetical world. Further, in a dynamic simulation of the past we construct such a hypothetical world at whatever point the game in question diverges from what actually happened. That is, we begin to construct such a world whenever in the simulation a decision is made that was not actually made in the past, or a chance event in the simulation "alters the course of history." Still, the simulation actually gives us much less than a complete hypothetical world. We leave many factors out of our simulation altogether on the grounds that they are not causally relevant to what happens within the simulation. Hence, the great gap between the dangerous counterfactual and the safe statement about the model lies in the possibility that some of these excluded factors might be causally relevant after all. In that case what happens in the simulation may diverge radically from what would have happened in the real situation.

Our earlier conclusion was that the use of counterfactuals not only involves hypothetical worlds, but that assumptions have to be made about the nature of these hypothetical worlds and their causal structures. While that conclusion still holds true, we are now setting up a systematic basis for the generation of counterfactuals. Our model now allows us to generate a whole range of hypothetical worlds by altering any one of a large num-

223

ber of decisions that were actually made. Having generated them, the model allows us to decide what happens in each of these hypothetical worlds. In this way we can derive any number of counterfactuals from the model, but it is no longer the case that each such counterfactual makes its own unique presuppositions. On the contrary, it is now the model that makes presuppositions, and the assumptions needed to justify the model are then adequate for any counterfactual derived from that model. Hence, we now have a single set of assumptions which apply to a whole range of counterfactuals. When we considered the statement, "If that ball had been hit three feet higher Jones would not have caught it," we had to try to see what assumptions would have to be made in order to justify that statement. Our new approach, on the other hand, would be to simulate the game of baseball, as played under certain conditions, and we would then be able to establish or refute that statement, among many others, relative to the assumptions of the model. The assumptions of the model will generally be to the effect that such-and-such a factor is not relevant. Or we may assume that a factor is relevant in general but that very minor variations in it are not relevant. For example, we may decide that whether or not it rains is relevant to the outcome of a battle, but also assume that the exact degree of humidity is not relevant. When we derive counterfactuals from the model in this way we are not talking just about the model; we are trying to say what really would have happened, but we are doing it in a more systematic way.

Actually, when someone makes even an ordinary counterfactual statement he has some idea what the hypothetical world involved would be like, and if these ideas could be made explicit enough, they would exclude certain models and be compatible with others. Any of the models concerned would allow us to make other counterfactuals beside the one that was actually made. So it is now a matter of choosing a basis for counterfactuals as opposed to choosing particular ones to assert. This is really presupposed where we have any systematic investigation of a subject or problem which is going to involve counterfactuals. There is no point in making them one by one intuitively in such a case. This methodology fails to fit our ordinary making of counterfactual assertions only to the extent that these counterfactuals are disjointed, unrelated to one another, and ill-founded. The modelling business is really the only way there is of being scientific about counterfactuals, except perhaps, deducing them directly from laws. But in history we simply do not have the very detailed sorts of laws that would be required.

This new methodology for counterfactuals does not, of course, eliminate the need for making assumptions which go beyond the ones required for ordinary induction. Thus, it does not protect them against some of the doubts which we raised earlier concerning counterfactuals in general. However, it does have one great advantage. As long as we assert counterfactuals one by one giving no great thought to their basis, we have no assurance that the various assumptions we would make in the course of asserting different counterfactuals would all be consistent. In fact, if we think of each new counterfactual as posing a new problem which is unrelated to the others, the chances are that in the long run we will end up making counterfactual assumptions which are inconsistent with one another. But if we derive all our counterfactuals from a single model, and only one set of assumptions goes with that model, it is relatively easy to make sure that these assumptions are all consistent with one another. It is in general much easier to show that any theory is consistent if it is systematized. The same thing is true of the making of counterfactuals which is essential to historiography.

6 *Historical Understanding*

We have long since seen that historical understanding does not consist simply in gathering facts. The historian has to interpret the facts that he has uncovered, and he has to explain some of them with respect to others. It is here that counterfactuals are essential. But it now appears that historical understanding is not exhausted even by the combined gathering of facts and the establishing of the counterfactuals which relate them. Even when the historian is dealing with the kings of ancient China, he is usually not content just to establish what few facts he can and offer a few explanations. If at all possible, he tries to make the people concerned come alive and give some insight into their feelings, hopes, and fears. For instance, he may know that the king concerned resisted attacks by barbarians, and that these attacks caused the king to adopt certain domestic policies, thereby explaining the existence of these policies. However, his reader will also want to know something about the motivation and attitudes of the king and his advisers. They might have looked upon themselves as trying to defend sacred Chinese soil from defilement by barbarians, or they might have been concerned lest the barbarians capture fertile land and dangerously decrease the food supply, or they might have been trying to defend certain holy places. Or they might not have particularly cared about the land itself, but have regarded it as a useful base from which to mount future attacks against the barbarians. It makes quite a difference whether these men were acting blindly in accordance with tradition, or acting on advice from astrologers, or were practical people who were trying to make military and economic plans. All this speculation is involved in historical understanding. The gathering or inferring of facts and the establishment of counterfactuals are aids to gaining that kind of insight, but neither the facts nor the counterfactuals provide it in themselves. To understand a historical figure the historian must gather all the factual information he can about the historical milieu, but he must then put himself in that milieu in order to understand the actions of his historical figure. In short, the historian must give himself the sort of training which would enable him to act effectively in a situation similar to the one actually encountered by the historical figure. Collingwood seems right when he says that the historian must sympathetically identify himself with the historical figure. This sympathetic identification amounts to more than just knowing what would have happened *if*; an essential part of it is the feeling of stresses and strains as one surveys the possible courses of action from the point of view of the historical figure and eventually chooses one. We have just seen that a simulation may be used as a method of training future leaders to make decisions under the best possible approximation of the conflicting demands that are likely to besiege them. In the same way, the historian can best put himself in the past situation by actually playing a game in which that situation is simulated as closely as possible in the relevant respects. Thus, historical understanding is not just a matter of learning, but also a matter of experiencing. The dynamic simulation of the past can help the historian in both these ways.

In fact, the historian may be able to understand the historical situation much better than the participants themselves did. First, he may have information which could not have been available to anyone living at the time, and, secondly, he has access to the dynamic computer simulation, which may enable him to play the game that the historical figures were playing, but play it better with a deeper appreciation of the tactics and strategy involved.

227

This being the case, we now have to ask whether we should simulate the situation on the basis of knowledge that was available at the time, or simulate it on the basis of all the knowledge that is available now. The first method promises us maximum sympathetic identification with the historical participants since we will be playing the game in the way that they had to play it. The second method promises us maximum understanding of the historical situation as it actually was. Both kinds of simulation are important, and they are interrelated in the ideal of historical understanding.

When we make the rules of the game reflect only the information that was available in the past we not only maximize sympathetic identification, but find it possible to evaluate the performance of the historical participants and make ethical judgments concerning them. We will be playing essentially the same game that they played, and we will be able to evaluate their performance in the way that we can assess the performance of partners or opponents in a game. The second kind of simulation, which we will call an "objective" as opposed to a "sympathetic" simulation, gives us a poor basis for making ethical judgments of any kind. For example, the designers of the *Dreadnought* and her immediate successors had no way of knowing that aircraft would play a significant role within the projected useful life of the ships. The possession of this knowledge would have affected the design of the ships, but it is unfair to expect the designers to have acted as they would have if they had had information that was available only later. It is not always a black-and-white case of a historical figure's either having a piece of information or lacking it. Statesmen and others sometimes act on the basis not of particular facts but of general principles. But a general principle is not necessarily something one either knows or fails to know. At one extreme one can state the principle explicitly and one can say exactly when one is making use of it. On the other hand, one may not be able to state the principle explicitly, but still have some vague knowledge of what it involves and conform to it in practice. Further down the scale, one might intuitively act according to the principle, unaware that any principle at all is involved and consequently unable to state it. For example, current statesmen are very often guided by economic principles having to do with deficits and balances of trade and other such concepts. Further, one may also notice that Elizabethan statesmen often acted from economic motives and seemed intuitively to try to obtain a favorable balance of trade. Since the science of economics did not exist at that time, one cannot blame them for not being familiar with it, but one can nevertheless compare various statesmen of the time in order to see to what extent their intuitive decisions accorded with ones that might be made in the light of present-day economics. When we simulate the historical situation, we can make our simulation more or less sophisticated depending on how many of these principles we import into it. At one extreme we can set up the game in such a way that the rules would all reflect statements representing common knowledge in Elizabethan times, or representing the background information and beliefs of some of the key figures insofar as these can be determined. Or we can set up the simulation in such a way that it makes use of all the relevant information which we now have, even though some of the principles might be far too technical for any of the historical participants to apprehend. Even when we are doing a sympathetic simulation, we would probably want to build into the simulation enough of these principles so that someone who acts intuitively according to them would have an advantage over someone who does not. In such a case the sympathetic simulation would differ from the objective simulation largely in that certain constants, such as, for example, the exact rate of growth in the gross national product of England in the sixteenth century, would be treated as imponderables in the sympathetic simulation and determined by chance; in the objective simulation we would try to approximate such constants as closely as possible by historical methods.

Thus while the sympathetic simulation does not pretend to tell us what actually would have happened under other circumstances, it both gives us sympathetic identification with the historical participants, and it allows us to make ethical evaluations. Actually, the ethical evaluation of historical figures, even under the ground rules laid down earlier, is a bit more complex than this. When we start seriously to evaluate a figure like Neville Chamberlain we always wind up asking not only how well he did, but also how much he had it in his power to do and what sorts of information he had to act upon. In order to determine how much power the individual had we have to look to the objective simulation, which incorporates all the relevant information that we have. With the advantage of hindsight, it is easy to suppose that a historical figure had more power than he actually had, and hence to blame him for not doing things that he could not have done in any case. However, if our objective simulation is sufficiently complete, we will be able to discover how much power and how much information the historical participant actually had. Having estimated these, we can then set up the sympathetic simulation in such a way that it truly reflects the position of the historical participant. In this way the sympathetic simulation presupposes the objective simulation in that information gained from the latter is essential to the setting up of the former. Returning to Chamberlain's dilemma, one of his problems was assessing the likelihood of Germany's going to war under varying conditions. We now have a great deal of information to the effect that the German armed forces were not prepared for war at the time of the Munich crisis, and this information should, of course, be incorporated into the objective simulation. But it may be that the information Chamberlain was getting, both from official and unofficial sources, indicated otherwise, and in that case we must also simulate the situation substituting a stronger *Wehrmacht* for the actual one. In studying this sympathetic simulation we might then discover that Chamberlain played the game as well as it could be played. Thus, the ethical evaluation can only follow on the prior determination of these other factors.

While the sympathetic simulations help us make ethical judgments, these ethical judgments do not seem to constitute the most important part of historiography. The more important function of the sympathetic simulation consists in its helping us gain sympathetic identification with the historical participants, hence its name. One way of gaining historical understanding, then, is to play games which simulate the situation of the participants in more and more detail until one finally gains proficiency. At that point one is prepared to act in the situation in which the historical figures did act.

There are two important parts in the construction of a dynamic simulation: first, establishing and collecting the needed facts, and secondly, devising the rules for the game using the information previously gathered. It would seem that anyone who devises the rules for a game would be able to play the game well because of his intimate understanding of it. However, he need not be the best player of the game. Suppose, for instance, that one is discomfited by one's inability to play a good game of chess and that one consequently invents a variant of chess where, for example, the bishops can bounce off the sides of the board and keep going. One might thereby hope to upset all the traditional chess strategies so that someone who has never practised them is no longer at a disadvantage. Of course, even the inventor of such a game might very well lose to a good chess player. Insofar as the understanding of the rules is distinct from skill in using them, the former is crucial to historical understanding. However, the connection is an intimate one, and one could not have a good understanding of the rules and be totally incapable of taking advantage of them.

On the other hand, it is quite easy to imagine that someone who collects minor bits of information on which some of the rules depend would turn out to be a poor player of the game. Thus, there appears to be a more intimate relationship between historical understanding and the setting up of the simulation than there is between historical understanding and the collection of information on which the simulation is based. Nevertheless, it is easy to exaggerate the difference. Collingwood thinks that a scientific historian, however specialized and detailed his investigation may be, always approaches the evidence with certain questions in mind and sifts through it until he finds something that bears on those questions. He does not go blindly through masses of evidence and copy it down, but knows both what he is looking for in advance and what its significance will be. Putting it in our way, he already has some idea of the kind of game played by the historical participants and is looking for things which will help specify the rules of that game. It probably never occurs to such a historian to set up a simulation of the past situation, but his understanding of the dynamics of the past situation puts him in a position where he could proceed at least part way with such a simulation if he wished.

We cannot, then, divide historians into two classes —the lower data-collectors as opposed to the aristocrats who put the data together and make sense out of it. Still, there are degrees of science in history and some useful information can be unearthed and gathered by persons who have relatively little historical understanding. For instance, almost anything that relates to Winston Churchill is obviously important, and one might, say, unearth an interesting correspondence between Churchill and a foreign diplomat in the thirties without having any understanding of the period. These small bits of the jigsaw puzzle are collected mainly by professional historians, as in our examples of piecemeal history. However, the professional historian is not usually content with unrelated bits and pieces; he usually wants to fit them together. In our view, this urge, if carried far enough, will lead to the setting up of a simulation. Hence, there is a certain amount of historical spade-work which someone has to do to make historical understanding of certain periods and events possible. That having been done, it is then possible for other persons, who have not done this work, to achieve historical understanding by becoming adept at the game so constructed. The one thing that such an expert player would not have is knowledge to the effect that he does indeed understand the past, since, for all he knows, the game might be nothing more than a game and might not be a simulation of an actual situation. Hence, the historian who has collected the information *and* set up the game *and* is adept at playing it has both historical understanding and knowledge that he has historical understanding. This is the ideal of historical understanding which is being promulgated in this book.

One of the peculiarities about history that we noted earlier is now explained. The net upshot of historiography reaches the public in a way that scientific results do not, and also in a way that articles in the historical journals do not. The reason is simply that one can understand a game and know how to play it without having had anything to do with the setting up of the game. Hence, the astute reader of history can understand the kind of game that, say, Gladstone was playing and know what kinds of moves he could have made and whether he did well or badly without being able to produce any kind of evidence for any kind of statement he might make about von Papen. He might not even know where to look for such evidence apart from looking at the bibliographies of the books he has read. But despite this handicap, if historical understanding, in the way we have defined it, is the end and everything else is the means to the end, then the evidence that a game really is a simulation is valued only because it allows us to say that we really *do* understand and is not valued for its own sake.

In saying that to understand a historical situation is to so prepare oneself that one could have acted in that situation, I do not, of course, refer to physical action. One does not have to train oneself in throwing spears or in haranguing crowds to understand the past. Further, one does not have to have or acquire the courage, moral or otherwise, that might have actually been required in the historical situation for the making of the crucial decisions. It must be recalled that the test for the kind of action that I have in mind is the playing of a game of the sort where action always consists merely in making decisions. What is required is to be able to play a *decision* game which simulates the actual situation. The close connection between decision games and action games, and the means of converting one kind of game to the other have been noted earlier. What I am saying here is that historical understanding consists in training oneself so that one could make the kinds of decisions that the actual historical figures were called on to make, and to make them wisely, taking into account the sorts of factors which actually did influence the historical figures.

In a decision game as opposed to an action game, there is relatively little difference between "knowing how" and "knowing that." In an action game like golf one can know exactly what sort of swing will produce a good shot, and still not be able to produce anything but dreadful ones. But in a decision game like chess, knowing what the consequences are of any of the alternative moves one might make, will thereby enable one to play the game, and, if one's knowledge of these consequences is extensive enough, one will then play the game well. This is

why there is an intimate connection between the function
that a dynamic simulation has in generating counterfactuals and the function that it has in enabling the historian to train himself to act in past situations. Once he
discovers enough of the counterfactual facts about a past
situation, he then knows the consequences which the
various alternative decisions would have had. Once knowing *that,* he is then in a position to have made the decisions in a rational manner. Since it is a decision game that
is simulating the past situation, the only actions to be performed are the making of decisions and the moving of
markers, or the recording of the decisions in some other
fashion. Moreover, even the action being simulated is
generally a decision that has been taken by some important person. This person himself usually engages in
relatively little physical action; he may merely give an
order or tell some subordinate that he has decided to do
such-and-such. Historians are usually much more interested in the persons who make decisions and sit in
chairs than in individual persons who throw spears and
shoot guns, but only follow orders. Hence, I conform to
historical tradition in defining historical understanding in
terms of the ability to have made the decisions as opposed
to the ability to have performed the physical actions.
Nevertheless, despite the fact that there is relatively little
difference between "knowing how" and "knowing that"
here, it still seems to be the former that is crucial. It is
this knowledge which allows us to identify sympathetically with the historical participant and see things from
his point of view as opposed to viewing everything from
the outside.

The subject matter of history proper consists of
human activity which is directed towards solving problems. Sometimes, of course, human activity occurs on
the instinctive level, as when a primitive man picks a
berry and eats it. One cannot really call this kind of
activity action directed at solving a problem, as it is

very like the behavior of animals, and does not really belong to history proper. Human instinctive capabilities and basic behavior tendencies may enter into our simulation, but they are not what we want to study or understand in a historical way. If these were to change over time, the historian would have to take account of them, but he would be taking account purely as a means to making historical understanding possible. When we are dealing with higher-level human activity directed at solving problems, we can always simulate this activity with a game. It is in the nature of a problem that there is one outcome, or a set of outcomes, which is desired over the others, and also that there are various approaches or strategies, some of which will be unsuccessful. If the problem is a solvable one, there will be at least one course of action which does lead to some degree of success. Further, given any sort of problem, the outcome that occurs is determined to some extent by the moves made to solve the problem. Hence, it is always possible to simulate problem-solving behavior dynamically. In historical understanding the important thing is not, of course, the solving of the problem. If it was not solved in history, it is too late to solve it now. Rather, what counts is knowing what it is like to try, in a realistic way, to solve the problems that did arise, which amounts simply to being able to deal with the problems arising in the dynamic simulation of the past situation.

The analysis of historical understanding in terms of the ability to play certain games makes it obvious that there will be degrees of historical understanding. Almost anyone can play almost any game to some degree. To play well, apart from winning most of the time, is to cultivate versatility and thus achieve the desired outcome in a variety of situations. A good chess player is one who can take advantage of favorable opportunities and one who can get himself out of trouble. From this point of view, it does not matter too much if we set up our simulations in such a way that they have just one player or more than one player. One can learn the game of eighteenth-century international commercial competition by choosing a country and making the moves for it while others make the moves for other countries, but one can also learn it by choosing a country and making the moves for that country while predetermined strategies have been assigned to the other countries. In either case the important thing is to be able to make the moves for any one of the countries involved and to be able to make them despite the moves made by the other countries. This can be achieved if one player contends with several who continually vary their strategies, but it can be more systematically achieved where one player plays from every position and plays against every possible strategy.

Actually, of course, one can achieve historical understanding without playing a game at all. The person who sets the game up probably has a good idea of what each country should do in varying situations, and he might never need actually to play the game.

The same situation might hold for someone who studies the game carefully without playing it, and it might even be that a person who is familiar with the period, and who never thinks in terms of games at all, would still be very good at the game if he were to play it. All these people would have historical understanding, and the kind of knowledge that professional historians ordinarily have counts as historical understanding under our re-definition. However little thought they may give to the sorts of games we have described, the sort of training which historians give their students and themselves fits them to play these games. Hence, what ordinarily counts as historical understanding will still so count under our re-definition.

The practical suggestion here is that historical understanding can be perfected and carried further than it usually is if we do resort to the setting up and playing of dynamic simulations. It is almost the universal experience of anyone who has ever tried to simulate any complex situation that as one goes along questions arise which are completely unanticipated. The computer needs instructions at every step, and one ultimately has to formulate a set of rules governing every relevant aspect of the situation simulated. One has some of the more obvious and more important rules in mind before beginning, but a host of supplementary rules is needed just to play the game at all (so that the players never arrive at a point where there are simply no rules telling them what to do next). Sometimes these other questions more or less answer themselves once they are raised, but often they force us to go back to our original sources with new questions which we did not think to raise before. Additional historical research will then be required to answer these questions. The setting up of a dynamic simulation thus forces us to make a more complete historical investigation than would have been made without the guidance of the simulation. Once the simulation has been set up, these new rules that had to be added along the way themselves generate unanticipated strategic subtleties. For example, someone might look at a chess board and learn the ways in which the pieces and pawns can move without dreaming of the complexities involved in chess strategy. Similarly, one may think that one understands a historical period very well, but in playing a dynamic simulation of that period, finds himself forced to make all sorts of unanticipated choices, which in turn requires a more thorough understanding of the historical period if they are to be made wisely.

It will be observed that this methodology preserves and emphasizes the many similarities we have found between the procedures used in history and those characteristic of the empirical sciences. Any proposed simulation constitutes a hypothesis in the strict sense of that term, and the predictions generated by the simulation are testable—thus history actually becomes an applied science. Of course, the extant historical evidence may not *justify* us in setting up a model as *detailed* as most models in the natural and social sciences. However, when it is not known whether a given statement about the past is true we can set up alternative models which are identical except that this statement is true in one and false in the other. In such a case we may be able indirectly to adduce evidence for or against the statement by seeing which model makes most probable *other* events which are known to have taken place.

We can now see something of the special relation between history and the social sciences. It is often pointed out that the historian studies the same sorts of situations in the past that the political scientist, the economist, the sociologist, and others study in the present. However, there is an obvious difference of method in that the other social scientists are attempting to discover general laws while the historian does not seem to be doing so. We have to some degree supported Hempel's contention that the historian gives explanation sketches in which case he will also be dealing with laws, but laws which are much vaguer than those dealt with by the other social scientists. There does seem to be something in the opposed position that historiography differs in kind from the other social sciences and does not just do in a vague way what they do in a precise way. Further, the relationship between history and the social sciences does not seem to be that the historian merely provides data on the basis of which the others formulate general laws. While one may find instances of sociological or economic principles in history, the providing of such instances seems to be more or less incidental to the purposes of the historian. We just mentioned that the historian does have to do a certain amount of data-collecting, but he does it as a means to historical understanding and not as a means to the formulation of, say, sociological laws.

In setting up a dynamic simulation of the past the main object is to formulate the rules governing that situation. Some of the more specific rules may be discovered directly by historical methods in that the historian may notice certain cycles of events or certain patterns in the behavior of some of the key figures. However, the most general and most important rules governing human behavior and institutions are the ones usually presupposed by the historian in every step of his inquiry. He assumes, for instance, that any nation, except in very special circumstances, seeks to expand its territorial holdings, and that almost any government tries to perpetuate itself in power in certain characteristic ways depending upon the sort of government it is. These general rules have to be drawn from the other social sciences and, as he proceeds with the dynamic simulation, he is bound to presuppose more subtle and more interesting laws of this sort. In fact, it would be virtually impossible to construct a dynamic simulation of a past situation without presupposing a great number of laws drawn from a great variety of fields.

My contention, then, is that while both historian and social scientist deal with laws governing human behavior and human institutions, the historian's work is distinct from the social scientist's in that he seeks to use rather than to discover these laws. He seeks to use them not *just* for the purpose of giving explanations and deriving counterfactuals, but for the setting up of models which also make possible sympathetic identification with persons living in the past. It is then that historical understanding is achieved. Hence, history really does have a unique position among the social sciences even though its subject matter may almost entirely overlap that of the others.

NOTES

Part 1

1. R. G. Collingwood, *The Idea of History,* New York: Oxford University Press, 1956.
2. Marcel Granet, *Chinese Civilization* (1930), New York: Meridian Books, 1958, adapted from the edition published by Barnes and Noble Inc., 1957. Parenthetical text references in sec. 1 are to Granet.
3. *Ibid.,* pp. 167–168. Granet's extended quotations here refer to the *Li Ki,* except for the last, which refers to the *Tso Chuan.*
4. *The Idea of History,* p. 283.
5. Alan Bullock, *Hitler, A Study in Tyranny,* New York: Harper & Row, 1964. Parenthetical text references in sec. 3 are to Bullock.
6. Franz von Papen, *Memoirs,* London: A. Deutsch, 1952, pp. 226–227.
7. *Memoirs,* p. 218.
8. Oscar Parkes, *British Battleships,* London: Seeley, Service & Co. Ltd., 1956. Parenthetical references in sec. 4 are to Parkes. Fisher-Gard design "E" is reproduced from Parkes, p. 473.
9. Charles Loch Mowat, *Britain Between the Wars 1918–1940,* Chicago: University of Chicago Press, 1955. Parenthetical references in sec. 5 are to Mowat.
10. A. M. MacIver, "Historical Explanation" in *Logic and Language,* 2d ser., ed. A. G. N. Flew, Oxford: Clarendon Press, 1959.
11. C. G. Hempel, "The Function of General Laws in History," in *Theories of History,* ed. P. Gardiner, Glencoe, Ill.: Free Press, 1959.
12. There is in the literature an extensive controversy over these points involving Hempel, William Dray and others. Rather than attempt-

ing to cover it here in detail, I will be content to let my own point of view emerge in Part II.

13. In the last sample (sec. 12, below), Crane Brinton gives us sketches of laws.

14. One point of view is expressed in the translation of the *Tao-te-ching* by J. J. Duyvendak, London: John Murray, 1954; the other is contained in Arthur Waley, *The Way and Its Power*, London: G. Allen and Unwin, 1934, which also contains a translation of the same text. Parenthetical references in sec. 6 are to these sources.

15. Paul Carus, *Lao Tzu's "Tao-Teh-King"* (1898), La Salle, Ill.: Open Court, n.d., p. 147.

16. Translation by Orde Poynton, in *The Great Sinderesis*, Adelaide, Australia: Hassell Press, 1949, p. 37.

17. Translation by Isabella Mears, in *Tao Tsŭ*, London: Theosophical Publishing House, 1922, p. 7.

18. Translation by Witter Bynner, in *The Way of Life According to Lao Tzu*, New York: John Day Co., Inc., 1944, p. 25.

19. Translation by R. B. Blakney, *The Way of Life*, New York: New American Library, 1955, p. 53.

20. Charles Tilly, "The Analysis of a Counter-Revolution," *History and Theory*, 3 (1963), 30–58. Parenthetical references in sec. 7 are to this source. A fuller account of the Vendean counterrevolution is given in Tilly's book, *The Vendée*, Cambridge: Harvard University Press, 1964.

21. These tables are separated in Tilly's text, appearing on pages 52, 53, and 55 respectively. Reproduced by permission, Weselyan University Press.

22. E. G. Campbell, *The Reorganization of the American Railroad System, 1893–1900*, New York: Columbia University Press, 1938. Parenthetical references in sec. 8 are to Campbell.

23. *Ibid.*, pp. 36–37. Campbell here cites S. F. Van Oss, *American Railroads as Investments*.

24. Chapter VII, "The Political and Military Value of Chivalrous Ideas," in J. Huizinga, *The Waning of the Middle Ages* (1924), Garden City, N.Y.: Doubleday Anchor Books, 1954, adapted from the original edition published by Edward Arnold Ltd. Parenthetical references in sec. 9 are to Huizinga.

25. Wolfgang Frank and Bernhard Rogge, *The German Raider Atlantis*, New York: Ballantine Books, 1956, p. 105.

26. J. A. Nixon, "Health and Sickness in the Slave Trade," Appendix to Chapter 11 of *The Trade Winds*, ed. C. Northcote Parkinson, London: G. Allen & Unwin, 1948. The statistics and the quotation from Barker's pamphlet are found on pp. 276 and 277 respectively.

27. L. B. Namier, *Diplomatic Prelude, 1938–1939*, London: Macmillan, 1948. Parenthetical references in sec. 11 are to Namier.

28. *Ibid.*, p. 159. In a note at the end of this passage Namier remarks that on May 10 Chamberlain himself had described the negotiations as being "of the greatest importance and of real urgency."

29. Crane Brinton, *The Anatomy of Revolution*, New York: W. W. Norton, 1938. Parenthetical references in sec. 12 are to Brinton.
30. While there is presently no *general* revolution of exactly the kind that Brinton has in mind, current events in America (and perhaps in China) illustrate many of Brinton's theses. The main thing that seems to separate the black militant movement from a revolution is that, as of this writing (1971), it cannot muster enough people to overthrow the government. Campus revolts, on the other hand, come much closer to being genuine revolutions, albeit on a miniature scale.
31. We can refer here to C. L. Stevenson, *Ethics and Language*, New Haven: Yale University Press, 1944; P. H. Nowell-Smith, *Ethics*, London: Penguin Books, 1954; and R. M. Hare, *The Language of Morals*, Oxford: Clarendon Press, 1952. In particular, Stevenson treats a moral judgment as an ethical judgment with extra persuasive strength and Hare treats such a judgment as a judgment made about a man where the reference class is the class of men. Even in Plato we find the doctrine that the man who knows the good will attempt to achieve it. One can then, in effect, make a moral judgment about a man by saying that he knows the good, and this minimizes the difference between moral judgments and those ethical judgments which assess someone's degree of rationality. It is these latter sorts of judgments which are particularly likely to occur in historical writing.
32. It might be supposed that to judge the rationality of a historical figure is simply to judge whether the arguments he used are deductively valid—a relatively simple matter. However, there is much more to such a judgment of rationality than this. Even when one is concerned just with arguments, one cannot say that a man is rational just because his arguments are all deductively valid. He may, for example, take perfectly wild statements for his premises, and not attempt to justify them in any way at all. To say that someone is rational is to say something very complicated about his whole system of beliefs, and it is extremely difficult to say in detail what features a rational system of belief would have to have. Further, when we are talking about a historical figure and say that he was rational, we would ordinarily have in mind not only arguments and beliefs, but also *actions*. It is even more difficult to say exactly what a *rational action* consists of, but it implies at least taking reasonable steps to achieve a reasonable goal. Obviously the terms used here are value-laden even though their analysis may be very difficult. Still, we use this sort of evaluative language every day in our ordinary speech, and there is no reason why the historian should not use the same sort of language.
33. There is, in fact, quite a striking parallel between history and literature in this respect. See W. Todd, "The Ethical Functions of the Novel," *Ethics*, 75, 3 (1965), 201–206. I have there argued that fictional characters are logically incomplete but that we are gener-

ally told just those things about them that allow us to evaluate them ethically and morally. The historian, on the other hand, tends to tell us what we need to know about a historical figure in order to evaluate his rationality and efficiency, if not his morality.

Part 2

1. Collingwood even compares the process to that of a detective trying to reenact a crime from the point of view of the murderer (*The Idea of History*, pp. 269–274).
2. Part of the material in this section is taken from W. Todd, "Counterfactual Conditionals and the Presuppositions of Induction," *Philosophy of Science*, 31 (1964), 101–110. See also my "Causal Laws and Accidents," *Theoria*, 31, 2 (1965), 110–124, for a discussion of some related problems.
3. J. L. Austin, *Philosophical Papers*, Oxford: Clarendon Press, 1961, p. 166n.
4. For a discussion of general inductive assumptions see A. W. Burks, "On the Presuppositions of Induction," *Rev. of Metaphysics*, 8 (1955), 574–611.
5. This brings up the question of the size and composition of the class concerned, which in turn involves the distinction between a causal law and an accidentally true generalization. Nelson Goodman discusses this distinction under the heading of "The problem of law," in "The Problem of Counterfactual Conditionals," *Journal of Philosophy*, 45(1947), 113–128. On this point see also Roderick Chisholm, "The Contrary-to-Fact Conditional," *Mind*, 55(1946), 289–307; and A. W. Burks, "The Logic of Causal Propositions," *Mind*, 60(1951), 363–382.
6. Goodman, pp. 120–121.
7. For an alternative way of handling Goodman's problem, see Wilfred Sellars, "Counterfactuals, Dispositions, and the Causal Modalities," in *Minnesota Studies in the Philosophy of Science*, vol. 2 (Minneapolis, 1956), pp. 240–248, especially.
8. I have in mind here an analysis of causal law similar to that of Burks in "The Logic of Causal Propositions" (above, n. 5). If one takes an extensional analysis the second assumption will be unnecessary.

INDEX

Accuracy of dynamic simulation, 174-75

Acts: Addison and Unemployment, 56, 58-59, 60-63, 65

Annals Written on Bamboo, 17, 18, 21

Arithmetical models, 165

Arms race, 43-44

Assumptions: 27, 183; about hypothetical world, 217-18; about revolutions, 150; historical, 69, 121; Namier's, 131-32

Austin, J. L.: determinism in "could", 207-8

Berchtold, Count, Austro-Hungarian Foreign Minister: his appointment, 117, 118-19

Brinton, Crane: 133-152; assumptions, qualified, 150; causality in, 135, 144-50; counterfactuals in, 135, 137-38; counterfactual (specimen), 156; ethical evaluation in, 134, 156; method of, scientific, 135-36, 141, 152; psychological question of, 148-49;

and social sciences, 133; uniformities in, 141-44

Bullock, Alan: 29-39; causal connection in, 64-66; counterfactual (specimen), 154; ethical evaluation in, 34; historical question of, 30; method of, 38-39, 80; method of hypothesis, 37, 38-39; and Mowat, 56; and Parkes, 41-42. *See also* Papen, Franz von

Burks, A. W., 244nn4, 5

Campbell, E. G.: 91-99; causality and counterfactuals, 94; counterfactual (specimen) 155; economic history, 91-92, 94-95, 98, 99, 105; economic laws, 98; ethical evaluation, 157; method of cumulative statistics, 92; and Mowat, 94. *See also* ECONOMIC HISTORY; Norfolk and Western Railroad

Causal connection: historical vs. scientific, 60-63

Causality: in Brinton, 141-50; and counterfactuals, 94; in Bullock, Parkes and Granet, 65-66; in ex-

Causality (*continued*)
planation sketches, 65; in Mo-
wat, 60-61, 65-66; in uniform-
ities, 141-44
Causal laws: and determinism,
219; limited, 218-19
Cavendish, Henry, M.P.: diary of,
119-20
Chamberlain, Neville: British
Prime Minister, 123-25; motives
of, 128, 129; social situation,
122, 123-25, 128, 129-31
Chance: 191-92; and human decisions, 191
Chinese history. *See* SCIENTIFIC
CHRONOLOGY; SOCIAL HISTORY
Chisholm, Roderick, 244*n*5
Chivalry: ideas of, 99, 100-103,
105, 106, 111-12
Choice: in action and decision, 52-
53
Choices: free, 201-2; and games,
182
Chronology, ancient Chinese, 16,
17, 18-19, 21-22
Collingwood, R. G.: 9, 13, 27-28,
53-54, 79-80, 161-62, 227; imaginative reconstruction, 79-80;
scientific history, 232; scissors-
and-paste history, 53, 54
Committees (historical): 41-42,
48-49
Common sense: and sympathetic
identification, 39; psychological
generalization of, 101; and
causal laws, 218-19
Comparative statistics: method of,
90, 91
Computers: 194, 199-200; and
operations research, 199
Construction of dynamic simulations: 201-2, 231
Cotenability: and actual causal
laws, 219
Counterfactual assumptions, and
evidence, 211
Counterfactuals: 179, 204-5, 206,
209-11, 213-15, 219, 221; and
decisions, 234-35; and economic
laws, 98; and ethical evaluations, 132; historians' use of,
138; implied, 122-23; in Brinton, 137-38; and scientific laws,
215-16
Counterrevolution, French, 83, 84-
86, 87-88, 89
Cumulative statistics, method of,
92

Decision and action games, 185-86,
188-89
Decisions: in historical game, 234-
36; and operations research, 197
DETAILED POLITICAL HISTORY, 29-
39
Determinism: and causal laws,
219, and counterfactuals, 206,
207
Dispositional analysis: of J. L.
Austin's example, 208, 209
Disputes: historical and scientific,
judging, 75-79, 79-80
Dreadnought, first modern battleship, 40, 42-43, 44-46, 47, 49-
51
Dumb simulation: 173; no counterfactuals in, 171-72
Duyvendak, J. J. L.: 66-80, 158-
59; counterfactual (specimen),
154; dispute, 67, 74, 75-80; ideology of text, 67, 78, 79; interpretation, 68; method of, 75-80;
sources, use of, 69, 70
Dynamic simulation: 171, 173-74,
180, 185, 191, 228-31, 236; 238-
39; as a game, 181, 187; and
counterfactuals, 172-73; ethical
evaluation in, 176; and events,
189-91; and goals, 179-80; and
historical understanding, 174; in
war games, 202; of past, 180-81,
199, 202-3; and oneself, 203;
rules of, 175-76, 238, 240

ECONOMIC HISTORY, 91-99
Economic history: 94-95, 99, 105; and cumulative statistics, 92; methods of, 91; and military, 91-92; position of, 98
Economic laws and counterfactuals: more specific, 98
Ethical evaluation: 129-30, 134, 159, 200-201, 230-31; and counterfactuals, 122-23; discussion of, in Brinton, Bullock, Huizinga, Mowat, Nixon, Parkes and Wank, 156-58; example of, 122; in Namier, 129-31; lacking in Tilly, Granet, Thomas, Waley and Duyvendak, 158-59; nonmoral, 156-57; and rationality, 157; and simulation, 176
Ethical judgment. *See* Ethical evaluation
EVALUATIVE HISTORY, 122-32
Events left to chance: in dynamic simulations, 189-90
Explanation sketch: 64-65; and explanation, 63-64; Hempel on, 239

Factors excluded from simulations, 223
Fisher, Sir John, First Sea Lord; and naval theory, 40, 41-43, 44-46, 47, 48-49, 50-51
Football play simulation; 168, 169, 172-73
French Revolution: factors relevant to it, 139-41

Games, historical: 182-83, 184, 189; as simulations, 189; and competition, 183-84; and computers, 227; and counterfactuals, 179; decision and action, 185-86; 188-89; decisions in, 234; and historical understanding, 231, 233, 234-35, 237; Wittgenstein on, 181
GENERAL HISTORY, 53-66

General laws, in economic history, 98; in Mowat, 98
Goals: in dynamic simulations, 179-80; in games, 182
Goodman, Nelson: on counterfactuals, 219 and 244nn5, 6
Granet, Marcel: 16-29, 55, 65-66, 158-59, 165; and Collingwood, 28; counterfactual (specimen), 153-54; ethical evaluation, 158-59; ideology, 16, 24; methods of archaeology, 17, astronomy, 21-22, psychology, 19, 20, 28, and science, 19-23, 27; social situation, 24-25; sources, use of, 16-17; sympathetic identification, 20, 25-29

Hare, R. M., 243n31
Hempel, C. G., explanation sketches, 63-64, 239
Historians: 233; in Tilly, 84-86; modern, 14; specialized, 55
Historical accident: in Parkes, 49-50; in Campbell, 95-96
Historical account: complete, and Namier's, 127-28
Historical individuals: 79-80, 129-30; Chamberlain, 129; Fisher, 41-42, 48-49; goals of, 171; in groups (Mowat, Granet), 66; own assumptions, 177-78; von Papen, 34-35
Historical investigation: and dynamic simulation, 238
Historical simulation(s): 197, 228, 238-39; testing accuracy of, 198
Historical understanding: 173-74, 227; degrees of, 236; and dynamic simulation, 174; game useful to, 237; and models, 162
Historical writing: 9-10, 65-66, 139, 156-57, 223, 224-25; and non-specialist, 139; and other social sciences, 239; sub-history of Granet, 23; and uniformities, 152

HISTORY OF IDEAS, 99-116
History of ideas: 52-53, 112, 163; and laws of human activity, 240; subject matter of, 235-36
HISTORY OF TECHNOLOGY, 39-53
Huizinga, J.: 99-116; counterfactual (specimen), 155; ideological history, 103-4, 112-13; method of, 99-100, 103-4, 112-13, 114, 116; and motives, 101, 103, 107; and sociology, 114; sympathetic identification, method of, 104, 115; and Tilly, 99, 116
Human decisions: and chance, 191; and operations research, 200
Hypothetical world(s), 209-11, 214-15

Ideology(ies): 16, 83, 107–8; for new actions (revolutions), 82-83; hypothetical, questioned, 84; in ancient texts, 24; in Huizinga and Tilly, 99; motives stemming from, 103; possible, in *Tao-te-ching*, 80-81. *See also* HISTORY OF IDEAS
Imaginative reenactment. *See* Sympathetic identification

Laws and counterfactuals: economic, 98; in historical writing, 65-66

MacIver, A. M.: levels of explanation in history, science, 63
Mass actions: in Huizinga, 113-14; problem of, Tilly, 84
Mass ideology: and polling, 81; questions about, 81; Tilly's discovery about, 86
Method(s): 167-68, 238-39; adequate historical, 162; of Brinton, 135-36; of Bullock, 80; of Bullock vs. Mowat, 56; of cumulative statistics, 92; of economic history, 91; of Granet, 19-23; of

Huizinga, 99-100, 103-4, 116; of Mowat, 55-57, 59, 99-100; of Namier, 128; of Parkes, 51-52; of Piecemeal, 117, 119-21; of scientific, 14; of sociology, 114; of Toynbee vs. Brinton, 134
Method of hypothesis: applied to history, 37, 38-39
Methodological framework: 161, 162
Model(s): 162-63, 164, 167-68, 195-96, 203, 222-23; and historical understanding, 162
Motives: choice of, 101; for historical actions, 107; and intuitive judgment, 107; statistically established, 129
Mowat, Charles Loch; 53-66; and Bullock, 56; and Campbell, 94; causality in, 60-63, 65; counterfactual (specimen), 154; and Granet, 54-55, 66; and Huizinga, 99-100; mass movement in, 81; method of, 55, 56-57, 59, 99-100; pattern in, 57; sources, use of, 53-54, 55; sympathetic identification, 66

Namier, L. B.: 122-32; and alternative assumptions, 131-32; counterfactuals, 122-23, 132; counterfactual (specimen), 155-56; ethical evaluation, 122-23, 128, 129-31, 132; historical accounts, 127-28; method of, 128, 129; sources, use of, 123, 125; sympathetic identification, 128
Nixon, Professor J. A.: 120-21; counterfactual (specimen), 155; ethical evaluation, 156-58; historical assumption, 121; method of, 121; sources, use of, 120-21; statistical method, 120-21
Norfolk and Western Railroad: economic situation of, 92, 94-95, 96-97; failure of, 94; historical accident, 95-96. *See* ECONOMIC HISTORY

Nowell-Smith, P. H., 243*n31*
Numerical indices: 141, 145-50;
scientific and historical, 161
'Objective' and 'sympathetic' simulations, 228-31
Operations research: and decisions,
197, 200; for historical understanding, 12; and historical conclusions, 198-99; and models, 12,
162-63, 195-97

Papen, Franz von: 29-39 passim;
his veracity or lack of it, 31-32,
33-34, 35-36, 37; motives and
intentions of, 80; and secret political meeting, 31; social situation of, 29-30; and von Schröder,
31-32, 36-37
Parkes, Dr. Oscar: 39-53; committee, analyzed, 41-42, 48-49, 50-
51; counterfactual (specimen),
154; ethical evaluation, 156-58;
Fisher, Sir John, key figure, 42,
47, 51; historical accident, 49-
50, 51; historical question, 41;
method of, 51-52; sources, use
of, 41-42
PIECEMEAL HISTORY, 116-22
Plausibility: of counterfactuals,
205, 221
Policies (historical): 118-19; and
general principles, 228-29
Problem-solving: behavior, dynamically simulated, 236; by computer and by brain, 194
Proposed method of historical
writing, 9-10, 223, 224-25
Psychological general laws: implicit, 20; unsupported by science,
161
Psychology, 19, 20, 28, 82, 101,
148-49
Public figures. *See* Historical individuals
"Pure" history: in Brinton, Namier,
Huizinga, Tilly and Granet, 138-
39

Rationality: and ethical judgments,
157, 243*n32*
Revolutions: four samples of, 133-
34, 150; assumptions, qualified,
150; factors relevant to, 139-41;
uniformities in, 141-44
Rule-determined events: in dynamic simulations, 191
Rules of dynamic simulations, 175-
76, 238, 240
Rules of a game, 182, 183

Samples of historical writing here:
controversial, 14; all "scientific",
13; counterfactuals in, 11; evaluative judgments in, 11-12
Schröder, K. von. *See* DETAILED
POLITICAL HISTORY
SCIENTIFIC CHRONOLOGY, 16-24
Scientific historical method: 14, 21,
22; in Brinton, 136; in Colling-
wood, 15; in Granet, 21-22; in
Waley and Duyvendak, 77-80;
needs a system of concepts, 141.
See Collingwood
Seamen on slavers, 120-21
Sellars, Wilfred, 244*n7*
Sequences of events: patterns in,
56-57
Simulation(s): and games, 181;
many sources of, 169; model
ship, 166-67; real situation of,
195; situation with mouse, 167
SOCIAL HISTORY, 24-29
Social psychology, and use of
questionnaires, 82
Social sciences and history, 239
Social scientist's model, 165-66
Social situation: in Bullock, 29-30,
55; in Granet, 24-25; in Mowat,
80-81; in Namier, 123-25; in
Nixon, 120-21; in Tilly, 88-89;
in Wank, 117; political pattern
in, 57
Sociological history. *See* Statistical
method
Sociology, method of: 53-63, 86-

Sociology (*continued*)
88, 90, 114; polling, 81; and statistics, 57, 62
Sources, use of: 15, 41-42, 54-55; as checks, 120; Collingwood's vs. Mowat's, 53-54; conclusions from (Wank), 118-19; credibility, 31-34, 36; Granet, 16, 17; Granet's vs. Mowat's, 54-55; Waley's and Duyvendak's, 69
Speed in battleships: speculation about, 46-47
Ssu-ma Ch'ien, anicent Chinese historian, 16, 18
STATISTICAL HISTORY, 80-91
Statistical method: 92, 114, 129; for intentions, 86-88; in Nixon, 120; and polling, 81; Tilly's use of, 80-91
Stevenson, C. L., 243*n31*
Sympathetic identification (imaginative reenactment): 104, 128, 162; and common sense, 39; definition of, 227; for interesting hypotheses, 152; and historic individuals, 79-80; in Collingwood, 28, in Granet, 25-27, 29; and objective simulations, 230; peculiar form of, 66
SYSTEMATIC HISTORY, 133-52

Tao-te-ching, 67, 68, 70, 71-75, 75-79
TEXTUAL CRITICISM AND HISTORICAL TRANSLATION, 66-80
Thomas, P. D. G.: 119-20; checklist, 120; counterfactual (specimen), 155; ethical evaluation,

158-59; method of, 120; sources, use of, 119-20; and Wank, 120
Tilly, Charles: 80-91; counterfactual (specimen), 154-55; historical question, 86; and Huizinga, 112-13, 116; ideology, 82-83, 84-85, 86; and mass action, 84; and Mowat, 81; psychology, social, 82; social situation, 84-85, 88-89; sociology, 81, 86-88, 112-13, 116; statistical method, 81, 87-88, 90-91
Toynbee, Charles: and Brinton, 134

Unactualized possibilities, 173-74, 176-77
Uniformities: 137-38, 152; historical vs. scientific, 143
Unquestioned assumptions: as rules, 182-83; and "impossible" possibilities, 177

Waley, Arthur: 66-80; etymological method, 68-69; ideology of, 67, 69; method of, 67, 77-80; social situation, 67, 69; sources, use of, 69. *See also* Disputes; Duyvendak
Wank, Solomon: 117-19; counterfactual (specimen), 155; ethical evaluation of, 157; method of, 117, 119; sources, use of, 118-19; and Thomas, 120
War game: played by operations research, 196
Wittgenstein, Ludwig: disquisition on games, 181

William Todd received his A.B. degree from Harvard College in 1955 and his Ph.D. from the University of Michigan in 1959. He is professor of philosophy at the University of Cincinnati.

He contributes frequently to philosophical journals here and abroad, and is editor of the new *Journal of Philosophical Linguistics*. His *Analytical Solipsism* was published in 1968.

The book was designed by Joanne Kinney. The type face for the text is Linotype Caledonia designed by W. A. Dwiggins in 1937; and the display face is Optima designed by Hermann Zapf.

The text is printed on Oxford Paper Company's Book Text paper and the book is bound in Columbia Mills' Fictionette cloth over binders' boards. Manufactured in the United States of America.